TOM PETTY

AN AMERICAN ROCK AND ROLL STORY

BY NICK THOMAS

GUARDIAN EXPRESS MEDIA
Green, Ohio U.S.A.

Library of Congress Control Number: 2014932838
ISBN: 978-0980056198

Library of Congress Cataloging-in-Publication Data
Thomas, Nick
    Tom Petty: An American Rock and Roll Story
    Includes bibliographical references
    ISBN 978-0980056198
    1. Rock music – Bio-bibliography.
    I. Title

We would like to thank the following individuals and organizations:
Tom Hanson, Andrea Schroeder, the Tulsa City-County Library, the Library and Archives of the Rock and Roll Hall of Fame and Museum, and the Music Library and Sound Recordings Archives at Bowling Green State University. Additionally, we are grateful to all of the individuals who consented to our interview requests.

Please contact the publisher to report any errors or omissions. Organizations and other groups interested in purchasing quantities of this book should contact the publisher.

Tom Petty and the Heartbreakers, their managers, their representatives, and their record companies did not participate in the writing, editing, production, or publication of this book. This is not an official or authorized work.
Cover photo © Mark Spowart / 123RF.com

Guardian Express Media
P.O. Box 205
Green, Ohio 44232

www.guardianexpress.com
Printed in the U.S.A.

▶ TABLE OF CONTENTS

TOM PETTY

AN AMERICAN ROCK AND ROLL STORY

▶ INTRODUCTION

Leaning into his microphone as he strums a 12-string Rickenbacker guitar, Tom Petty pounds his left foot to the beat of the music. Dressed in dark jeans, a slim suit jacket, and a colorful neckerchief tied loosely around his weathered neck, Petty leads his tight, melodic band on spirited performances of "Free Fallin'" and "American Girl." Wearing a satisfied smile, Petty is greeted with a loud sing-along from the crowd. As one of the most reliable performers in the world of rock and roll, Petty has entertained audiences for more than four decades.

Over the years, Tom Petty has been branded with many labels. He has been called a disciplined bandleader, a classic rock icon, a principled artist who stood up to the record industry, "one of rock music's most durable and dependable artists," and even "a surlier version of the Scarecrow from Oz's cornfields."

Documentary maker Peter Bogdanovich said of Tom Petty, "I found him so in the American grain." A music journalist commented: "He admits he's neither the most gifted guitarist nor the best singer. Some might even argue that he's not the cleverest songwriter. But the sum of his parts is astounding." A *Rolling Stone* writer declared: "It's easy to take Tom Petty for granted. Among his generation of Heartland-rock heroes he's conspicuous for not having cultivated a clear public persona. Neither a blue-collar poet like Bruce Springsteen nor an outspoken maverick like Neil Young, Petty is most familiar to us in the dryly goofy, self-effacing guises he adopts in his videos – the Mad Hatter haplessly burping into the camera or the adoring oaf dragging around Kim Basinger's corpse."

In Petty's hometown of Gainesville, "People told Tommy he'd never make it as a rock star. They said he didn't have a good-enough voice. Wasn't a good-enough guitar player. And, frankly, he wasn't good-looking enough, either. He was too gaunt and his teeth were too big." But Petty would humbly admit: "I didn't get into this to be a pinup. I wanted to be taken seriously as far as writing songs, making music.... Some people are so good-looking they can't help it. But I'm certainly not... saddled with that problem."

Tom Petty's musical adventure began in his teenage years. After a momentary but pivotal encounter with Elvis Presley, Petty was destined to pursue a life in rock and roll. But with an abusive and unsupportive father, Petty was maligned at home for his artistic pursuits, his long hair, and his streak of independence. At school, his teachers also discouraged the budding musician from pursuing his goals. These incidents would shape Petty's outlook as an adult: "I developed a problem with authority. Any time that authority was... unjust, I stood up to it, and that became my personality."

Remaining ambitious his entire life, Tom Petty possessed an iron focus. Whenever he was pushed into a corner, he always pushed back and would not surrender. In his most famous battle, Petty stubbornly refused to back down when MCA Records acquired his recording contract in 1979. Producer Jimmy Iovine observed: "Tom's the kind of proud guy who will not bend past a certain point. He's not going to do anything he doesn't believe in. But over the years I've realized that the really great ones don't have to compromise. Tom is definitely one of the great ones."

During his formative years, Tom Petty was shaped by a number of musical influences: "When I was coming up, I tried to emulate great rhythm guitarists like John Lennon, Mike Pender of the Searchers, and Keith Richards. The rhythm guitarists in '50s and '60s country music were amazing. And just listen to Elvis' stuff from the Sun Records period. His guitar was very loud in the mix, because it was bleeding into the vocal mic. Scotty Moore is great, but Elvis really carries those records."

In the first few years after forming the Heartbreakers, Tom Petty was accused of copying the Byrds. But Bob Dylan said of Petty: "People talk about how he sounds a little like Roger McGuinn, but playing with him and seeing what he does to a crowd, I think he's more in the Bob Marley area. He's real good."

This book will explore how a gifted singer-songwriter raised on a steady diet of Elvis and the Beatles would leave the safe confines of northern Florida to pursue a music career in the chaotic record industry hub of Los Angeles. With his journey taking various twists and turns along the way, Petty would thrive as the leader of the Heartbreakers, a co-founder of the rock supergroup the Traveling Wilburys, a member of the reformed Mudcrutch, and a solo artist. All the while, Petty would continue to maintain his musical integrity.

▶ CHAPTER 1
RAISED IN GAINESVILLE

Raised in an unremarkable, working-class home that was devoid of extravagance or luxury, Tom Petty experienced his first significant musical memory at age four when he heard Bill Haley & The Comets' pioneering rock and roll hit, "Rock Around The Clock." During Petty's early childhood, there was a radio but not a record player in the house. Although he never felt deprived, Petty realized at a young age that his family was neither wealthy nor even middle-class.

Tom's father, Earl Petty, was born in Argyle, Georgia, into a family of poor, hardworking laborers. Earl's parents, William and Sallie Petty, farmed and did backbreaking tasks in the region's lumber camps. In 1926, William "Pulpwood" Petty moved his entire family, including six-year-old Earl and his two brothers, ninety miles south to Florida. Their decision to leave Georgia was triggered by a violent encounter. Tom Petty recalled, "My dad's mother was [a Cherokee] Indian; she was a cook in a logging camp, and she married a logger, and they got into a fracas over interracial marriage." As Petty recounted, "They were attacked on a logging road in their wagon. And my grandfather took a logging ax and wound up killing one of the guys in the fight. And they fled during the night to Florida."

Although the vast majority of Cherokees had been driven from their Georgia homeland by the Federal government and forced to relocate west of the Mississippi River, Petty's Indian ancestors refused to leave. But Petty's Indian heritage was not a subject the family would openly discuss and was certainly not a source of pride in 1950s and '60s suburban America. In fact, Petty's grandmother would eventually deny her Indian heritage.

Escaping repercussions from both the law and the victim's family, William Petty and his family endured but did not prosper in their new environment near Gainesville. Continuing to work in the logging industry, the elder Petty also labored on the family's small farm. During World War II, Earl Petty would quit school to join the Air Force. While stationed in Egypt, he was positioned as a groundsman. After the war ended, he returned to Gainesville and worked as a delivery driver.

Meanwhile, Tom's mother, the former Katherine Johey Avery, was called "Kitty" by both family and friends. Born in Sycamore, Georgia, of French and British descent, she was the youngest of the three daughters of John and Troas Avery. The more stable and nurturing of Tom's parents, Kitty was in many ways the total opposite of her brash and uncultured husband. Tom Petty later pondered, "How they hooked up I can't imagine – they were completely different people."

In 1947, Earl and Kitty married, he was 27 and she was 24. They settled into a small house in Gainesville. On October 20, 1950, Earl and Kitty welcomed their first child, Thomas Earl Petty. Three years later the family would move several blocks away to the Debra Heights allotment on the northeast side of Gainesville. Tom Petty later said of the modest two-bedroom dwelling: "It was a cinder-block house in a subdivision. Hot as hell. No air conditioning." In 1957, Tom's only sibling, Wayne "Bruce" Petty, was born. But while Tom was enthralled with music from a young age, his brother repeatedly rejected Tom's offer to teach him how to play the guitar. In fact, no one else in Petty's family played a musical instrument.

Working a variety of jobs to support his young family, Earl occasionally attempted to go into business for himself. But as a violent, hard-drinking man who liked to gamble and take risks, he did not succeed as an entrepreneur. Tom Petty later recalled, "I never felt safe as a child. There is so much about my dad looking back that I like but I was so afraid of him. My father was such a loose cannon. I was never too at ease around him."

For a time, Earl Petty operated a small grocery store in the black section of Gainesville, which the locals referred to as "Colored Town." The neighborhood was also the birthplace of Gladys Horton, who later became the lead singer of the Motown group, the Marvelettes. (Ironically, at age 11, Tom Petty's first record purchase was a 45rpm record by the Marvelettes, "Playboy.")

Closing the grocery store, Earl then launched Petty's Wholesale Dry Goods Company, a small-time wholesaling operation that sold cheap merchandise to small mom-and-pop stores across northern Florida. Then after his wholesale business went bust, Earl took a job selling policies for the National Standard Life Insurance Company. He would remain with the company until his retirement. Meanwhile, Tom's mother, Katherine, worked as a clerk in the city tax department.

With both parents working, Tom and his brother would usually come home after school to an empty house. Oftentimes, they were met by their maternal grandmother, who lived nearby and tried to help out in the Petty household.

*   *   *   *   *   *

The area that became Gainesville was originally inhabited by the Timucua Indians, a regional tribe of 50,000 that farmed the productive land. But when Spanish explorers arrived in the early 16th century, they enslaved or murdered the local natives. Florida – which was named by conquistador Juan Ponce de León – would remain part of Spain for most of the next three-centuries, until 1819, when the region was ceded to the United States for a mere sum of $5 million. During this period, a huge population of non-native American Indians would displace the very last of the Timucuans. Coming mostly from South Carolina and Georgia, these Creek Indians "were called seceders, runaways, renegades." In their own language, they called themselves Seminoles. Finally, on March 3, 1845, Florida was admitted into the Union as the 27th state. Despite statehood, the U.S. Army continued to battle Indian tribes across Florida until 1858.

In 1854, Gainesville – which early residents sometimes spelled "Gainsville" – was established during the construction of a train line that stretched for 155 miles from the town of Fernandina near the Georgia line to Cedar Key on the Gulf Coast. Gainesville, which was platted with a central train depot, quickly became a busy shipping hub. During the Civil War, a thirty-mile stretch of the railroad was destroyed by Northern troops.

Gainesville was situated in the rolling hills of north-central Florida, a region dotted with small lakes, marshes, rivers, and large sinkholes. Nicknamed "Gatortown" and "Hogtown," the city bordered the southern edge of the massive gator-infested Okefenokee Swamp.

Soon, Gainesville became the county seat of Alachua County, which took its name from the Indian term for a local landmark, the Big Jug. Also known as the Alachua Sink, the Big Jug was an enormous, muddy sinkhole just southeast of the city, where a teenage Tom Petty and his friends often spent their days playing hooky from school.

Like much of northern Florida, Gainesville was eventually populated by settlers who arrived in the late-19th century from neighboring Alabama, Georgia, and South Carolina – lured by cheap, open land that was suitable for farming. Over the next several decades, Florida would remain a sleepy, low-populated state. But in the 1920s, a land boom brought an influx of developers, wealth, and a flourishing tourist industry. But after the state suffered a pair of devastating hurricanes in 1926 and 1928, the newfound prosperity appeared to be over.

Gainesville's continued growth was attributed to the arrival of a large public university. When the Florida legislature passed *The Buckman Act* in 1905, the state's system of colleges and universities was reorganized, and several small schools in northern Florida were merged into a new institution, the University of Florida. The school was lured to the Gainesville area with the pledge of 500 acres of land and free city water in perpetuity.

Tom Petty later observed: "There's two parts of Gainesville. There's the college in the middle and around it are just rednecks, farmers. My family didn't have anything to do with the college until I started playing gigs." With millions of American men choosing to sit in college classrooms rather than fight in the jungles of Vietnam, the university experienced a dramatic increase in enrollment during the period when Petty began performing around the campus. In the late-1960s, the enrollment at the university hovered at just under 20,000 students. For Petty, living in a college town exposed him to the opportunities of the outside world, thousands of miles away from the swamps and alligators of Gainesville.

Although Florida is celebrated for its palm trees, pink flamingos, and tourists smothered in suntan oil, Gainesville was a world away from the luxury spots of Tampa Bay, Miami Beach, and the Florida Keys. Located more than an hour away from both the Atlantic and Gulf coasts, the inland city of Gainesville was not blessed with the state's wealth of magnificent, sandy beaches. In fact, travel guides like *Frommer's Florida* often ignored Gainesville completely. As a result, for many years a sign at the small Gainesville Regional Airport welcomed visitors with the message, "The Other Florida." Even Orlando, 120 miles south of Gainesville in central Florida, was not a tourist destination until Walt Disney picked the region as the site for his Magic Kingdom amusement park.

Despite the fact that Gainesville shared in Florida's warm weather, one former resident described the seasonal changes in less than glowing terms: "The climate was hot and swampy, the air thick with mosquitoes. In the winter, it was dispiritingly cold and wet." Although the city's streets were lined with palm trees, the occasional winter frost made the commercial farming of citrus fruits unfeasible.

▶ CHAPTER 2
ELVIS & TOM

Tom Petty's childhood friends would remember him as "a quiet Southern boy with a quirky sense of humor and a serious mind for music." While attending Howard Bishop Junior High School, Tommy – as he was then called – sang in the school chorus. Struggling to sight read sheet-music and overly conscientious about how his unique voice stood out instead of blending in, Petty quit the chorus. Then at the insistence of his domineering father, young Tom also tested his capabilities in various sports. After failing in baseball at age ten – his coach would not let him bat – Petty played football in junior high. But as a skinny, small-sized teen, he did not possess the muscular physique needed for sports. As Petty later recalled, "I was a very poor athlete [but] my brother was athletic."

Instead, Petty would join the residents of Gainesville in supporting the local college football team every Saturday afternoon. In the 1960s, when Petty was growing up, college football was a major sensation in Gainesville as the Florida Gators played in both the Sugar and Orange Bowls. As Petty later explained, "when you grow up there, everything has a gator on it. My earliest memories are of going to the big pep rallies in the stadium the night before [the games] – they called them the Gator Growl – so, yeah, I always pulled for the Gators."

Soon, a brief, fleeting event would completely transform Petty's life. For just a few moments, a wide-eyed Tom Petty would stand face-to-face with America's king of rock and roll, Elvis Presley. Petty later recounted the fateful, life-changing episode: "Everything became pretty clear at that moment.... [Being a rock singer] looked like a great job."

In 1961, Presley would spend several months in northern Florida to shoot his first-ever comedy feature, *Follow That Dream*. It was Presley's ninth film and the followup to his box office success, *Blue Hawaii*. The previous year, Presley had finished a two-year stint in the U.S. Army and was eager to restart his music and film careers.

But Presley had already managed to make an impression on the residents of northern Florida. On May 13, 1955, a riot broke out at his concert in Jacksonville – which had attracted 14,000 shrieking, mostly female fans – when at the end of his performance he made an off-the-cuff comment. After he shouted, "Girls, I'll see y'all backstage," all hell broke loose when "hundreds of girls accepted the invitation, chasing him into a locker room, where they tore Elvis's shirt to shreds, ripped his jacket and took his socks and shoes before police rescued him."

Just a few months later, in August, Presley returned to Jacksonville and was met by Judge Marion Gooding, who threatened to arrest the singer if he shook his hips on stage. The controversy was reported by *Life* magazine, which openly sided with the judge. Taking the threat seriously, a restrained Presley shook only his pinkie finger during the six scheduled performances.

That same year, a pair of Florida songwriters – schoolteacher Mae Axton from Jacksonville and musician Tom Durden from Gainesville – composed "Heartbreak Hotel." Elvis would take the song to the top of the charts in 1956 after he left Sun Records for RCA. In exchange for recording "Heartbreak Hotel," Presley was given one-third ownership of the song.

Despite his past troubles, Elvis had no qualms about returning to sunny Florida to shoot a feature film. Meanwhile, Petty's uncle, Earl Jernigan, was hired as a propman and assistant set director for the Presley film, which was primarily shot on location in the towns of Inglis, Yankeetown, Inverness, and Ocala. Jernigan was a jovial and hard-working film afficionado who operated his own business in Gainesville, Jernigan's Motion Picture & Video Service.

The filming began during the first week of July. In a change of pace from his previous movie roles, Presley portrayed an uneducated bumpkin named Toby Kwimper, who outwitted a group of Chicago mobsters as well as a number of snooping government bureaucrats.

One afternoon while Earl Jernigan was working on the set of the film, young Tom was asked if he wanted to visit his uncle and possibly meet Elvis. Petty was driven by his aunt to the courthouse in downtown Inverness, which had been cordoned off during the filming. One newspaper later reported, "Teenagers screaming 'We want Elvis' lined the courthouse square. Girls covered the fins of Elvis' Cadillac with lipstick kisses." One local 16-year-old girl who managed to get a kiss on the cheek from Elvis said of the swivel-hipped rocker, "He talked Southern, like he was the guy from the next town, but it didn't matter if you were a baby or 100 years old, he'd charm you."

Petty would later recall: "One day my uncle, who worked on a movie crew in Florida, took my cousin and I down to the set where Elvis Presley was filming.... My uncle took us into the trailer and introduced us to Elvis. I remember all those good-looking girls losing their heads over him. He looked fantastic you know? That hairdo and those sleepy eyes. From that moment on I became a fanatic about Elvis.... It gave me something to do. I mean, I was in the 5th grade and not into Little League." Petty's father also vividly recalled that day, "He got home and told us all about it. He was so excited. And he wanted... a guitar."

Then in a twist of fate, Petty suddenly found himself with a sizeable collection of Elvis Presley records. Petty recalled, "This guy who lived down the street – I'm telling him about Elvis, and he says, 'Well, you know my sister that used to live here and moved out used to dig Elvis,' and he says, 'Look at this,' and he pulls out this box, and in the box he's got nothing but 45s, and they're all mint 45s of the perfect period, like '56 to '60, just perfect. And he even had a couple Suns in there, and he had Jerry Lee (Lewis) in there and Little Richard, Buddy Holly. Everything was in there. I couldn't have handpicked it better." In a quick trade, Petty netted dozens of rock records in exchange for a Whammo slingshot and a couple of mail-order albums of pop music from Lucky Strike cigarettes.

Petty's collection of Elvis records would continue to grow. As one of Petty's boyhood friends fondly recalled: "By the sixth grade, we'd ride our bikes to the Gainesville Shopping Center and go to Neisner's and Grant's to look through the Elvis record albums. [Tom] had all of them." The young Petty played those rock and roll records – day in and day out – on his cheap, portable record player without realizing that one day he would be making his own records.

Petty later recalled, "I can't tell you how much rock 'n' roll consumed me. It wasn't a matter of choice. It was something that came over me like a disease. It was all I lived for.... For the next two years all I did was sit in my room and listen to those records. My dad was worried about me because I didn't go outside, I didn't play sports, I didn't do nothing but listen to those records." To the dismay of everyone around him, Petty had entered into a lifelong commitment: "And that was the end of doing anything other than music with my life. I didn't want anything to fall back on, because I was not going to fall back." Sadie Darnell, Petty's cousin who later became the sheriff of Alachua County, told an interviewer: "He was completely, completely enthralled.... And Tommy told us as a family that he was going to be a rock star." Many years later, Petty would admit: "It's a strange thing to say out loud, but I felt destined to do this. From a very young age, I felt this was going to happen to me."

At age eleven, Petty began to grow his hair and grease it back just like Elvis. But he would soon stick out from the other students at his school, which inevitably led to frequent taunts.

But Petty was obsessed with his rock and roll records for another reason. He later admitted: "Music was a safe place to be. I think that in many ways I had a pretty tough childhood, and the music actually became a safe haven for me. That was where I escaped to. It really is the only true magic I've found in this world."

Years later, Petty would describe his encounter with Presley in almost religious terms: "When I met Elvis, we didn't really have a conversation. I was introduced by my uncle, and he sort of grunted my way. What stays with me is the whole scene. I had never seen a real mob scene before. I was really young and impressionable. Elvis really did look – he looked sort of not real, as if he were glowing. He was astounding, even spiritual. It was like a procession in church: a line of white Cadillacs and mohair suits and pompadours so black, they were blue."

On April 10, 1962, *Follow That Dream* had its gala opening at the Marion Theatre in Ocala, about 40 miles south of Gainesville. Although the film's stars were not present, the premiere was a major media event that was attended by local and state dignitaries, with all the glitz and glamour you would see in Hollywood. Petty had to wait a few weeks for the film to open in a Gainesville theater.

Like many boys his age in the 1950s and early '60s, Tom Petty was also fascinated by Western films and was particularly enthralled by singing cowboys. The showmanship of the modern rock guitarist has a basis in the silver-screen singing cowboys like Gene Autrey and Roy Rogers, who wore fancy Stetson hats, sat on majestic white horses, and would celebrate the capture of cattle thieves or horse rustlers by pulling out a guitar and crooning a sentimental ballad next to a warm campfire. Petty later recalled, "When I was really young, I liked cowboys who played guitar. That's why I thought the guitar was cool – the guitar just always seemed like a kind of rebellious instrument to me. And then Elvis came along – he was kind of like a cowboy, too." In fact, two of Presley's early films – *Love Me Tender* and *Flaming Star* – were Westerns that featured Elvis playing his guitar.

Soon, Petty was not satisfied with merely listening to records – he wanted to create his own music. Deciding he wanted to be a musician, Petty began pestering his mother for a guitar. Spotting an acoustic model in a Sears catalog, he convinced his mother to contribute the $38.50 down payment, with the promise that he would pay the monthly installments by mowing lawns and performing other odd jobs around town. Petty recalled: "We were country people, and my mom aspired to be a city person and become a little more sophisticated. She encouraged my interest in the arts, bringing me books and records, and would pay for me to go to the movies. My father couldn't see the sense in that; I don't think he ever went to the movies."

Petty also began hanging out at local instrument stores. Although there were places like Marvin Kay's Music Center in Jacksonville, Petty preferred to stay in Gainesville, where he would frequent Lipham Music. Opened in 1954 by a father and son team, Lipham's originally carried mostly guitars and sheet music. At Lipham's, Petty enjoyed the vibe of being around *real* musicians, including future Heartbreakers keyboardist Benmont Tench, who beginning at age 11, could often be found playing a piano in the store.

Petty became friends with one of the employees at Lipham's, a young guitarist named Don Felder, who would later gain fame in the 1970s as a member of the Eagles. Felder had initially taken the job to pay for a second-hand Fender Stratocaster he spotted in the store's front window. Felder's duties at Lipham's soon expanded to giving private guitar lessons. In his autobiography, Felder said of the job: "Before I knew it, I was teaching ten-year-old snot-nosed kids who whined all the time because their fingers hurt and they thought they'd be able to play like Elvis the minute they picked up the guitar their parents had just bought them.... One of my students, however showed some real promise. His name was Tommy Petty, and he was my star pupil. Tommy was three years younger than me, skinny, with buckteeth and an awful guitar. I went over to his house to give him lessons, and he had a microphone set up and was belting it out, standing in his living room, singing and playing for all he was worth. I was impressed. Tommy wasn't an outstanding guitar player, but he had a voice somewhere between Mick Jagger and Bob Dylan, and a whole lot of nerve."

The Continentals, Felder's band at the time, were one of the leading rock acts in Gainesville during the 1960s. Also in the band was another future star, Stephen Stills, who had attended Gainesville High School and was later a member of the marching band at the University of Florida. When Stills left the group, he was replaced by Bernie Leadon, another future member of the Eagles. Soon after, the Continentals would evolve into a British Invasion-inspired outfit, the Maundy Quintet.

▶ CHAPTER 3
THE BRITISH INVASION HITS GAINESVILLE

On February 9, 1964, the American musical landscape was reshaped when the Beatles made their triumphant debut on *The Ed Sullivan Show*. Watching that Sunday evening was 13-year-old Tom Petty, who like 73 million viewers across the country, was instantly captivated by the Fab Four. Exactly three months later, the Beatles would hold down all five of the top-five positions on *Billboard* magazine's Hot 100 chart.

Beatlemania had arrived and young Tom was in the grip of its seismic revolution. "They came out and just flattened me. To hear them on the radio was amazing enough, but to finally see them play, it was electrifying. They did those three songs at the top of the show and then you had to wait till the end for them to come back on. It felt like an eternity, watching these comedy skits and, like, guys spinning plates – and remember, this is the biggest show on TV, but to us kids, we wanted the Beatles, so to have to watch a guy spinning plates, it was total torture. Plus, the girls screaming – I never seen or heard anything like that in my life. Girls were going insane, crying and waving. You just knew the TV studio was being turned upside down," Petty recalled.

Overnight, the Beatles were everywhere, their hit songs were everywhere, and their influence was everywhere. Often lost in history is the fact that America had another reason for embracing Beatlemania. A dark and ominous shadow had fallen over the country after President Kennedy had been murdered in Dallas two months earlier in December 1963. For weeks afterward, many radio stations abstained from playing upbeat, cheerful songs. It was the overwhelmingly optimistic, light-hearted, and innocent nature of the Beatles' early hits that signaled to America that life must go on.

American record companies were caught unprepared by the British Invasion as act after act was pushed off the charts, with syrupy girl groups and teenage ballad singers displaced by modern, guitar-driven rock groups. In reaction to the Beatles' domination of the music charts in 1964, the nervous heads of American record companies began searching for untapped British bands or, at the very least, domestic guitar-oriented groups that looked or sounded British.

But as America was entering the most turbulent decade in its history, the country's social fabric was undergoing profound changes. As author Grace Pallandino observed, "The rise of Beatlemania coincided with a real shift in middle-class teenage behavior. By the mid-1960s, even college-bound, suburban teenagers were defying their parents' authority, not only behind their backs (as countless teenagers had done for decades) but right in front of their faces. Boys were growing their hair too long, girls were wearing their jeans too tight, and teenagers were talking back to parents and teachers as if they had every right in the world to contradict their elders. Others went even further, adopting a personal style that advertised their contempt for conventional life. By 1964, some of the best and brightest teenagers were fascinated with living life at the margins."

Suddenly, Petty's youthful adoration of Elvis Presley had been replaced by his new teenage passion for the Beatles. Then shortly after he first witnessed the Beatles on television, Petty attended a local concert and experienced yet another revelation. He recalled: "It was the Escorts, Gregg and Duane Allman's first band. They were playing Gainesville. They were already pretty good, but what knocked me out was their hair – it was already long! This was only a few weeks after the Beatles played. Change was happening so fast, you could barely keep up with it." Another budding local musician, Mike Campbell, was equally impressed by the Beatles: "Once I found the guitar... everything else stopped, nothing else interested me any more – well, girls – I was completely engrossed."

Following in the path of the Beatles, Petty began to let his hair grow even longer, "which made me the freak around town," he recalled. Petty's hair was also causing him trouble with his school teachers: "They threw me out of school because my hair was so long. As long as it was greased back Elvis-style no one knew how long it really was but when the Beatles and their bangs came along I let my hair fall naturally. They took one look at me in junior high school and kicked me out." As one of Petty's cousins later explained: "That was a time of intense conformity. He was a long-haired person in a short-haired person's world."

The fight over the length of Tom's hair would continue at home, where he was often berated by his father. Tom Petty later recalled, "He was very abusive. I had a couple of bad experiences. There was one big fight where he came in and smashed up a lot of records. But it didn't stop me. Music was in my blood. I couldn't quit. I never had any choice about what I was going do." On the other hand, Tom's mother said little about his hair and was far more encouraging: "[She] was a complete angel. She was cool." But despite his mother's backing, she also felt intimated in her own home. As Petty later recalled, "My mother... never stood up to him. She couldn't, because he was frightening."

After the arrival of the Beatles, Petty switched from the acoustic to the electric guitar. Purchasing a Beatles songbook from Lipham's, Petty taught himself to play a number of Lennon-McCartney compositions: "I basically just studied Lennon's playing, even in the films, just watching his right hand and how it worked. Stuff like 'And I Love Her' has an amazing rhythm pattern; I learned a lot from that." Paying the one-dollar admission at the Florida Theater in downtown Gainesville to watch *A Hard Day's Night*, Petty was in awe of his new musical heroes. The black-and-white film had a simple plot: when the Beatles were not performing upbeat songs like "She Love You" and "Can't Buy Me Love," they were running from large groups of hysterical young women. But what really caught Petty's attention was the teenage girls in the darkened theater who began screaming at the celluloid images of the Beatles on the screen, as though the film was an actual concert.

The British Invasion would soon generate a number of guitar-based groups, and Petty took notice: "The Beatles came out. And then the Stones. I was stuck. I must have listened eight hours a day to the record player. It was my world." Explaining his fascination with British rock groups, Petty said: "In the mid-Sixties, the British had a more romantic view of rock and roll than the States did. We didn't take it seriously. The energy that came with the British Invasion was the difference – these guys brought the guitar to the fore. You weren't getting guitar off the Shirelles."

▶ CHAPTER 4
SO YOU WANNA BE A ROCK & ROLL STAR

At age 14, while in the 8th grade, Tom Petty assembled his first rock band, the Sundowners. He formed the group in an attempt to impress a female classmate at a junior high school dance. As Petty recounted: "some song came on, I think it was 'The Game Of Love' by Wayne Fontana and the Mindbenders. She says, 'I love this song,' so I said my band played that song. I stretched the truth a little. I didn't even have a band. I had just met this [drummer]. She told me she was in charge of the school dance that was coming up the next week. She wanted my band to play during the deejay's break. I said we would be glad to do it. I left the dance to find the kid with the drums.... I told him we had a gig next week, even though we didn't really have a band. It took almost the whole week to get four people to be in the band." During that week, Petty and his new bandmates spent hours practicing in his living room. The aspiring musicians plugged their instruments into one "enormous Sears amplifier with six inputs, and just started wailing away. It was such an incredible rush," Petty recalled.

Arriving at the school dance in matching blue shirts, Petty and his bandmates played their first gig without using a single microphone. As Petty remembered: "[We] went to the dance, extremely nervous. And then the break came, and we came up to play, and it went over so well we had to play the same three numbers three times."

After making an impression on the deejay, the Sundowners were asked if they would be interested in playing a gig at the nearby college. Jumping at the opportunity, the young musicians purchased a microphone and learned more songs. However, back in school, Petty's big plan to win over his pretty classmate had failed. Petty recalled: "The girl wasn't impressed. After all that, she didn't go for me."

Over the next two years, the Sundowners performed in teen clubs, at area schools, at the local Moose Lodge, and for an entire summer, on a beach. Not surprisingly, the members of the group were earning a good amount of money. Petty recalled the reaction at home: "My mom was flabbergasted at the money I was making. I mean, honestly, when I think back on it, there were probably times in my teenage years when I was making as much as my dad. That was probably real insulting."

Eventually, the group found its way to the fraternity row of the University of Florida campus. Don Felder recalled: "Those frat parties were wild. It was just like Animal House, with everyone drunk out of their minds.... Those boys knew how to party, and we were more than happy to provide the soundtrack to their madness." Future country-pop stars David and Howard Bellamy, later known as the Bellamy Brothers, were also regulars on the university's frat circuit in the late-1960s. But while fraternity parties and college bars provided a steady income for dozens of rock bands during the school year, it was a far different situation during the summer months when school was out and Gainesville reverted to a quiet burg.

Although the original lineup of the Sundowners consisted of three guitarists and one drummer, Petty switched to the bass. The group – which included drummer Dennis Lee, rhythm guitarist Richie Hinson, and the oldest member, 18-year-old lead guitarist Robert Crawford – was initially limited to playing only instrumentals. But with Petty emerging as the lead vocalist, the Sundowners began performing more British Invasion material.

Despite his newfound success as a musician, Petty's popularity did not extend to school. As his friend Marty Jourard would later recall, Petty "was one of the guys... that was getting hassled by rednecks and big football player dudes." John Densmore, the drummer for the Doors, said of this era: "It was not yet cool to be a musician. If you were a football player, you were definitely the coolest. Basketball was second in 'Cool,' then baseball, track, and finally tennis. The jocks with their lettermen sweaters got the girls."

The Sundowners had the luxury of practicing in their own private rehearsal space. Tom Petty's father had built a small enclosed structure – made of wood and cement – against the back wall of the family's house, which meant the neighbors could hear the blaring, amplified rock and roll music whenever the group practiced. As a result, the Sundowners did not always find appreciative audiences. As one local resident later recalled: "I could hear loud music coming from the Petty backyard. Later that night, my mother, who was at the time a very conservative and strict Baptist, instructed my sister and I to 'walk on the other side of the street,' because 'who knows *what* is going on in that backyard with that older Petty boy and his music!'"

Following one particularly heated dispute with the drummer of the Sundowners, Petty quit the band in October 1965 and joined another local outfit, the Epics. A cover band that played both Southern soul and British Invasion hits, the Epics consisted of Dickie Underwood, brothers Rick and Rodney Rucker and, joining the following year, Tom Leadon – the younger brother of Bernie Leadon. Rick Rucker later recalled, "We realized Tom was the real musician of the band. But it took him a while to figure it out."

Petty had previously performed with the Epics as a substitute bass player and had an open invitation to join the group. Although he would usually remain in the background, Petty provided the lead vocal on a pair of songs, "Love Potion No. 9" and "Like A Rolling Stone."

In many ways, joining the Epics was a major career move for Petty, who at just 16-years-old, was now playing with older musicians, most of whom had already graduated from high school. While the Sundowners and the Epics were similar in terms of the music they played, the Epics embraced a rock and roll lifestyle. And unlike the Sundowners, Petty's new band had its own van, booked shows that were hundreds of miles away, and often stayed in out-of-town motels for the night. In these motel rooms, Tom Petty was first exposed to the adult world of all-night parties with beer and women.

Still attending high school, Petty was discouraged from pursuing a career in music by his art teacher, who said things like, "There's no money in it; this is no way to make a living; these are shaky people." In addition, the teacher "urged [Petty's] friends not to hang around with him because he was too consumed with his music and wouldn't amount to anything." Eventually, Petty was sent to a school psychologist. Asked to explain why he focused his attention on music rather than schoolwork, Petty boldly replied, "Rock is more fun." Years later, Petty recounted: "Once I got in a band, how could I take [school] seriously? This guy worrying about my hair touching my ears is going to teach me something?"

At 17, Petty left home and rented an apartment. But unhappy with living in a decrepit, run-down building and tired of the responsibility of paying rent every month, Petty moved back home a year later. During this period, Petty took a series of jobs, including a salesman position at his favorite hangout, Lipham's. "He came in one day and said 'I'd like a job.' He wanted to be a salesperson. He was really tenacious. If you came in here, you'd better watch out, 'cause Tommy was like a bulldog. He would not let you go 'til you bought something," recalled the store manager. Then in the spring of 1968, Petty attended a concert on the campus of the University of Florida that would help shape his musical outlook. Headlined by the Beach Boys and featuring Buffalo Springfield and the Strawberry Alarm Clock, the concert showcased both the established and emerging music scenes of Los Angeles.

After briefly dropping out of high school, Petty continued to tour with the Epics. However, sensing he had made a mistake, Petty resumed his studies at Gainesville High School and graduated in 1968, despite missing 42 days of school. In his senior yearbook photo, Petty appeared almost clean-cut in a suit and tie; he had been forced to cut his long hair before he could return to school. But while Petty's classmates were at a graduation ceremony, dressed in caps and gowns to receive their diplomas, Petty was hundreds of miles away in south Florida, on a nightclub stage with the Epics. Petty would later admit, "High school was the most bitter experience of my life."

Soon after, Petty had another concern. Like millions of young American males who graduated from high school in the 1960s, he faced the prospect of being drafted and shipped to a dangerous battle zone in Asia. Part of Petty's lifelong distrust of authority was rooted in what he witnessed on the University of Florida campus in 1968. As the war raged in Vietnam, students engaged in large, organized protests. The city of Gainesville emerged as the base of youth protests in the Southeast part of the country, more so than even Atlanta. University of Florida professor Marshall Jones recalled, "Gainesville was the only place south of Virginia and east of Texas that had a serious student movement in the '60s."

Later, the protests in Gainesville turned violent as 2,000 students blocked a highway in front of the university for three days. When a fire truck was set ablaze, the protestors were targeted by state and local police with tear gas and billy clubs. Although Petty did not participate in the protest activities, he was fully aware of the anger against the unpopular war.

Restless and wanting to test the musical waters outside of Gainesville, Petty packed a guitar and boarded a bus, southbound to Tampa. After settling into a fleabag motel, he had no better luck in his new surroundings. Working as a dishwasher at a restaurant to pay his bills, Petty found little success on the local music scene.

Making his way back to Gainesville, Petty took a short detour before returning to music on a full-time basis. With Earl Petty convinced that his son had the potential to become an architect or graphic artist, Tom briefly attended a pair of community college. Finally, Tom Petty pleaded with his father: "Daddy, if you'll just leave me alone, I'll be a millionaire by the time I'm 35." But Petty's father continued to discourage his son from pursuing a career as a musician: "I thought he was going to starve to death in the music business." Not surprisingly, Tom Petty would never see eye-to-eye with his father on any subject. Years later, Petty admitted: "My father was a very charismatic guy, like Jerry Lee Lewis with no talent. He was a very good story-teller, and maybe I inherited some of his ability."

After Petty's mother was stricken with a serious neurological illness, Petty's father acquired a wandering eye. Tom Petty recalled: "My father used to have many mistresses. I never made a specific trip to meet them. But my dad was – he was hell on wheels, you know. He was quite a character, and he was one of those people that... somehow remained likable although he was really a cad." During this time, Petty's grandmother took over many of the duties in the Petty household.

Meanwhile, northern Florida and adjacent southern Georgia and Alabama soon became the breeding ground for a new musical genre called Southern rock. Jacksonville – a mere 70 miles northeast of Gainesville – was the epicenter of the movement. Rickey Medlocke, the leader of the group Blackfoot, remembered: "Jacksonville was a transient town. It had three Naval bases, a steelworks, the Anheuser-Busch brewery, the shipyards – an industrial town that liked to blow off steam, so it became a hotbed for musicians." The region would spawn a number of Southern rock groups including Lynyrd Skynyrd, the Allman Brothers, Molly Hatchett, and .38 Special.

Although Petty appreciated the country and blues roots of Southern rock, he grew to dislike the genre's endless, meandering guitar solos, which were far too prevalent, especially on stage. Trained in the Elvis and early Beatles school of rock, Petty preferred shorter, three or four minute songs with memorable hooks and few guitar solos.

Despite the fact that very few Gainesville rock groups had jumped on the Southern rock bandwagon, the city's music scene continued to thrive. Petty recalled: "There was something in the water in Gainesville.... Everybody wanted to be in a rock 'n' roll band and everybody seemed to find a place to play. The cream rose to the top, the better players were obvious right away. There was a second tier coming in all the time. They were great days really." Other popular bands in north-central Florida during this period included the Jades, the Rare Breed, the Certain Amount, and the Nightcrawlers, a group from Daytona who scored a national hit with "The Little Black Egg," one of the finest examples of 1960s garage-rock.

Because of Gainesville's relative isolation from the large cities of Florida, Petty was limited to what he heard on the radio. Although there were four local AM stations that played rock music, Petty favored WGGG-1230, which adopted a top-40 rock format in 1968. The only local FM station at the time played mostly classical music. But with nighttime AM radio signals capable of traveling hundreds of miles, Petty would tune in distant stations from Chicago, New Orleans, and Memphis, where he discovered a separate world of blues and soul music from Bo Diddley, Muddy Waters, and B.B. King. Petty recalled: "At night we could get WLS. There, you got to hear all that great R&B and stuff. I had to listen to everything." (Eventually, a second FM station in Gainesville, WGVL, began broadcasting in 1970, and adopted a progressive album-rock format the following year.)

Meanwhile, Petty would experience a revelation about his future while attending a concert in November 1969. Dubbed the Woodstock of the South, the three-day West Palm Beach International Music and Arts Festival was staged over Thanksgiving weekend, four hours away in southern Florida. Petty recalled: "I got to see the Byrds... with the Rolling Stones. In the beginning, that was the original blueprint for the Heartbreakers – we wanted to be a mix of the Byrds and the Stones. We figured, 'What could be cooler than that?'" But Petty's vision would have to wait.

▶ CHAPTER 5
HERE COMES MUDCRUTCH

In 1970, the Epics had evolved into Mudcrutch. Although there are several stories explaining the origin of the group's new name, Tom Petty and his bandmates simply wanted a moniker that conveyed a psychedelic, West Coast flavor. Tom Leadon recalled, "I think we liked it because it just sounded sort of dirty and decrepit. We thought it was funny sounding; I don't think it really means anything. It just projected a certain image, and we liked that at the time." But years later, Petty would describe Mudcrutch as "the band with the worst name in the history of show business."

However, after just a few months, Mudcrutch fell apart. Wanting to continue the group, Petty and Leadon auditioned a number of musicians who had responded to a flyer posted on the wall at Lipham's. Initially, Jim Lenahan, Petty's high school classmate, was hired as the group's vocalist. After playing a few shows as a trio, the men realized they needed to expand the group.

After leaving his business card on the wall at Lipham's, drummer Randall Marsh – a native of Bushnell, Florida – was asked to audition inside Lenahan's garage. Still not an official member of the group, Marsh was auditioned for a second time at a house he shared with two roommates, including a 20-year-old guitarist named Mike Campbell. With Petty and Marsh needing a guitar player for the audition, Marsh asked Campbell to join in for a few songs. Although Marsh was aware that Petty wanted to hire a second guitarist, he did not believe that his roommate – a very rock-oriented player – was a good fit for Mudcrutch.

But when the three men broke into a rendition of the Chuck Berry classic "Johnny B. Goode," Petty was impressed by Marsh, but blown away by Campbell. Although Marsh was eager to be a part of Mudcrutch, Campbell was attending the University of Florida and was not interested in joining a full-time, working band. But after a few months, Campbell eventually gave in to Petty's pleadings. "I took my tuition and bought a guitar. That was it," Campbell later recalled. Soon after, the house shared by Marsh and Campbell would be nicknamed "the Mudcrutch Farm."

*   *   *   *   *   *

A native of Panama City, Florida, Mike Campbell (born Michael Wayne Campbell) grew up in the Atlantic Coast city of Jacksonville. Campbell's father – an electrician by trade – had embraced rock and roll in the 1950s. As Campbell recalled, "My dad was a big Elvis and Johnny Cash fan, and he always played those records."

Picking up the guitar at age 16, Campbell was inspired to master the instrument after hearing Bob Dylan's breakthrough chart-topping hit, "Like A Rolling Stone." Campbell recalled, "My mom got me my first guitar, a Harmony acoustic for $30 that was unplayable. The strings were so high and I would struggle like crazy and my fingers would bleed trying to play the damn thing."

But when he borrowed a high-end, solid-body electric guitar, Campbell was amazed by the instrument: "I went to a friend's house one day and he had a Gibson SG, and I could not believe how easy it was to push the strings down. So I started on that Harmony acoustic and later on my Dad got me my first electric guitar, a Goya. I wish I still had those, but I gave them away over the years." (Campbell was playing that cheap $80 Goya when he auditioned for Petty.)

Over the next few years, Campbell would teach himself to play the guitar: "Back then we didn't have cassette players or anything, but I would sometimes slow the records down and listen real close and try to figure out how the guitar player was doing certain things. I had a couple of guitar books too. There was one I had, I wish I still had it – it was *How To Play The Guitar With Carl Wilson* [of the Beach Boys], and it had pictures of his hands." Eventually, Campbell applied to a music school but was rejected due to his lack of a formal musical background. Other than a few accordion lessons as a sixth grader, Campbell would receive no musical instruction.

Looking back at his musical influences, Campbell recalled, "The stuff that got me into the guitar.... the Stones, the Kinks, the Beach Boys, the Animals, all those '60s bands, had real simple guitar parts to go around the song as opposed to guitar solos that interrupted the song."

After graduating from Ribault High School in 1968, Campbell enrolled at the University of Florida in Gainesville. For a time, he dropped out of school to work as a musician on a full-time basis. In the late-1960s, Campbell had joined Randall Marsh in a psychedelic-styled, blues-rock trio called Dead Or Alive. On stage, the group often veered into extended jams of Grateful Dead songs. But after the bass player quit, the group was forced to disband. During this period, Campbell also worked as a book sorter at the local library.

Constantly worrying about his future, Campbell was fiercely determined to finish his college education: "Our families were just scraping and barely making ends meet." So when Petty asked Campbell to join Mudcrutch, it was not easy for him to quit school.

Meanwhile, two other Gainesville musicians were working on their own separate career paths: Stan Lynch and Ron Blair. Although the two men knew each other from the local music scene, they never expected to later join forces in California.

*   *   *   *   *   *

A native of Cincinnati, Stan Lynch (born Stanley Joseph Lynch, Jr.) moved with his family to Gainesville at age five. Lynch's father was a UPS worker who later became an educator; Lynch's mother was also a teacher. As a young child, Lynch took musical lessons on three different instruments – violin, trumpet, and piano. Then after moving to Miami at age 11, Stanley, as he was called at the time, took up the drums as a means of releasing some of his aggression. Exposed to a wide variety of music in his early years, Lynch later explained: "I think [my] attraction to drums was visual. I couldn't take my eyes off the drummer."

Returning to Gainesville, Lynch grew up in a working-class neighborhood. A less than stellar student, he realized at a young age that college was not in his future. At age 13, Lynch joined his school band, where he would set his sights high: "I remember playing in the Westwood Junior High Band, walking home for miles convinced that my destiny was to one day be a big time rock 'n' roll drummer." But just like the situation in Tom Petty's home, Lynch's father discouraged his son from pursuing a career in music.

Just before Lynch turned 15 in 1970, he bought an expensive drum set on credit – without either of his parents co-signing for the purchase. The owner of Lipham's was impressed by Lynch's drumming skills and was confident in the ability of the young musician to find work and make the payments. Around this time, Lynch and his friend Marty Jourard joined a shortlived five-man band, Flash and the Cosmic Blades. Lynch and Jourard were classmates at P.K. Yonge Developmental Research School, an experimental public school affiliated with the University of Florida.

Later that year, Lynch would meet future Heartbreakers bandmate Ron Blair for the first time. But their initial encounter was less than pleasant when Lynch accused Blair of trying to steal his musical gear. Lynch recalled: "I was gigging pretty heavily during high school, working the bars, and my bands had recorded a little bit. So I was learning from the recordings. I got to hear how crummy I was playing. I could pick out my problems a little better."

But while performing around Gainesville, Lynch often got into physical altercations with other musicians. Lynch explained: "I used to get in fights with people I was in groups with all the time.... I'd get pissed off and go beat up the bass player." (Years later when Lynch joined the Heartbreakers, Tom Petty had to lecture him about fighting: "Look man, you can call anybody anything you want.... that they suck, and you can say it loud, but you can't lay a hand on anyone in this band.") Then while celebrating his 16th birthday, Stan Lynch first met future Heartbreaker, Benmont Tench, on a street corner in Gainesville.

In 1971, Lynch joined a popular Gainesville cover band, Styrophoam Soule. Shortly afterwards, the group traveled to Orlando to record a few tracks, including a stripped-down rendition of Chicago's "Make Me Smile." But after an argument about his stage clothes, Lynch quit the band.

Shortly after turning 17 in 1972, Lynch spent his summer break in the power trio, Road Turkey. In a promotional photo of the group, Lynch wore a sailor's cap and sported muscular arms and a large mane of hair. The two other members of the group – bassist Marty Jourard and guitarist Steve Soar – wore towering afros and wrap-around chin beards. A track recorded by group, "Out On The Shreads," would appear on an obscure, Atlanta-based compilation album, *Almanac*.

Still getting into brawls, Lynch was frequently suspended from school. As a result of his temper, Lynch attended three different high schools before graduating in 1973. During his senior year, Lynch took a short course in the history of rock music. For a field trip, the class attended an on-campus performance by Tom Petty's band, Mudcrutch. But a minor calamity occurred during the concert – which was Benmont Tench's first-ever appearance with the group – when Petty and his bandmates managed to crack the auditorium ceiling as a result of their excessive volume. The school authorities were not amused and threatened to sue the group for the cost of the repairs.

Eventually, Road Turkey was hired as the house band at a go-go club called Trader Tom's. During this period, Road Turkey often played on the same bill with Mudcrutch, sometimes for weeks at a time. At one point, Petty hired Lynch as the replacement drummer for an out-of-town show.

After Road Turkey disbanded, Lynch relocated to Los Angeles with the goal of furthering his music career. Although not yet 20-years-old at the time, Lynch was already a seasoned professional. The following year, the other two members of Road Turkey would follow Lynch to the West Coast.

$$*\qquad*\qquad*\qquad*\qquad*\qquad*$$

Another future Heartbreaker, Ron Blair (born Ronald Edward Blair) was raised in a military family. A native of San Diego, he was frequently uprooted. While living in northern Florida, he was drawn to surf music – particularly the Beach Boys – and spent several summers mastering his skills on a surfboard. Blair recalled: "Then sometime in 1964, my dad got stationed overseas. Next thing I knew, we were on a boat headed for Japan. When I got there it was like going back in time; it took a long time for music to get over to Japan, so they were somewhat behind."

Returning to northern Florida a few years later, Blair began playing the drums. But after his father bought him a Japanese-made Guyatone electric guitar, Blair switched instruments. Then out of necessity, Blair began playing the bass: "After I got back to Gainesville, I started jamming with a few bands. I had some friends in a band, two brothers who didn't get along, and one of the brothers had to go. So my friend asked me, 'Would you be into playing bass?' I went down to Lipham's Music Store – where we used to hang out – and I borrowed a bass. Then

I got a hold of a little psychedelic substance and tripped out all night playing bass... By morning, I went, 'I'm a bass player!' Back in those days the bass wasn't a romantic instrument. You really had to talk someone into playing bass."

After graduating from high school, Blair enrolled at the University of Florida in Gainesville, specifically selecting the school to be with his girlfriend at the time. While pursuing a degree in engineering, he spent much of his free time playing in bands. Blair recalled, "Around 1968, my dad got stationed in Hong Kong, but I stayed [in Florida] and lived with the family of one of my band members, a group called the Mojos." Bored with his college studies, Blair dropped out of school during his third year to pursue a full-time career in music.

By 1970, Blair began crossing paths with Tom Petty on a regular basis: "I got into a band that did gigs at places where Mudcrutch would play. Around that time I met a great girl who turned out to be Tom's wife's best friend. We used to go over to his little apartment above a laundromat, so I became acquainted with Tom then. I liked him as a friend before we ever started playing together." Blair also became a fan of Mudcrutch: "They were into a different kind of rock than the band I was in. But they were real good, and they had their own following around there. We did, too, but maybe a little more of the degenerates." Blair was also amused by Petty's stage antics during this time: "Tom used to impress me because he had kind of a beard, he was a real scraggly guy. He looked like he drank a few beers, just really loose onstage. He looked like he was on the edge of looseness – like 'this guy's gonna fall off the stage!' but then he'd keep it together and rock the whole set."

Blair eventually joined a hard-partying Gainesville-based group, RGF. The band featured two lead singers and two lead guitarists, including Jeff Jourard. Blair later described the group's sound as "like the Who, or a little nastier." After building a strong local following, RGF decided to test the waters outside of Gainesville. But as an unknown act trying to score gigs, sight unseen, in nightclubs hundreds of miles from home, the group fared poorly and disbanded in 1972 after a performance in Boston.

Relocating to Macon, Georgia, Blair passed through a variety of bands and was one of many musicians who hung out at "the Big House," which was the Allman Brothers' version of the Mudcrutch Farm. The members of the Allman Brothers wrote a number of their songs inside the aging Tudor-style mansion, including "Ramblin' Man" and "Midnight Rider." (While the Allman Brothers' headquarters was later renovated and converted into a museum, the Mudcrutch Farm was demolished to make way for a housing development.)

Blair became close to the Allman family after his younger sister, Jann, married Gregg Allman in 1972. Janice "Jann" Blair – a budding singer at the time – was the subject of Gregg Allman's solo track "Queen Of Hearts." In his autobiography, Allman recalled: "Janice was so gorgeous, and I was completely in love. I just worshiped that woman. She's the one on the *Laid Back* sleeve, riding a horse I'd bought her not too long after we met. We got married in 1973 and started living together in an apartment in Macon. Just like the others, though, it didn't last." After the couple divorced in 1975, Gregg Allman would marry singer Cher.

In late 1974, a restless Ron Blair headed for Los Angeles to visit a friend. Deciding to stay in Southern California, Blair would join a series of top-40 cover bands.

▶ CHAPTER 6
THE MUDCRUTCH FARM

After Mike Campbell and Randall Marsh joined Mudcrutch, the group quickly grew into a cohesive unit. Needing somewhere to live after disbanding their previous band, Campbell and Marsh were joined by friend William "Red" Slater (an engineering student who attended the University of Florida) in renting a run-down farmhouse at the end of a long dirt road, on the outskirts of the city limits. The three men split the $75 monthly rent. The small, one-story, tin-roofed, box-style building was in desperate need of a paint job, lacked hot water, and was overrun with untrimmed shrubs. Nicknamed the Mudcrutch Farm, the humble building would serve as the group's home base.

Although Campbell and Marsh were the only members of the group who actually lived there, the entire band used the house as a practice space and for late-night parties after gigs. Eventually, the Mudcrutch Farm grew in reputation and "became the hangout for every hippie musician that passed through Gainesville." Tom Petty later described his daily routine during this period: "My transportation was not what it should've been. I had to wake up every day and figure out how to get to Mudcrutch Farm. I hitchhiked, I rode on a bicycle. I had this terrible little Ford Cortina that I could strap together with coat hangers – sometimes it would make it."

Unlike Petty's previous rock-oriented groups, Mudcrutch also embraced various elements of folk-rock and classic country. Drawn to the innovative folk-rock fusion of the Byrds, Petty was particularly influenced by Florida native Gram Parsons. When Parsons joined the Byrds in 1968, he took the group in a more country-flavored direction on the album, *Sweetheart Of The Rodeo*. Before joining the Byrds, Parsons had performed throughout central Florida as a member of the Legends, a group that also included future, solo pop singer, Jim Stafford.

The Mudcrutch Farm was situated on several acres of land. The property included a large open field, which was suitable for outdoor performances. Petty and his bandmates decided to take advantage of the site and constructed a makeshift stage. On weekends, Mudcrutch and other local rock bands would perform for free, hoping to build a fanbase. Photographs from this period show Petty striking a rocker's pose and looking much like a young Gregg or Duane Allman with a full mustache, pork-chop sideburns, and long, straight hair parted down the middle.

One evening, the members of Mudcrutch got into a discussion about Woodstock, and then decided to host their own similar event, but on a much smaller scale. The motivation to stage a music festival was partly fueled by the local university's decision to ban Mudcrutch from performing at an outdoor space on campus, due to the band's excessive volume.

The Mudcrutch Farm Festival was planned for December 13, 1970. Handmade posters promising "Live Bands – Free Food – Hogtown Food Co-op" were placed all around town. But while the festival was scheduled to take place on a Sunday, many of the bands and their fans began arriving on Friday.

The festival drew fellow musicians, artists, college students, and hippies in tie-dyed shirts from around the area. To the group's surprise, the event was a bigger success than expected, with more than 1,000 attendees making their way to the farm.

Although Mudcrutch became the target of local authorities and angry residents who lived near the farm, Petty and his bandmates enjoyed newfound fame around Gainesville. Cashing in on the publicity, the suddenly in-demand group was booked by club owners all around the city. Soon, Mudcrutch was playing at venues such as the Keg, Mad Monk's Inn, Cin City, the Rathskeller, and their soon-to-be home base, Dub's, which was conveniently located just one mile from the Mudcrutch Farm.

Dub's was operated by James "Dub" Thomas, a brawny former bouncer who had made his fortune by investing in a West Coast fast-food chain. When Thomas purchased the club, it was a steakhouse that occasionally featured musical acts. In 1966, Thomas changed the business's name from the Orleans to Dub's Steer Room. The large rectangular building was constructed of plain concrete blocks and had high ceilings. During this period, a 30-foot high, streetside sign attracted patrons with the promise of "liquor, lounge, dancing."

By the late-1960s, Thomas began booking more rock bands in order to cater to the growing college crowds. One popular band at Dub's, the Royal Guardsmen from nearby Ocala, would score a national top-10 hit with the novelty single, "Snoopy Vs. The Red Baron." In 1967, Thomas financed the recording sessions of a blue-eyed soul singer from Gainesville, Linda Lyndell. Her second single, "What A Man," was a minor R&B hit. But decades later, the song gained notoriety when it was recorded by the hit duo Salt-n-Pepa.

But Dub's also began featuring topless dancers and needed local rock bands to back the "entertainers." Mike Campbell recalled: "We played there for several months, five nights a week, five sets a night, so we became really tight and got an education in the real world. There were go-go dancers, drunks, rednecks and music lovers – it was a great environment." Much like the early Beatles in Hamburg, Germany, Petty and his bandmates were forced to work long hours in a less than ideal environment. But it was this relentless daily routine that forced the members of Mudcrutch to become solid musicians.

Petty, who wore Beatle-style boots on stage, was simply happy to be making a living as a member of a rock and roll band. At first, Petty sang the lead on just one song, but slowly assumed more of the vocal duties. On occasion, Mudcrutch would split the bill with another area band, Lynyrd Skynyrd, which Petty described as "more like a heavy metal group than a boogie band in those days."

In the summer of 1971, Mudcrutch recorded their first single. The recording sessions were financed by a pepper and peanut farmer from nearby Bushnell, Florida, named Gerald Maddox. Maddox's son was a close friend of the group's drummer. Traveling to Miami, Mudcrutch recorded at the prestigious Criteria Studios. Tom Leadon recalled, "[My brother] Bernie told me exactly how to do the basic tracks, the overdubs, how to mike my acoustic guitar. We set up in this club we were playing in and spent the whole afternoon rehearsing the instrumental tracks. When we went down to Criteria, we nailed the first song... in one take. The [producer] was really surprised! We wasted no time, and got both songs done in one day."

Petty, who wrote both sides of the single, later recalled, "We had never really been in a studio before, and we did 'Up In Mississippi Tonight' and one other song ['Cause Is Understood'] in four or five hours. They were done really fast, put on a 45, and released in the

Gainesville area [and] 'Mississippi' did pretty well on the radio. For a local group, we got a lot of play on it, which was cool, because we got to raise our prices a little bit. But we were just kids, and how we did it I have no idea." At Criteria, the group had worked with Ron Albert, who produced and engineered the two tracks. The previous year, Ron Albert and his brother, Howard, engineered the hit album, *Layla And Other Assorted Love Songs* by Derek and the Dominos.

The Mudcrutch single was issued on the Red Pepper label, which was meant as a tribute to the band's investor. In addition, Gerald Maddox was also listed as the record's executive producer. In all, just 500 copies of the record were pressed.

But despite scoring a local hit that received radio airplay, the group fought with nightclub owners over the issue of playing original material instead of top-40 hits. Petty recalled: "There was a point with Mudcrutch, around '71, where we made a commitment: Let's really try to make our own music. We wanted to do our own songs and find an audience for it." In addition to the two tracks from their single, Mudcrutch began performing a number of self-composed songs such as "Silver Dagger," "Unheard Of Kind Of Hero," and "Depot Street." But the band would soon pay a heavy price for following its artistic principles. "It got very hard to [find] work at that point. It made the gigs a lot more select," Petty remembered.

Meanwhile, the second Mudcrutch Farm Festival was staged in 1972. On the poster promoting the festival, Mudcrutch was billed as "Gainesville's No. 1 Boogie Band." The all-day event drew even bigger crowds than the first festival.

But with the throngs of visitors parking their cars and motorcycles on both sides of the roads leading to the Mudcrutch Farm, the local police arrived to investigate. With Petty and his bandmates arguing that permits were not required for the free event, the authorities relented and allowed the festival to continue.

Ultimately, angry neighbors finally convinced the farm's owner, who lived in Tampa, to evict the group. Suddenly, the members of Mudcrutch were left without a home and practice space.

Eventually, the group settled into a rented house northeast of Gainesville. Describing the band's new headquarters, Petty recounted: "We didn't have a TV, but in the living room we had a record player set up between two big guitar amps, and we each got to pick an album and put it on and everyone would sit and listen and discuss it. And I mean, we really listened and that was our music education. Randall would put on a Hendrix album, Tom [Leadon] might bring Doc Watson, Mike might have Chet Atkins."

The following year, Mudcrutch experienced a series of line-up changes. Tom Leadon was fired after he got the group booted from their longtime gig at Dub's. Leadon then headed for California in an attempt to break into the music industry. Managing a fair amount of success, he worked with Linda Ronstadt, scored a top-20 hit in 1976 as a member of the country-rock group Silver, and co-wrote a song recorded by the Eagles, "Hollywood Waltz."

Lead singer Jim Lenahan would also leave Mudcrutch. Returning to college, he earned a degree in Theatrical Scenic Design from the University of Florida. Years later, he rejoined Petty as the stage director for the Heartbreakers.

Lenahan was replaced in Mudcrutch by multi-instrumentalist Danny Roberts. As a former member of a regional band called Power, Roberts had opened for dozens of national acts including Fleetwood Mac and Frank Zappa. But after spending a full year recuperating from a serious hand injury, Roberts was booked as the opening act for Mudcrutch at the University of Florida's annual Halloween Festival. Playing a set of acoustic blues for a boisterous crowd of nearly 10,000 students, Roberts impressed both the audience and the members of Mudcrutch. As he was coming off the stage, Powers was invited by Petty to join Mudcrutch.

Joining the band, the talented Roberts played the guitar and bass, began composing songs, and assumed much of the lead vocal duties. Soon, Petty and Powers emerged as a powerful team with their close vocal harmonies. Also added to the band for a short time was Rick Rucker, Petty's former bandmate from the Epics.

Then in April 1973, Mudcrutch would experience an important personnel change with the addition of keyboard player Benmont Tench. But Tench initially joined the band on a part-time basis.

*   *   *   *   *   *

A native of Gainesville, Benmont Tench (born Benjamin Montmorency Tench III) began performing with Mudcrutch whenever he was home from college. The son of Circuit Court Judge Benjamin M.

Tench, young Benmont was deeply rooted in the culture and traditions of the Deep South. Tench's great-grandfather had served as a major in the Confederate Army during the Civil War.

A child prodigy who gave his first piano recital at age six, Tench recounted, "I started playing piano when I was 5 or 6 years old, and the Beatles didn't show up until I was 10 or 11 and I was stuck." But Tench's fascination with the Fab Four often got him into trouble: "I'd hear the Beatles on the radio and start playing that by ear and neglect the lessons, to the immense frustrations of my teacher."

Soft-spoken and introverted his entire life, Tench remembered the first time he met Tom Petty: "He was an older kid. He had a good haircut and was in a band – very impressive and very intimidating.... He worked in a music store where I used to go mess around with all the instruments."

At age 12 in 1965, Tench spent a year studying classical music at the National Conservatory in Panama, joining his father who was an officer in the Foreign Service. Returning to Gainesville the following year, young Benmont resumed his lessons under the tutelage of a local music professor.

Later, Tench attended a prestigious, all-male boarding school in New Hampshire, Phillips Exeter Academy, which was originally established as a preparatory institution for students planning to enroll at Harvard. Exeter's famous alumni include Gore Vidal, Daniel Webster, and Mark Zuckerberg.

Tench later told a friend, "I don't think I ever cut a single class, but every moment that we weren't in class or doing homework we spent talking about music, playing music or listening to music." Tench fondly remembered: "There was a bit of a blues explosion and we just loved it. Though it was pretty silly for a bunch of guys at Exeter to be sitting around singing about the devil at the crossroads or 'Down On Parchman Farm,' we just thought it was good music." But he would characterize one of his groups at the school, the Apathetics, in less than glowing terms: "Our mission was to prove that white men can't play the blues."

While tuned to Boston radio stations like WBCN-FM, Tench was inspired by the British Invasion as well as a number of emerging rock bands from the late-1960s. Although the Summer of Love took place during Tench's second year at the academy, he did not embrace the movement or attend the Woodstock Festival, which was staged a mere four hours away.

After graduating from Exeter in 1971, Tench enrolled at Tulane University in New Orleans. He planned to attend the school for a year or two before transferring to a music college. While at Tulane, Tench formed a band, Tuna Fish Larry, with a guitar player who lived in his dorm. But the group was not successful. At one point Tench was arrested by overzealous police for performing on a public sidewalk. But after a few telephone calls from an angry Judge Tench, the young wayward keyboard player was released and the charges were dropped.

During his time back in Gainesville, Tench explored the local music scene and, on the advice of a friend, attended a Mudcrutch concert: "The guy who started my first band was a roadie for them... He called me and said, 'You've got to see this band.' He was right."

Soon, Tench would occasionally sit in with Mudcrutch. When asked to join the band on a permanent basis, Tench was initially hesitant and feared his father's reaction. But after a number of long discussions, Petty convinced Tench's father that his son possessed the talent to support himself as a musician. Eventually, Judge Tench gave his blessing and allowed his son to drop out of school – for the time being.

▶ CHAPTER 7
RESTLESS IN GAINESVILLE

Despite their eviction from the Mudcrutch Farm, Tom Petty and his bandmates staged a third Mudcrutch Farm Festival, this time drawing visitors from hundreds of miles away. If nothing else, Petty had proven himself as a successful concert promoter.

Now a regional band, Mudcrutch was performing in clubs across Florida and in the neighboring states of Alabama and Georgia, where the group was starting to build a following. During this period, Petty and his bandmates paid their dues by learning the hard lessons of the road. As Petty recalled, the group had to adapt to various situations: "It would depend on the county you were in as to just how late the night would go. Sometimes you'd play in a place until two A.M. and it would close, then you'd go down a couple of blocks to the bottle club where you brought your own bottle. Then that could stay open 'til dawn, so you'd just start all over again.... Boy, that was rough – but at the time I never really thought of it as rough. I just thought: 'This is what it is.'"

Dealing with nightclub owners was another frequent aggravation for the group. As Petty recalled: "I remember we drove one time from Gainesville to Birmingham, Alabama, and that's a long drive. We set up, got ready to play. And the club owner comes out and says, 'Hey man, you can't play wearin' tennis shoes. We've got tablecloths on the tables here.'" After exchanging words with the club owner, Petty recounted, "We walked out, packed up." During this period, the group flirted with the idea of changing its name from Mudcrutch to the more aggressive, Bullseyes.

Frustrated by the lack of record companies in northern Florida, Mudcrutch was forced to drive five-hours north to Macon, Georgia, for an audition at Capricorn Records, a thriving upstart label headed by Phil Walden. Although Capricorn had a number of successes with Southern rock acts in the 1970s, Mudcrutch refused to jump on the bandwagon in order to get signed. Petty recalled, "Wherever you turned there were dozens of slide guitars jammin' for what seemed like days on end. Things really got quite outta hand and degenerated into tuneless triple live boogie albums." More focused on melodies and memorable hooks, Mudcrutch had little in common, musically, with Southern rock bands such as Lynyrd Skynyrd and the Allman Brothers. As Petty later explained: "We went to the record company in Macon, and they weren't interested because [we] didn't sound like Marshall Tucker." Walden also felt that Mudcrutch sounded *too British*.

Around this time, the group faced an additional, unexpected obstacle. As Benmont Tench recalled: "About a year before we left, there was a really good, strong, creative music scene in Gainesville. And it started to die out when disco started up.... But we were trying to be the only band around that didn't play boogie and barbeque music." When the members of Mudcrutch refused to play disco songs, their days on the club scene of northern Florida were numbered.

Petty was forced to contemplate his career options: "Everybody started to leave because there really wasn't much opportunity to record down there.... So we said, 'Let's go out to California.' We figured it would be better to starve in the sunshine than go to New York and starve in the snow." Although Petty would always remain fond of Gainesville, he was also happy to leave: "Most people come to Florida to escape something – cold weather, their past, whatever. And they're very content about it. I was always uncontent. I ran a little faster than Florida. When I left Gainesville in '74, it felt like I was escaping."

In February 1974, Mudcrutch made a demo tape in Judge Tench's living room. Renting a mobile two-track tape system, the group recorded eight songs, including a composition written by Benmont Tench, "On The Street." The songs were recorded over two days at a cost of $200. Petty was convinced he could easily land a recording contract if he personally delivered the demo tape to record companies in Los Angeles.

In March, Petty made the long trek to the West Coast. With Danny Roberts driving, Petty was also joined on the long trip by the group's road manager, 21-year-old Keith "Duke" McAllister. Mike Campbell recalled, "I stayed behind because there wasn't enough room in the van. But I gave [them] my rent and food money for that month for the cause. I stayed back to sort of keep an eye on the girlfriends." Meanwhile,

Benmont Tench – who was hedging his bets in case Petty came back empty-handed – rode along in the Volkswagen van and was dropped off at Tulane University in New Orleans to resume his schooling.

Since Petty and his crew could not afford to stay in hotels, they drove for several days straight without stopping to rest. Petty later recounted the coast-to-coast trip: "Driving to L.A. was the funniest thing. I remember stopping the car in Arizona and getting out because we saw a cactus and couldn't believe it." In another incident, the three men were stopped in Texas by U.S. border agents who searched their vehicle for drugs. Fortunately, the authorities failed to find the group's hidden stash.

Finally arriving in Los Angeles, the men drove to the city's entertainment district. Petty was instantly captivated by the bustling, cosmopolitan atmosphere. He later admitted: "There's something magical about it. It just feels like all the people who want to escape their little small town hells and really don't fit into conventional life head for Los Angeles.... I do love Southern California and Los Angeles. It's always been the land of milk and honey for me." Even if Petty had failed in his mission to secure a recording contract, he had no desire to return to his mundane life in Florida.

Although Los Angeles is best known as the home of the fabled Hollywood film industry, the city has also served as an important base for rock music. In the 1950s, pioneering, independent record companies such as Aladdin, Imperial, and Specialty (which was the home of Little Richard) were crucial in the early development of rock and roll.

By the early 1960s, a number of Los Angeles-based rock acts such as the Beach Boys and Dick Dale gave rise to the surf music craze. Then in 1964 when Dick Clark relocated *American Bandstand* from Philadelphia to Los Angeles, his actions were intended to keep the program relevant as sunny Southern California became the epicenter of popular culture and musical trends. Suddenly, millions of young, red-blooded, American teens wanted to drive hotrods and hit the beaches with their surfboards. In the 1960s, Los Angeles was home to a number of important record labels such as Warner Brothers and A&M; Capitol Records – the American home of the Beatles – was headquartered in a circular, 13-story building that was shaped like a stack of records. In 1972, the city would also lure the legendary Motown label from Detroit.

With its multitude of record labels and nightclubs, Sunset Boulevard in Hollywood was the ultimate spot for hipsters and trailblazers, and was glorified on television by the hit series, *77 Sunset Strip*. By the mid-60s, the Sunset Boulevard scene would spawn groundbreaking rock acts such as Buffalo Springfield, the Byrds, and the Doors. The Strip was lined with dozens of trendsetting nightclubs including the Roxy Theater, the Starwood, the Galaxy, the London Fog, and most importantly, the Whisky-a-Go-Go. At the nearby Troubadour nightclub on Santa Monica Boulevard, John Lennon and his drinking companion Harry Nilsson were famously ejected for heckling the Smothers Brothers. Located just one mile north of Sunset Boulevard, the Hollywood Bowl hosted nearly every major rock act of the 1960s and '70s with the exception of Elvis Presley; the Beatles performed there three times.

Upon arriving in Los Angeles, Tom Petty continued on his mission: "We made our first rounds... from the addresses of record companies we'd written down from ads in *Rolling Stone*." Remarkably, while making calls from a telephone booth in front of a diner, Petty and Roberts found a discarded sheet of paper that listed the names, addresses, and phone numbers of the A&R bosses of twenty-five record companies.

During a week of meetings with record companies, Petty sparked the interest of seven different labels: "We told them we drove all the way from Florida to L.A. as if we were the first people to drive 3,000 miles to go to Hollywood." As Petty recalled, "I remember going into MGM Records. They wanted to make a deal for a single. The same day we went to London Records, they wanted to make an album." As the one-time record label of Petty's musical idols, the Rolling Stones, London Records represented the rock and roll dream. But without offering a written contract or monetary advance, London Records instructed Petty to relocate his band to Los Angeles. But while Petty had intended to sign with the label, fate would later intervene.

Convinced they had struck paydirt, Petty, Roberts, and McAllister made a return trip to Florida to organize a move to the West Coast. On the way back to Gainesville, the trio stopped in New Orleans to pick up Benmont Tench, who remained cautiously optimistic about abandoning his studies for a career in music.

Before returning to Los Angeles, the members of Mudcrutch decided to spend a few weeks rehearsing. Local musician Jeff Jourard later recalled, "It was not a sure thing. [Petty] didn't leave Gainesville as this conquering hero. He knew he had to go to L.A., because that's where the record companies were."

Two members of Mudcrutch had some important personal business to take care of before leaving for California. On March 24, 1974, Mike Campbell would marry his girlfriend, Marcie. Exactly a week later – one day before the band was scheduled to leave Gainesville – Tom Petty married his high school sweetheart, Jane A. Benyo. Petty had first met Jane when she was dating future Mudcrutch bandmate, Tom Leadon. More of a rocker than Tom, Jane would encourage her new husband to pursue his career goals in music. By getting married at age 23, Petty had forced himself to become grounded and was strongly motivated to succeed for the sake of his new wife. Years later, a rock critic would observe that Jane "could pass for" Tom's "twin sister."

After the members of Mudcrutch had packed their instruments and personal possessions, Petty received an unexpected telephone call from Denny Cordell of Shelter Records, one of the other labels that had shown interest in the group. Cordell made a generous offer to Petty and invited his group to take a slight detour to Shelter's recording studio in Tulsa, Oklahoma. There, the large entourage could rest for a few days and Mudcrutch could work on some additional demos.

Shelter Records had been established by several music industry veterans and was headed by Denny Cordell and Leon Russell. Tom Petty first became aware of the company after buying a copy of the 45rpm single, "Crazy Mama" by J.J. Cale. Petty recalled, "That was the first time I ever saw a Shelter Records label. It played no small part in me signing with the label." Cale would record four albums for the label.

Born in Buenos Aires, Argentina, but raised in England, Denny Cordell had a storied background in the music industry. In the early-1960s, while in his late-teens, he briefly managed jazz great Chet Baker. After moving to Jamaica, Cordell was hired by Island Records to manage a subsidiary label but left to produce the first Moody Blues album. Thriving as an independent producer, he would work with Joe Cocker, Georgie Fame, and a group that later included Jeff Lynne, the Move. A friend would describe Cordell as "a bearlike man who didn't seem to consider his appearance a priority. His jeans were expensive but worn and his shirts, though neatly pressed, appeared to have been thrown on.... His curly brown hair was tousled, even though he undoubtedly had it cut at one of the more expensive and trendy salons. With his 'take things as they come' attitude, he was one of the most fascinating people I'd ever met, a fabulously successful British record producer who at age twenty-four produced, 'Whiter Shade of Pale' for Procol Harum. That one song earned him five million pounds, or 'five cool and funky big ones,' as he liked to put it." With his prematurely graying hair, Cordell looked far older than his actual age.

In the late-1960s, Cordell met visiting American musician Leon Russell, who was in England for some session work. In addition to starting their own label, Cordell and Russell joined forces to help Joe Cocker organize the legendary Mad Dogs & Englishmen tour.

An American-born singer-songwriter, Leon Russell had relocated from Tulsa to Los Angeles at the age of 16 in 1959 to work as a session musician. Befriended by guitar virtuoso James Burton, Russell was soon playing on hit records by Herb Alpert, the Byrds, and Gary Lewis and the Playboys. As a member of the Wrecking Crew – an informal group of the city's top session players – Russell was in high demand. In 1970, Russell released his first solo album, which included guest appearances by members of the Beatles and the Rolling Stones. In 1971, Russell was invited by George Harrison to play the piano on Badfinger's third album, *Straight Up*. Also a prolific songwriter, Russell enjoyed a string of hits in the late-1960s including "This Diamond Ring" by Gary Lewis and the Playboys and "Delta Lady" by Joe Cocker.

In 1970, Denny Cordell asked Chris O'Dell – an employee at Apple Records and Leon Russell's then-girlfriend – to scout a building in Los Angeles as the headquarters for Shelter Records. O'Dell recalled: "I was so proud of myself when I found a funky old Hollywood house in the 'less desirable' part of Hollywood Boulevard, definitely in need of repairs but charming on the inside with built-in cabinets, gorgeous wood floors, and a screened sunporch. It had a down-home feel, which Denny and Leon loved, and we all agreed that I discovered the absolute perfect home for Shelter." The label's new headquarters was located next to a liquor store and across the street from an adult theater.

Eventually, Cordell and Russell opened a second office and constructed a recording studio in Tulsa. The studio was built inside an 8,000-square-foot former church and was appropriately named the Church Studio. Leon Russell hired former Muscle Shoals recording engineer Tom Russell (no relation to Leon) to oversee the 16-track studio. Embracing the ethos of the era, Shelter bought and converted six nearby homes as living quarters for the label's musical acts. Tom Russell recalled, "(Leon's) idea was to give the musicians and friends of his the opportunity to come in, do what they wanted to do and see what came of it. Anybody he found on the [West] Coast, they would bring them in, put them in the studio and groom them there, getting them ready to record." Leon Russell had other properties in Tulsa at the time, including two large homes and a nightclub, the Colony, which booked a number of Shelter artists including Dwight Twilley and J.J. Cale. And according to local lore, both Eric Clapton and George Harrison gave surprise performances at the small club.

*   *   *   *   *   *

On April 1, 1974, a caravan of three vehicles carrying nine people and a jumble of musical instruments left Gainesville for Los Angeles. After traveling just two blocks, their rented truck broke down. With repairs made, the truck, a station wagon owned by Benmont Tench's mother, and a 1969 Volkswagen van owned by Danny Roberts headed toward Oklahoma. The group brought along an 8-millimeter movie camera and a portable tape recorder to capture mementoes of the journey. After three days on the road, the group arrived in Tulsa. Then after a night's rest, the members of Mudcrutch spent the next twenty hours in the studio, recording some additional demos. During the sessions, Petty warmed up to Cordell.

A week later, the caravan reached Los Angeles, with the members of Mudcrutch still intending to accept the offer made by London Records. But after some additional conversations with Cordell, the group would instead sign with Shelter Records. Cordell had done something that London Records had neglected to do – he offered Tom Petty and his financially-strapped bandmates a quick cash advance to keep them afloat. Petty later said, "Cordell was a great guy, really smart, really talented. I dug him right away. I can say that he gave me a great education in the studios and stuff. He always had the right ideas musically. On the business side, I don't agree with anything that he wanted to do, but on the creative end, I have to appreciate that he did all that for us. So we said no to the others. 'We're gonna go with Denny because he talks like we do, and to hell with the rest of 'em.'" Similarly, Mike Campbell recalled, "it was a different time back then, and record companies were a little more concerned with artistic development and less concerned about the bottom line. Especially Cordell, who really had an artistic vision and who was really helpful to us.... He had made lots of records to be respected, and he really saw a germ of talent in Tom's songwriting. He really nurtured it, and kind of helped us filter out what was good and what wasn't good about what we were doing." Cordell was the first of several mentors who would foster Petty's creativity.

But on the other hand, the contracts Petty would sign during the next few months would come to haunt him later in his career. Petty explained the situation in the opening chapter of a guidebook on music publishing: "In the early '70s my bandmates and I arrived in Los Angeles, fresh and green.... Just old enough to get ourselves into some real legal trouble, my pals and I went for a [record] deal with the most money up front. A staggering $10,000. No small amount to us in those days, plus there was talk of buying us new amplifiers, and oh, first we had to sign something called a publishing agreement. This came up as we stood pen in hand around a desk, all set to close the deal of a lifetime.... But publishing was something that hadn't really come up in our discussions. [Our] lawyer had seen a quick thousand bucks and told us things looked good to him, so understandably there were some quiet stares between us as we sized up this deal-or-no-deal situation. Hell, why hold this thing up over publishing? Let 'em print the songbooks... So we all signed, and drinks were lifted." However, the publishing rights that Petty had signed over were a far different matter than just a few "songbooks." Petty had unwittingly signed over a significant portion of the earnings from his first few albums, a move that would ultimately cost him millions of dollars during his lifetime. Taking a philosophical perspective, Petty later said, "It's an awkward situation when you're starving and a guy says he'll buy you all the amps you want, just sign this. And then maybe you've got a hit record and bunch of amps and he's got all the money."

The music industry has never been concerned with the equitable treatment of performers or songwriters. As music historian Fred Goodman wrote, "It wasn't so long ago that an artist was tied to his label for life. Ten-album deals were the standard for new artists well into the '70s, and today's terms for an artist walking off the street aren't much better. Most labels still guarantee just one or two albums, while insisting on options for six or seven more should the artist succeed."

With each member of Mudcrutch getting an equal share of the $10,000 advance, Petty used his windfall on a car. He recalled, "We all had two grand apiece, and I spent mine on a little Opel GT, red. It leaked oil and nearly asphyxiated me, and that's what I got around in for a long time – till I had a hit record." Initially, Shelter Records was also paying to house Petty and the other members of Mudcrutch at a dirt-cheap, run-down motel in Hollywood. After complaining, the group was moved for a time to a large house with a swimming pool in Canoga Park.

Eventually, the members of Mudcrutch were moved again. Petty recalled: "Jane was with me. And then later on, [a daughter] Adria was born; I remember living in a Travelodge when she was a baby. We actually used to put her in a drawer in a Travelodge, for a crib. You don't forget stuff like that. It's a really down-to-nothing way to live. We just didn't have any money at all, and then I sent Jane and the baby back to Florida for a while, and then when I got more on my feet, they came back."

▶ CHAPTER 8
CALIFORNIA DREAMING

Although Tom Petty and his bandmates were veterans of the stage, they knew very little about the intricate complexities of the recording process. Consequently, the members of Mudcrutch were shipped to Shelter's studio in Tulsa, where they were schooled in the various aspects of recording and production.

After returning to Los Angeles, Mudcrutch was initially sent to the Village Recorder studio, which was located in a building that originally housed a Freemasons lodge in the 1920s. Produced by Denny Cordell and engineered by Galen Denogles, the sessions did not go smoothly. During this period, Cordell hired Al Kooper to tutor Petty in the studio. Coincidentally, Mudcrutch was Kooper's opening act earlier in the year at a nightclub in southern Florida. A talented keyboard player who co-founded Blood, Sweat & Tears, Kooper was better known for playing the opening organ riff of Bob Dylan's groundbreaking anthem, "Like A Rolling Stone." In 1972, Kooper had discovered another rock group from northern Florida, Lynyrd Skynyrd, and was familiar with the musical talent in the region.

Meanwhile, Mudcrutch was hired as the opening act for surf-music pioneers Dick Dale & His Del-Tones at the Whisky-a-Go-Go. A seemingly mismatched pairing, Mudcrutch was the opener for five performances in September 1974.

But back in the studio, the members of Mudcrutch had a difficult time adjusting to the rigors of the formal recording process. They also began bickering over the group's musical direction. It did not help that Mudcrutch had three songwriters, each of whom wanted to dominate the sessions. It was during this period that Danny Roberts quit after repeatedly proposing changes to the structure of the group. "They asked me to come back 15 to 20 times, every day for a while," Roberts recalled. Instead, he headed back to Florida and resumed his music career. (A few years later, Roberts returned to Los Angeles at the invitation of Denny Cordell to join Phil Seymour's backing band.)

Needing a quick replacement for Roberts, Petty remembered a talented musician back in Florida named Charlie Souza. Petty had met Souza, who was in a popular band called the Tropics, while playing on fraternity row at the University of Florida. Accepting Petty's invitation to join Mudcrutch, Souza drove across the country to Los Angeles. But with Souza playing the bass, Petty took over the rhythm guitar duties.

Changing environments, the group tried recording at Shelter's studio in Tulsa. Returning to Los Angeles six weeks later, the group struggled to find its focus. With frustration abound, Mudcrutch would soon implode. The breaking point came when one of the members wanted to record a song about a space alien, which caused Petty to abruptly quit the band. He later recalled: "There were too many cooks in that band and at least one real asshole. I learned that a band needed one real leader. It was also good if a band didn't have any assholes." Although the members of Mudcrutch had high hopes, the group self-destructed less than one year after arriving in Los Angeles. Despite being left without a band, Petty had no desire to return to Gainesville.

Mike Campbell later said of the experience, "There were personal things, and musically we were very frustrated – especially the rhythm section. We sort of became a burden to the label after a while, spending money in the studio on an album that wasn't working." In fact, Shelter Records had invested a great deal of resources on Petty and the band. Al Kooper later recalled: "We did half an album, and then it just stopped. And Tom and I were already starting to be friends. Then he disappeared for six months."

Although Mudcrutch had completed several tracks, Shelter released just one single from the sessions. In the February 15, 1975, issue of *Billboard* magazine, "Depot Street" was given a positive review and described as a "good reggae cut." Although the song had a tropical Caribbean feel, similar in flavor to Jimmy Buffett, it was not Jamaican reggae in the style of Bob Marley or Peter Tosh. Except in Petty's hometown of Gainesville, "Depot Street" would receive little airplay.

In the aftermath of the band's disintegration, Cordell convinced Petty to remain with Shelter, at least as a songwriter and session musician. As a proficient and talented songwriter, Petty had value to Cordell, who was a businessman at heart. Petty would sign with Shelter Records for an annual base salary of $6,000. In addition, Petty was also encouraged to record a solo album. Meanwhile, the other members of Mudcrutch would scramble to find work. For a time, Benmont Tench and Randall Marsh had joined forces to play at fraternity parties.

During this period, Petty and Campbell would discuss the possibility of collaborating on an album. Although much has been made about why Petty remained close to only Campbell, the two men both played the same instrument, related to each other as songwriters, and had already nurtured a strong friendship. Petty would make another change during this period when he shaved his Allman Brothers-style beard, leaving just a mustache. But the mustache would soon disappear as well.

Meanwhile, Leon Russell would contact Petty after hearing the Mudcrutch demo, "Lost In Your Eyes." Petty explained, "I was living in Hollywood at the Winona Hotel – kind of a hooker's place. The phone rings and it's Leon. He'd heard a song I'd written... and wanted to know if he could record it. I didn't know where tomorrow's rent was coming from. He said, 'Do you feel like writing?' And I said, 'Yeah, buddy! I'm ready right now!'"

Petty recalled what happened next: "Leon, who I'd never met, picked me up in his big Rolls-Royce and took me out to his house. There were quite a few people there, including Roger Linn, the man who invented the drum machine – I told him, 'You'll ruin music forever' – and Gary Busey, the actor, who used to play drums. We'd hang out and me and Leon would do something if he felt like writing."

Soon, Russell invited Petty to move into his mansion, which contained an impressive 40-track home studio. Russell had hoped to collaborate with Petty for an album's worth of material. Petty recalled: "[Russell] kept me on salary as a lyric writer.... If he needed lyrics, I was the guy. I never got credit – I didn't know about *that* – but it was a great education." But Petty had to adapt to Russell's unusual daily routine: "It was a real crazy schedule... we'd get up at nine in the evening, and I'd go in and work all night.... What Leon was doing was very sophisticated music for me."

When Russell left to go on a four-month tour, Petty continued to live in the mansion and was free to work on his own material in Russell's studio. Petty also continued to record solo tracks at Shelter Records, where he worked with various topnotch musicians including Jim Keltner.

But for whatever reason, the sessions went poorly and songs would not gel. Although both Cordell and Russell had envisioned Petty as a solo artist, that was not to be.

Realizing that working with session players was not the optimal method for creating music, Petty yearned for a full-time backing band. Petty recalled, "I tried making an album with studio musicians, but it sounded too sterile."

*   *   *   *   *   *

Around the same time that Mudcrutch had left Gainesville for Los Angeles, two future members of the Heartbreakers would make the identical westward trek. But unlike Tom Petty, Stan Lynch and Ron Blair both came to California without any specific plans or interest from record companies.

Arriving in Los Angeles, Lynch struggled to find work and a place to stay, but soon, "for $40 a month, he found the ultimate luxury of a Laurel Canyon basement [without a] kitchen and bathroom, and got a job at a record store." Unhappy working as a clerk, Lynch begged his boss at Tower Records to fire him so he could collect unemployment benefits. But after a few months, Lynch "quit when he found himself peering into the wrong end of a gun during a holdup."

Lynch got his first break when he joined a group that had relocated to Southern California: "I was working with this great heavy blues band from Texas called Slip of the Wrist. Their original drummer had played with Stevie Ray Vaughan back in Texas."

Then in early 1976, Lynch had a chance meeting with Benmont Tench when the two men "literally ran into each other on the street, and Benmont told Stan he was about to record some demo tapes in a 24-track studio, would he want to come and play? Without much else to do, Stan said sure, and he brought along bassist Ron Blair." During this period, Blair was a member of three different bands, one of which was close to signing a record deal.

At the time, Tench was working in a Motown-style soul revue and was hoping to land a recording contract as a solo act: "What happened was a friend of mine who was an engineer rang up to see if I had any songs I wanted to cut, because he could get me some [studio] time. So I called up all the musicians I knew, who happened to be from

Gainesville." Also present at the late-night session at the Village Recorder studio were Tom Petty and Mike Campbell, who had been invited separately. Tench explained, "I called Tom and I said, 'Do you want to come down here and give me some pointers on how to sing this demo?'"

After spending the day at Leon Russell's estate, Petty arrived at the studio and was surprised to see the cast of musicians that were assembled for the session. He recalled, "I knew everybody in the room but had never seen them in that combination.... We played together that first day, the next day I called them all and asked them if they wanted to start the band." Petty had convinced the other musicians to join him by pointing out the reality of the situation: "I have a record deal, so you can circumvent the whole try-to-make-it thing and go in with me." Instantly, a new rock group was born.

Petty's new backing group would retain Mike Campbell and Benmont Tench from Mudcrutch. Also added were two members from the Gainesville band RGF, bassist Ron Blair and guitarist Jeff Jourard. Rounding out the group was drummer Stan Lynch, who at 21, was the youngest member.

On the following night, the unnamed group met at the Shelter studio and added instrumentation to an existing, unfinished track, "Strangered In The Night," which had been intended for Petty's solo album. After hearing Petty and his new backing band, Denny Cordell gave his approval to the arrangement.

Although Petty had never intended to be the focus of the new group, it was simply a matter of convenience: "The whole reason my name got put in the thing in the first place was because I had a record deal. I'd already been through a deal with Shelter that didn't happen. They'd spent a fortune on this group (Mudcrutch), so they held me over as solo [act]." And instead of blending into the background as Mudcrutch's bass player and occasional vocalist, Petty was suddenly thrust to the forefront of the band as the singer, rhythm guitarist, and defacto leader.

At first, the group called itself the Gainesville All-Stars. But needing a permanent name, Cordell suggested "the Heartbreakers." Petty, on the other hand, wanted to call the group the King Bees, which was a reference to the Slim Harpo blues classic, "I'm A King Bee." Although Tom Petty was still called "Tommy" by both family and friends, the group was instead christened Tom Petty and the Heartbreakers. Agreeing to the change, Petty felt that Tom sounded much better than Tommy.

Over the next two years, Tom Petty and the Heartbreakers would spend a considerable amount of time in the office and studio of their new label, often just hanging out. While at Shelter, Petty became friends with members of another newly signed act, the Dwight Twilley Band, which in addition to Twilley, included the talented multi-instrumentalist, Phil Seymour. Besides the Dwight Twilley Band, Shelter would sign a number of Tulsa-based acts including singer-songwriter J.J. Cale and the Gap Band. Also on the label's roster were bluesman Freddie King and folk singer Phoebe Snow.

Although Petty was rooted in various musical traditions – the British Invasion, folk-rock, and 1950s rock and roll – he would soon be exposed to Twilley's brand of jangly Power Pop, which was clearly evident on the early Heartbreakers tracks, "American Girl" and "Listen To Her Heart." Petty recalled, "We were spendin' every day with Dwight and Phil at Shelter. It was great – there were a lot of ideas goin' on. And you had interplay among artists."

Then when the Dwight Twilley Band was invited to appear on a local, Saturday-morning television program in Tulsa, Twilley asked Petty to perform with the group. Dressed in black, Petty remained in the background as he played the bass. Petty would also appear on Twilley's second album, *Twilley Don't Mind*. Not surprisingly, Twilley and Seymour would reciprocate and provide some backing vocals on the Heartbreakers' debut album.

▶ CHAPTER 9
HERE COME THE HEARTBREAKERS

The first Heartbreakers album was recorded in just 15 days. Most of the recording sessions took place at Shelter's new studio, which was located on the second floor above the label's offices in Los Angeles. As Petty recalled, the setting was hardly ideal: "They were building a studio at the same time – it was still boards and wires."

The Heartbreakers initially finished "Strangered In The Night" and a holdover from the Mudcrutch period, "Hometown Blues." With Al Kooper present at some of the sessions, the Heartbreakers also recorded a number of cover songs including Bo Diddley and Slim Harpo standards, none of which were included on the album. Benmont Tench later recounted one memorable aspect of the sessions: "The engineers were *proudly* on acid. They would take an old rectangular strobe light and put tape on it, like an X, flash it at themselves and start mixing." Quickly, Petty and his bandmates fell into a daily routine. Petty would spend his afternoons writing songs. Then in the evenings, the entire group would assemble for the recording sessions. Petty later recalled: "When we did it, we'd only been a band for a week or so."

Early in the sessions, guitarist Jeff Jourard left the Heartbreakers, but not before appearing on one track. Petty felt the group did not need a third guitarist. Jourard would later team with his brother, Marty, in the Motels, a Los Angeles-based New Wave-inspired group fronted by singer Martha Davis. (In the 1980s, future Heartbreakers member Scott Thurston would also join the Motels.)

Meanwhile, entertainment manager Tony Dimitriades – a former attorney – was living in Los Angeles, where he was working with Ace, a rock band led by Paul Carrack. But when Ace disbanded, Dimitriades was eager to find a new client to represent. After hearing a song on the radio by the Dwight Twilley Band, Dimitriades visited Shelter Records where he was informed that Twilley was not in need of a manager.

Instead, Cordell suggested to the fellow Brit that he meet with another act at the label, Tom Petty and the Heartbreakers. Dimitriades was joined by Joe Cocker's former manager, Reggie Locke, in evaluating the group's unreleased debut album. Dimitriades recalled, "We went and listened to it, met Tom and became the managers of the band. It's amazing that we went in to listen to this particular album and it had 'American Girl' and 'Breakdown' on it." Short, serious-minded and possessing a thick British accent and an impressive blond mane, Dimitriades would take the stage to introduce the Heartbreakers at their early concerts. (Several months later, Locke would be dismissed from his co-managerial position.)

During this period, Leon Russell and Denny Cordell started to battle over the control of Shelter Records. But that was not the only crisis at the label. Shelter had broken its distribution deal with Capitol Records, which hurt the independent label's ability to place its records in stores around the country. Although Shelter had managed to reach the top-20 in mid-1975 with Dwight Twilley's single "I'm On Fire," the accompanying album went unreleased until the following year due to the turmoil at the label – a situation which ultimately damaged Twilley's career.

Finally, after signing a distribution deal with ABC Records, Shelter was in a position to release the debut Heartbreakers record. After an intense power struggle that included multiple lawsuits, Russell sold his portion of Shelter to Cordell in 1976. Russell would later start another label, Paradise Records.

But after Tom Petty and the Heartbreakers completed their debut album, the group began experiencing some identity issues. As Petty recalled, the "album was a real curiosity. 'Oh, this is what it is. How weird.' I remember taking it around to people and they'd just go: 'What is it?' Especially at ABC Records. It was like, 'We're not really sure what it is. This must be punk rock.'" Part of the confusion stemmed from Petty's vocal delivery. Unlike his musical contemporaries from the Deep South like Gregg Allman of the Allman Brothers or Ronnie Van Zandt of Lynyrd Skynyrd, Petty did not sing with a Southern dialect. In fact, on "Breakdown," Petty adopted an aggressive vocal delivery that was closer in style to the emerging punk movement of New York City than any rock act with roots in Florida.

The executives at ABC Records were not alone in believing that Tom

Petty and the Heartbreakers should be lumped into the punk rock camp. In its review of the group's debut album, *Billboard* magazine called Petty "another punk rock, black leather jacketed offshoot."

The album's artwork also perpetuated the punk myth. The front cover featured a moody, menacing shot of Petty with a disinterested facial expression. Petty later recalled, "When I did that album cover, that day I had on a leather jacket and some bullets, and there is this never ending stream of questions, like, 'Why are you wearing the bullets?' 'Are you in the punk-rock movement?'" Although Bruce Springsteen wore a similar leather jacket on the cover of his early album *Born To Run*, Petty looked more like a street-wise punk who would have been more at home on the cover of a Ramones album. Meanwhile, the back cover of the debut Heartbreakers album featured ominous photos of the group's members – two of whom were sporting oversized, biker-style mustaches.

But Petty sometimes liked to play the tough guy in public, and wearing a jacket adorned with bullets was all about making a statement. Courtney Love told music writer Jim DeRogatis: "I've heard this story about Tom Petty: When he was dealing with people, he'd take this knife and stab the desk when he wanted to make a point!" The story may have been an exaggeration but during one showdown with ABC Records, Petty took out a knife to "admire" the blade in a successful attempt to remedy a standoff with the label.

Similarly, Mike Campbell said in 1981, "Maybe the reason it's taken us so long to succeed is that Tom pisses people off. For as long as I've known him he's bugged people in authority. In the Mudcrutch days, it was the disc jockeys. Tom always rubs them the wrong way." But Petty would defend his actions, "I've found you can save a lot of time being direct and honest with people. I don't hold things in. I've seen people going around in circles for days and days just to avoid hurting each other's feelings." But decades later, Petty would explain his earlier outbursts: "I had a bad temper. I had a temper that could just flare up and take over. And I would stay mad for a long time." Identifying the origin of his anger, Petty revealed: "I had a tough childhood and took a lot of abuse. That rage was in me, and when it got away from me, I didn't know how to control it. But I could vent it in this music."

After a period of time, Petty grew tired of the punk label and began making statements that were critical of punk rock music. In an often-repeated quotation, Petty jokingly told the British press, "Call me a punk and I'll cut you." But Petty's anti-punk attitude would lead to a showdown with Johnny Rotten of the Sex Pistols. Petty recalled, "We were walking into our hotel lobby in England. I hear this snotty voice saying, 'Oh, it's the American pop star Tom Petty.' I ignore it, check into the hotel, and Stan [Lynch] and I start walking toward the elevator. We hear the same voice, kind of whining, 'There the hippies go. Bye-bye Tom.' At this point, Stan wheels around and starts heading for whoever it is. He wants to kill. Well, it's Johnny Rotten, surrounded by French journalists. Stan has to be restrained. I went over there and said, 'Who the... are you talking to?' Rotten immediately goes into his wounded-punk act, says nothing. There ain't no Robin Hoods in rock, man. All that punk shit was just a little too trendy."

But being labeled a punk band would also cause unexpected problems. As Petty recalled, "Those were wonderful days, though we really took shit from both sides. To the punks we were slow and wimpy and to the mainstream crowd we were too wild and original. Plus, they couldn't understand a band from Florida not playing 'Free Bird.'" Years later, Petty would adopt a less hostile opinion of the punk movement: "I liked punk but I wasn't gonna spike my hair up and pretend to be something I wasn't."

Then later after the punk label wore off, Tom Petty and the Heartbreakers found themselves referred to as a New Wave act. So it was no surprise when the group was given its own entry in the 389-page reference book, *The Trouser Press Guide to New Wave Records*. The term, New Wave, was popularized by Seymour Stein of Sire Records, who felt that "punk" had a negative connotation and could potentially harm an artist's career. At the time, Sire Record had a number of New Wave acts on its roster including Talking Heads and Depeche Mode.

In another misconception about Petty, some early biographies claimed he was born and raised in Tulsa. The mistake was even propagated by historian William W. Savage in the book, *A Short History of Popular Music in Oklahoma*, in which he called Petty "an Oklahoman." It did not help that Petty refused to identify his hometown in one early Heartbreakers press release, and called the information unimportant. As Dwight Twilley – himself a native of Tulsa – recalled, "A lot of people used to think Petty was from Tulsa. It used to really bother him." Perhaps it was his desire to distance himself from the city, but Petty would not perform in Tulsa until decades later in 2010.

▶ CHAPTER 10
THE DEBUT ALBUM

A few weeks before the release of their debut album, Tom Petty and the Heartbreakers returned to Florida for a brief respite and to play a few shows. Because the locals had not forgotten Mudcrutch, but were unfamiliar with the Heartbreakers, the band was occasionally billed as Tom Petty and Nightro, a name they had briefly used in California. One of the group's first Florida shows was staged at a small club in West Palm Beach. An employee of ABC Records went backstage and observed: "Petty was the most reserved member of the group, though he clearly possessed a star's charisma."

Petty was looking forward to his future, not reliving his past, when he told his hometown paper at the time, "Since I've been back here I've heard a lot about Mudcrutch, but I've forgotten about that band and I don't think about it at all. But every gig I've played in Florida so far, Mudcrutch has come up and it gets a little old."

Issued on November 9, 1976, the group's self-titled debut album, *Tom Petty And The Heartbreakers*, was initially a very slow seller. Petty, who had turned 26 a few weeks earlier, wrote all ten of the album's songs, two in collaboration with Mike Campbell. All of the tracks were less than four-minutes in length.

The Heartbreakers were anxious for the record to be released because without a physical, tangible product, few nightclubs were willing to book the band. Not surprisingly, Petty heard "Breakdown" on the radio for the very first time when he was in Gainesville. The single was issued shortly after the release of labelmate J.J. Cale's self-composed track "Cocaine," which later became a far bigger hit for Eric Clapton.

Launching their first *official* tour, Tom Petty and the Heartbreakers opened up for Kiss at the 3,900 seat Municipal Auditorium in Columbus, Georgia, and then headed to the Northeast. This would be the first time in Petty's life he would experience snowfall.

The Heartbreakers' debut U.S. single, "Breakdown," was initially ignored by radio. Petty explained the genesis of the song: "I wrote 'Breakdown' in the studio [around 1975], and the first version was seven minutes long, with this long guitar solo in the end. Everyone had gone home, and I was sitting there listening and in walks... Dwight Twilley. Right in the fadeout of the song... Twilley turns to me and says, 'That's the lick, man! How come he only plays it once at the end of the song? It's the whole hook.' I listened back, and he was right." Mike Campbell explained, "When I came up with that lick, I had been trying to add a slide part, but most of it didn't work. Somewhere near the end [of the song] I played that lick, but I never gave it a second thought. Tom called me later that night... and he made me get out of bed and go into the studio to record it right then." The revised version of the song was recorded in just a few takes.

In mid-December, Tom Petty and the Heartbreakers performed in New York City for the first time. Ironically, the group was booked at CBGB's, the city's famed punk mecca in the Bowery. As a rising but unknown West Coast band, the Heartbreakers drew members of the press and plenty of record industry insiders but few others to the Tuesday night show. Dressed completely in black, Petty and the Heartbreakers were well received by those in attendance. But while in the Big Apple, Petty first learned of the *other* Heartbreakers, a punk band established in May 1975 by two former members of the New York Dolls, Johnny Thunders and Jerry Nolan. Although Petty's Heartbreakers refused to change their name, the other band soon started calling itself Johnny Thunders' Heartbreakers. But over the next two years, some members of the rock press occasionally confused Tom Petty's group with the other Heartbreakers.

In early 1977, Shelter Records was concerned with keeping the Heartbreakers in the public spotlight. While the group was on the road in support of its debut album, Shelter decided to issue a promotional album, *Official Live 'Leg*, which consisted of tracks from a performance at Paul's Mall nightclub in Boston. The album was released in limited quantities without Petty's knowledge, and he was not pleased. This would mark the first of many times Petty would battle with his record label. (Ironically, the album – which was purposely meant to look like an unauthorized, bootleg release – was itself heavily bootlegged.)

Petty said afterwards: "Yeah, the *Live 'Leg* is really historical. I get letters all the time from people offering me outrageous sums of money for a copy. The thing is that it was recorded at our sixth gig ever. Al Kooper was in town, and he played with us, and it was fun. We just played this little dive, and somebody taped it on a four-track for radio. I never thought about it at all. Then, the radio [station] taped it, and [Shelter] decided to press it for radio stations. I never considered it an album at all. To me, it was just kind of silly. When I hear it, it sounds like the band getting together, and that's all." The album featured tracks from the first Heartbreakers album as well as an unreleased song, "Dog On The Run," and a cover version of an obscure Chuck Berry tune, "Jaguar And Thunderbird."

Returning to Los Angeles, Tom Petty and the Heartbreakers would soon prove themselves on the stage of the city's most important concert venue for up-and-coming rock acts. With some assistance from Robert Hilburn, the outspoken rock critic of *The Los Angeles Times*, the Heartbreakers landed a coveted slot at the legendary Whisky-a-Go-Go. The group was booked as the opening act for an emerging New Wave band, Blondie. With the Heartbreakers still considered a New Wave act by much of the rock press, on paper it looked like a smart double-bill.

But with the mismatched pairing, it was no surprise that Tom Petty and the Heartbreakers were met by a mostly disinterested audience on the first night of the weeklong residency. Instead, the majority of the crowd had paid to see blond bombshell, Debbie Harry. But Petty described the evolving situation: "We had enough buzz to play the Whisky-a-Go-Go, and we started playing [there] as an opening band for Blondie, who were also unknown, and, really, by the end of that week it just exploded. There were lines around the block." A *Rolling Stone* reviewer said of Petty's performance at the Whisky, "When he sings his 'Fooled Again' like Van Morrison in delirium, you believe him. His pinched face and wispy blond hair, ablaze in a crimson light, heighten the tension in the Heartbreakers' music. It's all powerful testimony, and the audience fans the spirit with a volley of exhortations and clenched fists." Phil Spector, the eccentric producer, was in the audience for a number of the performances.

While Petty has often spoken fondly of his time with Debbie Harry, she has rarely mentioned her weeklong stint with Petty in published interviews. After their successful shows at the Whisky, Tom Petty and the Heartbreakers continued to draw large crowds during a stint at the nearby Starwood club.

But Petty was still not comfortable as the main focus of the group. During this time, he rarely stepped away from the microphone and kept his stage banter to a minimum. As a result, the rock press began describing Petty and his bandmates as "moody."

▶ CHAPTER 11
AMERICAN GIRL

In February 1977, Shelter Records issued "American Girl" as the Heartbreakers' second U.S. single. Although the track would receive some airplay on AOR radio, pop stations mostly ignored the record. Unhappy with the timing of his label's actions, Petty later argued: "'American Girl' would have made it if its release had been planned right. It came out right when we went to Europe so we weren't around to support it at all."

Nonetheless, "American Girl" initially broke out on legendary Los Angeles radio station KROQ, which was the first major-market station in the country to focus on punk and New Wave music. Petty was later invited to the station for an on-air performance, but instead spent most of his time playing classic 1960s records by artists such as Wilson Pickett and the Rolling Stones.

Fittingly, Petty had composed "American Girl" on the nation's bicentennial, July 4, 1976. Petty later explained, "I wrote 'American Girl' really fast on the piano on that Fourth of July, and it's just a song about this chick. I remember the night well; the air-conditioning broke down and it was really hot. That was the same night we took the photos for the album cover. Anyway, we [worked on] 'American Girl' all night long, and it never occurred to me that it sounded like the Byrds."

The lyrics of "American Girl" mentioned U.S. Route 441– also known as 13th street when it passes through the city of Gainesville – which was the location of Mudcrutch's longtime musical base, Dub's. On the track, Stan Lynch admitted he was attempting to replicate what is known as "the Bo Diddley beat," but with limited success. He would later describe his playing as "my sorry attempt to sound like him." Over the years, Petty was forced to repeatedly squash a myth that the song was based on the death of a coed at a dormitory on the University of Florida campus.

A month after the triumphant string of shows at the Whisky, Tom Petty and the Heartbreakers returned to New York City for a three-day stint at the Bottom Line as the opening act for Roger McGuinn of the Byrds. Then after some dates in the Midwest – including a stop at the legendary Cleveland Agora, a venue known for booking promising new acts – the group returned to the West Coast.

On April 23rd, Tom Petty and the Heartbreakers performed a concert that was broadcast on KSAN in San Francisco. As Petty recalled, "Just before the band left America, we did a session at the Record Plant in Sausalito, San Francisco. We were doin' a radio concert and what you do is you go in, it's 24 tracks, you get a sound, there's a small audience of about 30 people in the studio, and they play it over the radio. The day before I was going down, Al Kooper called and said, 'Hey, can I come down and see that everything goes right?' So this was sort of Al's baby. He sat in and he did a great job. There was nothing you could overdub and it came out really well. And I got this really paranoid feeling that someone was going to press it up and start sending it around."

The following day, the Heartbreakers played an auditorium show for only the second time in their short career. Reviewing the concert, Robert Hilburn described the Heartbreakers as "a classic rock 'n' roll band, one whose sound hasn't been polluted by the excesses so common in today's recycled pop scene. There's a purity in the group's music that combines the shadowy, like-night compulsion of the Rolling Stones' *Exile On Main Street* with the classic American immediacy that can be traced back to Elvis and Eddie Cochran. The tone is urgent, defiant, desperate. Rather than overstate, his music leaves room for the imagination. His themes touch on familiar rock experiences but are free of the usual calculation and pretense. The emotion comes across as genuine and gripping."

Also that month, a music critic at *Sounds* magazine declared, "You can quote me on this: Petty's going to be a big star, the new Heartbreak Kid of rock."

But despite their modest success, the Heartbreakers were in the middle of a whirlwind of activity. As Stan Lynch later recalled, "The next thing I knew, the record was out and we were going to Europe. It all happened mystically in a way. There was no plan for any of this. All that was going on in 1976 was disco and we were coming out of left field.

We were making a very inexpensive, crude rock 'n' roll album with a record company that barely existed. Somehow we lucked out and... something happened."

Flying to Britain during the first week of May, the Heartbreakers began a two-week tour as the opening act for Chicago-born guitarist Nils Lofgren. To everyone's surprise, the Heartbreakers were an overnight sensation. As Petty recalled, "There were riots 15 minutes into the first gig. It's an incredible high – you're scared, you're excited, and you're pleased.... We'd never had people on stage knocking kids back down, and the girls breaking through, knocking us around and grabbing us around the waist while we're trying to play."

But with the sudden success came problems. The road crew for the headlining artist felt slighted by the attention showered on the little-known opening act. In retaliation, Lofgren's roadies would not allow Stan Lynch to set up his drum riser. Then with Tom Petty and the Heartbreakers continuing to garner strong audience response, Lofgren's roadies reacted by pushing the Heartbreakers' stage gear into a decreasingly smaller space on the stage. Petty ended his tour with Lofgren on May 26, with a performance at the 3,500 seat Apollo in Glasgow, Scotland.

Surprisingly, Tom Petty and the Heartbreakers were invited to perform on the prestigious BBC television program, *The Old Grey Whistle Test*. Petty, who had let his sun-bleached hair grow especially long during this period, was unusually animated, particularly during a passionate rendition of "Fooled Again." Around this time, Shelter issued a Heartbreakers single – "Anything That's Rock 'n' Roll" – in Britain, but not in the U.S.

Meanwhile, as legend would have it, Roger McGuinn heard "American Girl" on the radio shortly after its release. He later recalled: "the first time I heard of Tom was in 1976 when my manager played 'American Girl' and I joked with him and said 'When did I write that song?'" But a few months later, McGuinn decided to record a reworked rendition of the track for his 1977 album, *Thunderbyrd*.

But Petty had to deal with some unforeseen consequences after McGuinn recorded the song. Petty told an interviewer in 1978: "He rang up the office and asked me to come over, and I went over and just started playing. So he said, 'show me how that song goes,' and I showed him, and overnight it was on their album. Ever since, I've read reviews about us that say, 'and they did a great version of the Byrds' old hit, 'American Girl,'' and it bugs the hell out of me. I wrote it!" Although Petty's version of the song appeared to feature a jangly 12-string Rickenbacker guitar – which was McGuinn's signature sound in the Byrds – Petty and Campbell achieved a similar effect with just two 6-string guitars.

But nonetheless, Petty remained in awe of McGuinn and the Byrds. Now living in the same city as McGuinn, Petty attended a number of concerts by the Byrds offshoot group, McGuinn, Clark & Hillman. Al Hersh, the trio's road manager, recalled in the book, *Mr. Tambourine Man*, "Tom Petty was a real groupie. I can't tell you how many dressing rooms I threw him out of. He was sending me music for years and I thought it was really good.... I was trying to get Roger [McGuinn] to record some Petty stuff because no one was recording [Petty's songs] at the time and Roger wasn't writing shit. I thought it would be the perfect match. Tom Petty became what Roger could have been if he continued to create. Instead he resented it. We ended up recording one of his songs, but it was a really tough thing to record it. Roger even changed some of the words. He always felt that Petty wouldn't amount to anything and was a cheap imitation of him. And we all know what happened."

Eventually, Petty would tire of the comparisons between the Heartbreakers and the Byrds: "We've always been cast in the twelve string sound; those Byrds comparisons. I know we sound like them at times, and God knows I've tried not to, but I get a bit tired of hearing them now." But Mike Campbell gave a more straightforward explanation: "The problem with doing a 12-string [guitar] solo is that it's extremely difficult to not sound like Roger McGuinn... Soloing a 12-string just leads you into that style." But in a short period of time, the Heartbreakers had forged their own musical identity and the comparisons with the Byrds were no longer valid.

*   *   *   *   *   *

Following their British tour, Tom Petty and the Heartbreakers played several shows across Continental Europe. At the annual Pinkpop Festival in Geleen, Netherlands, the Heartbreakers were on a bill that included Nils Lofgren and several other acts including the Kinks and Golden Earring. Petty performed just four songs and closed his short set with "Breakdown." In mid-June, the Heartbreakers decided to return to

Britain and stage their own tour. The group traveled around in a rented bread van for what was dubbed the Terminal Romance UK Tour. The group's manager Tony Dimitriades recalled, "We went around Europe, then came back to England and did a headline tour of the same venues we'd just opened in." The influential rock magazine *Melody Maker* put Petty on its front cover and described the Heartbreakers as "one of the most in-demand bands currently playing in this country."

Then during a return trip to mainland Europe for a performance on the German television show *Rockpalast*, Tom Petty and the Heartbreakers were suspected of transporting hashish. Traveling from Holland – where possession of the drug was legal – the group was stopped after a customs agent discovered a hash pipe in Stan Lynch's suitcase. Reacting quickly, Ron Blair managed to swallow the large chunk of hash he was carrying in his pocket. Then after inspecting the group's bottles of aspirin and vitamin pills, the overzealous agents accused the Heartbreakers of trying to smuggle cocaine and LSD. After the Heartbreakers were stripped-searched and questioned for nearly four hours, a panicked producer from *Rockpalast* convinced the agents to release the group. Eventually, the Heartbreakers made it to the television studio in time for their scheduled performance. But a dazed and glassy-eyed Ron Blair barely made it through the group's 12-song, hour-long set.

Meanwhile, the two Heartbreakers tours across Britain had paid off when both "American Girl" and "Anything That's Rock 'n' Roll" reached the lower portions of the U.K. top-40 that summer. Additionally, the group's debut album would peak at #24 on the British charts, a respectable achievement for a new act. An American rock critic reported that "the European tour gave [the Heartbreakers] their first real taste of monster success. Crowds were large and ecstatic wherever they played.... The English papers decided that Petty was going to be The Next Big Thing and one German paper ran a headline that" called Tom Petty the "new Mick Jagger."

Petty recounted: "We got on the covers of the music weeklies and [the leading rock paper] *NME*, and we did *Top Of The Pops* on the TV. We were beyond thrilled. By the time we left England, we were a headlining band, and then we flew home and got off the plane, and you're nothing again." Echoing Petty's assessment, Stan Lynch recounted that the tour across Europe meant "big hotel rooms and lots of women. And then it was back to California, and I was back living in the basement." Petty later admitted, "We probably would've been dropped [by Shelter Records] if it hadn't been for what happened in England."

After returning to the U.S., the Heartbreakers demanded more promotion for their album, which was now a proven seller in Europe. Then in August, the Heartbreakers launched a West Coast tour, beginning with shows at the Old Waldorf in San Francisco and the Whisky-a-Go-Go in Los Angeles. Soon, the group was opening for a series of rock bands including Meat Loaf, the J. Geils Band, and Rush, as well as a number of New Wave acts including the Rubinoos, Be Bop Deluxe, and Elvis Costello & The Attractions. On the road, a number of the headlining artists – particularly Ray Davies of the Kinks – taught Petty about showmanship and how to handle an audience. During this period, Tom Petty and the Heartbreakers would often open their shows with "Surrender," an original composition that would not see an official release for nearly two decades.

But the bookings were sometimes haphazard. As Petty recalled, "We got to this gig in Chicago – it was a jazz club. We were on with Tom Scott and the L.A. Express. We walked out – we had these Vox amps – and somebody yelled, 'What is this, the Monkees?' That did not go well."

But eventually, Petty realized that the constant grind as an opening act was hurting the Heartbreakers' longterm success. Petty was now determined to headline shows as a means of growing the band's popularity – even if that meant performing for significantly smaller crowds. As Petty recalled: "One night with the Doobie Brothers, in Wheeling, West Virginia, was particularly bad. You had to take what you were given as far as stage room and monitors. I was so pissed. We played and went back to the hotel. I called a meeting and said, 'We're never opening again. We're just going to play for whoever comes to see us.'"

But Petty was later forced to modify his strategy. As Rick Derringer observed the following year, "Tom's a good example of people in trouble. I know him.... He had one album that got real big, created a name, put him out on the road... and now he's strugglin'.... He refused to be anything but a headliner on this tour, and all of sudden he had to rescind on that ultimatum and start being an opening act and take second billing.... He had to cancel three or four weeks of his dates 'cause he wasn't drawin' the people he thought he should." But Petty viewed the situation as a temporary setback. Soon, the Heartbreakers were again headlining shows.

*　　*　　*　　*　　*　　*

In September 1977, Tom Petty and the Heartbreakers enjoyed belated success when their debut album finally reached *Billboard's* Top 200 sales chart, a full ten months after its release. It took renewed interest in the track, "Breakdown," to ignite sales of the album. The song had received widespread exposure after its placement on the soundtrack of the movie, *FM*. Making a cameo appearance in the film, Petty was interviewed in the studio of a fictional Los Angeles radio station, Q-Sky. Although the film was hardly a blockbuster, the soundtrack album was certified platinum and several of the tracks received heavy airplay on album-rock stations across the country.

Peaking at #40 on the U.S. pop chart, "Breakdown" remained an enduring fan favorite throughout Petty's career. Although the recorded version of the track was a mere 2:44 in length, the live rendition often surpassed six-minutes and included an improvised monologue by Petty, during which time he would infuse a bit of theatrics by violently strangling his microphone.

Taking advantage of their newfound popularity among U.S. record buyers, Tom Petty and the Heartbreakers had performed nearly 200 concerts by the end of 1977. Petty explained at the time, "We knew the first album was really good and that's why we were playing constantly all last year. We refused for that album not to succeed. We could see that when we played the songs, we were getting a great reaction; so we tried to play all the time so the following would keep building. It accelerated the entire year."

Meanwhile, Petty was hit hard by the sudden death of one of his musical idols. On August 16, 1977, Elvis Presley was found dead on the floor of a bathroom at his Graceland mansion. Petty recalled, "It was a surreal day, it was black when I got up. I had just gotten out of bed and I heard there was an earthquake in Santa Monica. Then the phone rang and Elvis was dead. I went into a blur for maybe twenty-four hours."

▶ CHAPTER 12
TOM PETTY: SINGER & SONGWRITER

Tom Petty possesses one of the most identifiable voices in rock and roll. His unique voice has been called bluesy, expressive, and raw. But on numerous occasions, Petty has been accused of trying to sing like either Roger McGuinn or Bob Dylan. (Conversely, Bob Dylan has made a career of copying the vocal style of folk pioneer Woody Guthrie.) But a closer examination would reveal that Petty was more influenced by the vocal phrasings of his musical idol, George Harrison. But for whatever reason, Petty has rarely attempted to emulate the singing style of his first musical influence, Elvis Presley.

Petty's often anguished vocal delivery was perfectly suited for songs about lost love such as "A Woman In Love" and "Breakdown." The slight raspiness in his voice was the product of his lifestyle. Petty explained: "I'm not careful about my voice: I smoke and do other sorts of bodily harm to myself, I stay up all hours, I'm not like in training to sing better. The thing about vocals, the only thing about vocals for me is believability, it's not about being in tune or hitting a note, it's not doing anything except making people believe what you're singing." Similarly, Stan Lynch has observed: "Tom's always been a style singer. He's never gonna do Pavarotti, but he's a style man.... Tom has his own way of thinking, walking, [and] talking."

But Petty's strongest musical attribute is his proficiency as a songwriter. Even after the Heartbreakers had recorded two well-received albums, Petty still believed he was destined to succeed as a songwriter, not a performer. As Mike Campbell has said, "[Petty] was the only guy from Gainesville who could even come close to writing and singing songs of the quality of Lennon's and McCartney's."

Petty remembered his first songwriting attempt: "The first time I tried to write [a song] was when I was 14, after I got an electric guitar. I put a song together, and it wasn't that bad! The writing came natural to me. I thought everybody could do it." Petty would continue to write music as he passed through various groups.

In trying to identify the source of his musical creativity, Petty explained: "Songwriting is a hard thing to understand. Who knows where it comes from – it's kind of supernatural. It just appears. It's never the same; there's no formula for it. It just happens, you know? Some days you can pick up a guitar and it's very friendly to you, very sweet and good. Then there are other days I just put it away and don't try very much. But those 'friendly' days, when things are sounding good, songs tend to appear."

While Petty would originally compose songs whenever a creative opportunity arose, in the mid-1980s he decided to stop writing music while on tour. Instead, he preferred to craft songs at home or, more commonly, in the studio. As he explained, "[after a concert] I don't feel like playing the guitar. Some people go back to their room or carry portable studios on the road. I couldn't possibly do that. It's always after you come back from the tour and you feel like a civilian." Preferring to compose songs in a relaxed atmosphere, Petty observed: "I find that the less I think about them the better they are. When I bear down and think about writing a song, it usually sounds like a labored sort of thing. So I try to deal in things that will keep my interest but not overly labor me. I don't want to feel like I just dug a ditch."

But as Petty admits, a melody or lyric can strike him unexpectedly: "You're in the bathroom when it hits, or just walking around the house and it's comin' in, it's comin' in and you just pick up an instrument, and everywhere at home I've got these little cassette recorders, but – oh no! – there's no tape in it. So you look everywhere tryin' to find a tape. You go over to David Crosby's album [cover] or something and say, 'Sorry, David, but I gotta get this down!' I just get enough down so I can remember the idea when I wake up the next day, and that's how it goes. It's as random as that."

Stan Lynch revealed the inner workings of Petty's songwriting process: "He'll come up with real scattered ideas and sometimes you can see that he's like a songwriter in a supermarket with his ideas. Tommy's got a warehouse of ideas – some of them are like in the antique department; some of them are frozen – they're all over the store and he'll come in with just pieces. He doesn't really know where the feel, groove, or beat is going to be. It's not concrete in his head." But Mike Campbell described the process differently: "Tom's trip is based around his voice against his own rhythm part. He'll bring me a song, and before I even know what the song is, I'll start playing along. And usually before we've reached the chorus or second verse, I've got an understanding of what part will fit against what he's playing. We generally find the essence of the song in the first couple of run-throughs." Lynch added, "I've seen songs come in every possible way and under every possible condition. I've seen them come in as completed demos. I've seen them come in as an acoustic guitar riff that turned into a real electric guitar riff. I've seen them just come in as 'What the hell is that going to be?'"

Lyrically, Petty has repeatedly employed a proven recipe: "I'm real good with ambiguity. You've only got four minutes or so in a song. If you nail things down too much, it doesn't seem to hold up to repeated listenings. You wear out on it quicker if you get a narrative song and you stay with the storyline really close." Campbell added: "There's times I'll hear a line and I'll think, 'He must be writing that about Jane, or somebody.' But you can never really tell. We've all been hurt, you know. Tom doesn't write 'Good Day Sunshine.'" If fact, Petty wrote very few upbeat, optimistic songs during his early years with the Heartbreakers.

As for his grasp of language and the ability to pen meaningful lyrics, Petty admitted: "I never was a big poem reader. I didn't study poets. I always did really well in English in school. I don't know why I could do it effortlessly." Benmont Tench observed: "Tom doesn't want to sing somebody else's lyrics, he wants to sing about what's on his mind. He doesn't need any help."

Eventually, Petty would create characters within his songs such as Spike or Eddie Rebel. Warren Zanes, a member of the 1980s rock act the Del Fuegos and former Vice President of the Rock and Roll Hall of Fame, observed: "Petty's stories were distilled in such a way that it allowed you to identify with the protagonist in the deepest way." Petty's creativity as a lyricist also permitted him to write from a woman's perspective. As a result, Petty was able to attract a sizable female fanbase, from the start of his career.

Petty composed most of his biggest hits on a classic Dove model, Gibson guitar. He explained: "We tend to work from the guitar a lot, so I always move the key around to fit the voice. I'll say, 'You know, I'll have to push my voice up to that key because it doesn't sound right if I bring it down low.' Sometimes you gotta compromise a little bit because the guitar is unforgiving with the open strings. So most of what we did was based around the sounds we were getting on the guitar. I did move the keys around a bit quite a lot when we were starting out. We really got into the idea of 'Hey, we know we've got something here, so let's make it work.'"

After recording a basic demo, the Heartbreakers would experiment with various aspects of the track. But on some occasions, Petty was happier with the original demo than the final recorded version, which might have taken weeks to complete.

Remaining humble about his songwriting abilities, Petty admitted: "I'm pretty rough on myself, as far as giving a pat on the back. I get nervous, to this day, bringing a song to the band. They're tough. It runs the gamut, from being very quiet, not saying anything. That drives me insane.... They all liked 'Refugee'.... They didn't like anything on *Full Moon Fever*." Although the various members of the band would offer their suggestions during the songwriting process, Petty was always the final arbiter: the Heartbreakers were not a democracy and Tom Petty was clearly the leader.

Although Campbell has remained Petty's longtime songwriting partner, he has often been a reluctant collaborator. Petty recounted: "I have to go to his house and listen to everything he's done, because he won't offer up. And I've found some great songs. He wasn't hiding them, he just didn't think they were worth seeing." Later in his career, Petty would work with songwriters outside of the Heartbreakers including Bob Dylan, Jeff Lynne, Dave Stewart, and members of his other two bands, the Traveling Wilburys and Mudcrutch.

As singer-songwriter Kevin Devine concluded, "[Petty's] stuff is deceptively simple. It sounds easily arrived at, but it's totally flawlessly executed music, perfectly constructed songs, recorded and performed well." In his overall assessment of the songwriting process, Petty once proclaimed: "Once you have a good song, the rest of it is just making a record. Which isn't hard for us to do."

▶ CHAPTER 13
YOU'RE GONNA GET IT

After spending most of the previous year on the road, Tom Petty and the Heartbreakers were back in the studio at the start of 1978. But the group had to grapple with the turmoil at Shelter's partner label, ABC Records. Petty said at the time, "when we got back ABC Records had changed their personnel, they'd got a new president, and a whole new bunch of people, and a whole bunch of labels came in and it became like a real tug-of-war. All we wanted was to make sure the records were promoted – which had never been done, there had never been an ad at all. It did work out good, but it was a real drag for a while. We would have had another record soon after our return to the States but as a result of the legal stuff we couldn't record so we just stayed on the road."

But when the debut Heartbreakers album finally captured the attention of the American public, the group was caught by surprise and desperately wanted to return to the road as quickly as possible. Out of necessity, Petty and the Heartbreakers approached the sessions for their second album with a sense of urgency. Petty attempted to hire Jeff Lynne of the Electric Light Orchestra to produce the album, but was told, "well, he doesn't do outside projects." Although Denny Cordell would be credited with producing the second Heartbreakers album, most of the sessions were actually conducted by Noah Shark, with Petty receiving credit as a co-producer.

The album was recorded at the legendary Sound City studio in Van Nuys. Opened in 1969, the poorly-lit studio was infamous for its brown shag carpeting on the walls, rumpled couches, and beat-up equipment with stray wires. But countless A-list rockers booked time at the studio including Fleetwood Mac, Pat Benatar, Cheap Trick, Neil Young, Guns N' Roses, and the Red Hot Chili Peppers. The main allure of Sound City was a very rare Neve model-8028, custom-made, German mixing console. Dave Grohl, who later produced a documentary about Sound City, explained: "The Neve boards were considered like the Cadillacs of recording consoles. They're these really big, behemoth-looking recording desks; they kind of look like they're from the Enterprise in Star Trek.... and to any studio geek or gear enthusiast it's like the coolest toy in the world." (Decades later, Petty would acquire an elusive Neve for his home studio, after stumbling upon the mixing board during a visit to New York City.)

Recorded over a four-month period, *You're Gonna Get It* was originally titled *Terminal Romance*. Wanting to record an album that was different from their debut release, the Heartbreakers were more confident in their abilities this time around. Experimenting with sound, the group employed a number of odd effects including the whirl of a toy helicopter and noises from a pinball gallery.

Before arriving at the sessions, Petty had already written two of the album's tracks, "I Need To Know" and "Listen To Heart," both of which were already a part of the group's live setlist. Another track, "Magnolia," was intended for Roger McGuinn's 1977 album *Thunderbyrd*. But with McGuinn unable to record a satisfactory version of the song, Petty went back to Mike Campbell's original demo, which became the basis for the Heartbreakers' rendition. Meanwhile, the sessions were delayed for a short period when bassist Ron Blair was hospitalized. Then after the completion of the album, the Heartbreakers hired a second manager, Elliot Roberts.

For the cover of their second album, Tom Petty and the Heartbreakers demanded a group shot. But Petty was convinced to scrap the first version of the cover – an upbeat portrait of the band taken by famed photographer Annie Leibovitz – in favor of a simpler, more moody shot. But the album's cover did little to dispel the public perception that the Heartbreakers were a punk rock band: Petty and his bandmates posed with grim-faced expressions, with the normally non-confrontational Benmont Tench offering a particularly threatening stare.

Released in May 1978, *You're Gonna Get It* was quickly embraced by album-rock radio. Petty had written all ten songs, two in collaboration with Mike Campbell. The album's lead-off single, "I Need To Know," just barely missed reaching the top-40. Petty explained the song's origin: "I was trying to make a song like Wilson Pickett's 'Land Of 1000 Dances.' That's one of my favorite records. I actually wrote that at

Crescent Beach, Florida, at a friend's house."

The followup single, "Listen To Her Heart," was the victim of a mild controversy, with Petty refusing his record company's suggestion to substitute the word "cocaine" with "champagne." Unfortunately, it was that refusal which kept the song from being added to many top-40 playlists. The song's lyrics were inspired by an odd incident at the home of an infamous R&B singer: "My wife Jane had gone, with (producer) Denny Cordell, over to Ike Turner's place. And she had been kinda cornered by Ike Turner and barely got away. She was saying it was this wild experience. I don't really think I was writing to Ike. I think it gave me an idea and I took it from there."

Although Petty disliked appearing on television, he came to respect the power of the medium to attract new fans. As Petty once said, "The only good rock 'n' roll I saw on television was the Beatles on *Ed Sullivan*. That was about the last thing I remember that really impressed me." From a performance in May 1978, Tom Petty and the Heartbreakers appeared on the June 2nd episode of the weekly NBC music program, *The Midnight Special*. After country singer Crystal Gayle introduced the Heartbreakers, the group performed – and did not lip sync – three songs, "I Need To Know," "Listen To Her Heart," and "American Girl." While on the set, Petty enjoyed a memorable moment: "I actually *danced* with [the show's announcer] Wolfman Jack. Had a great time." Also on the bill were Chuck Mangione and Eddie Rabbitt. (Ironically, a video clip performance by Bob Dylan and his longtime backing group, the Band, would air on the same episode.)

Returning to England in mid-June, Tom Petty and the Heartbreakers again appeared on the BBC program, *The Old Grey Whistle Test*. The entire band was dressed in dark clothing; Petty wore aviator-style sunglasses and was far more self-assured than during his previous appearance.

Then on June 24th, Tom Petty and the Heartbreakers performed at the prestigious Knebworth Festival, just north of London. The group appeared on a bill with Jefferson Starship, Devo, Brand X, Roy Harper, the Atlanta Rhythm Section, and headlining act, Genesis. The Heartbreakers were booked as a replacement for Jeff Beck, who bowed out after he was unable to assemble a suitable band. Knebworth promoter Freddy Bannister had never been to a Heartbreakers concert but was still eager to book the band.

After a performance by the Akron-based New Wave act Devo – which was met with an unfriendly barrage of mud, bottles, and verbal abuse from the hostile crowd – Tom Petty and the Heartbreakers took the stage and were well received. At the start of his performance, Petty announced to the crowd that he was not used to playing in broad daylight. Wearing Beatle boots and a top hat that someone in the audience had thrown to him, Petty got his first taste of performing at a large British music festival. Petty later recalled, "I didn't want to do it, but we didn't have time to do a whole tour of the country.... The show was fine and everything, just pretty distant to me. I really felt distant from 100,000 people."

Three days later, the Heartbreakers played a surprise gig at London's famed Marquee Club, the location of the very first concert by the Rolling Stones in 1962. But not all went well for the Heartbreakers inside the small Soho venue. The concert had been oversold and the room was packed well beyond its normal capacity. In the middle of his performance, Petty passed out on stage from the intense heat. After screaming for the blaring stage lights to be turned off, Petty put his head in a bucket of cold water and finished his set.

Returning to the U.S., the group began to enjoy a new level of success. In July, *You're Gonna Get It* was certified gold by the R.I.A.A. with sales of half a million copies. Now playing in larger rooms, Petty was embraced by the rock press, especially *Circus* and *Creem* magazines, both of which began to follow the Heartbreakers' every move. But playing larger venues had a downside. As Petty explained at the time: "We haven't played bars in a while and I miss it. You can see everybody right there. I don't mind playing bars, they're fun."

Around this time, Tom Petty and The Heartbreakers were asked to star in the low-budget movie, *Rock 'n' Roll High School*. But the group had no interest in spending several months on a film project. Instead, Petty advised the film's producers to offer the role to the Ramones. Although the Ramones were paid a mere $25,000, the Heartbreakers had been asked to work for no salary – in exchange for the exposure.

Then in late-1978, the Heartbreakers introduced a new track from their upcoming album. The song, "Refugee," would take the group in a more mature, commercially-accessibly direction.

In what would be a strange year for Petty, he suffered a series of potentially career-ending mishaps in 1978. During a heavy rainstorm in

March, his kitchen ceiling collapsed, nearly injuring him. Then at a July concert in Miami – one of several shows as the opening act for Patti Smith – Petty was struck by a surge of electricity when he touched his microphone stand. Dazed and forced to leave the stage for several minutes, he eventually returned and finished his performance.

Then on December 30, 1978, during a performance at the Winterland Ballroom in San Francisco, one day before promoter Bill Graham would close the legendary venue, Petty barely averted serious bodily harm. As he stood at the edge of the stage, he was pulled into the audience. It took four fast-acting roadies to yank a dazed and shaken Petty out of the frenzied crowd and push him back onto the stage. In a matter of seconds, Petty had suffered a number of injuries: "I have a real heavy vest and they ripped that, my whole shirt went, I had a neckerchief tied real tight around my neck and... it's hanging down to my chest because it had been pulled and twisted. I lost handfuls of hair and my whole lip was busted. It was this weird sensation of falling and never hitting the ground and people diving in. They're crazy people when they're that worked up." Several years after the incident, Petty observed: "I've noticed that I can't get near an audience as Bruce Springsteen does. They rip me up. Bruce can walk through them. I think they look at him as their buddy. With me, there seems to be some violent or sexual vibes. I'm the last guy on earth to be violent."

▶ CHAPTER 14
I FOUGHT THE LAW

In late-1978, Tom Petty and the Heartbreakers made the realization that, creatively, they had gone as far as they could with Denny Cordell as their producer. Cordell also recognized that fact and in discussions with Petty, recommended Jimmy Iovine. But instead of Petty approaching Iovine, it was actually Iovine who discovered that the Heartbreakers needed a new producer and made the initial contact. Iovine recalled, "I heard Tom Petty's first two albums and then [music industry insider] Debbie Gold called me up and said that Tom's looking for a record producer. 'Not any more, he's not!' I said. I got Denny Cordell on the phone and said, 'Hey, man, I can make a hit record with this guy in a minute. In a *heartbeat*, okay?' I felt I knew exactly what to do to get him to the next step."

Iovine recounted his first meeting with Petty: "The first two songs he played me were 'Refugee' and 'Here Comes My Girl.' That doesn't happen every day. I always wait for someone to walk into my office and tell me they're playing me their new album and have two songs that [are as] good as [those] first two songs."

Petty recalled: "At the time, Iovine had only done the Patti Smith record [1978's *Easter*] as a producer. That's the reason I gave him the job – because I'd heard 'Because The Night' with those great tom-toms. The songs were pretty well written for [our] album when Jimmy showed up. That album was a whole rediscovery of the studio for me, because we'd had our own way of doing it, which was pretty amateur. Then (engineer) Shelley Yakus came in from New York, and these guys were really serious about this stuff. They'd be gettin' a drum sound for a week. And I'd be pullin' my hair out, goin', What is going on? We've never spent more than an hour with the drums.... So it was a real educational experience, and probably one of our better albums, really." At the start of the sessions, Stan Lynch had purchased some better quality drums at the urging of Shelley Yakus.

But soon, Petty had to deal with a far more pressing matter. He was about to engage in a costly and emotionally-ravaging lawsuit which could have permanently ended his music career.

*   *   *   *   *   *

The record business is just that – a business. And more often than not, it is an ugly, ruthless, and backstabbing business operated by smiling, fast-taking shysters in stylish suits who promise quick wealth and fame. The history of rock and roll is littered with grim stories of artists and songwriters who were cheated by their labels, their managers, and even their own bandmates. Pioneering rocker Little Richard sold his copyright to "Tutti Frutti" to Specialty Records for a measly $50. Buddy Holly offered the lucrative co-ownership of his compositions "That'll Be The Day," "Not Fade Away," and "Peggy Sue" to producer Norman Petty in exchange for a promise he would use his clout with music industry contacts in New York City. In the fictional film *The Five Heartbeats*, a singer who refused to sign a new contract with his record company was held by his feet, upside-down, from a window in a high-rise hotel; the episode was allegedly based on a real-life event in Jackie Wilson's tragic career.

Even a young Bob Dylan eagerly signed his first recording contract in 1961 without the aid of an attorney, simply because he was amazed that a major label was showing interest in him and his music. Dylan recounted the meeting with Columbia Records executive John Hammond: "He put a contract in front of me, the standard one, and I signed it right then and there, didn't get absorbed into the details – didn't need a lawyer, advisor or anybody looking over my shoulder. I would have gladly signed whatever form he put in front of me."

In 1975, Tom Petty had unwittingly signed over his publishing rights to Shelter Records. Publishing rights are long-term moneymakers in which one hit song could potentially generate hundreds of thousands of dollars. Therefore, record companies were eager to retain at least a portion of the publishing profits. Eventually, most musicians became wise to the financial aspects of the publishing side of music and made smarter choices. But Petty was not schooled in the inner workings of the music industry and became a victim of his own inexperience. Even with two solid albums under his belt, Petty was earning little money and remained heavily in debt to his label.

But the future of Petty's career was not entirely in his hands. In 1975, ABC Records had acquired the distribution rights to Shelter Records. Then in 1977, Shelter transferred the distribution rights of all its artists – except for J. J. Cale and Tom Petty – to Arista Records. ABC retained the rights to Cale and Petty. Then on February 1, 1978, Shelter and ABC Records issued a press release to announce that Petty had signed a new contract. But the following year, ABC would fully acquire Shelter Records. Then later that same year, ABC was itself sold to another label, MCA Records, for a reported $30 million.

However, in a surprise move, Tom Petty informed MCA that his contract was "non-assignable" and would not transfer upon the label's acquisition of ABC. At that point, MCA informed Petty that he had a contractual debt of $575,000, which could be repaid only if he remained with the label and promised to deliver an additional *six* albums. As one music writer observed: "it is no secret that the main reason the conglomerate bought ABC was to get Petty, Jimmy Buffett, and the Steely Dan catalogue, so they were not about to let one of those plumbs slip away from them."

Petty recalled: "It was the principle: the idea of being told to report to those guys really pissed me off. Plus it was the knowledge that we would remain under that old deal, which wasn't worth shit. I could work my ass off for the rest of my life, and for every dime I saw, the people that set me up would've seen ten times as much. And at that point, MCA's attitude was, 'We know your next album's going to be bigger than your last, and we got you, son: the deal's done.' .... [But] as soon as they thought my action might set an industry precedent, they rolled out the big guns. That's when I realized these guys were mean. It was like they were after me just because I had the potential to do something. For that, they would destroy me."

By challenging a powerful record company with deep pockets, Petty was risking his entire career. Other rockers had battled their record companies with mixed results. When John Fogerty tried to get out of an unfair contract with Fantasy Records – in which he still owed eight albums to the label – his recording career was sidelined for nearly a decade, until 1985, when he enjoyed a major comeback. Tom Scholz, the founder of the rock group Boston, engaged in a seven-year court battle with his record company, CBS, after the label sued him for $20 million and suspended all royalty payments because he had not delivered the group's third album on time. After spending millions in legal fees, Scholz eventually prevailed. And Don Henley attempted to break his contract with Geffen Records by citing a 1944 legal precedent in a lawsuit involving actress Olivia de Havilland, which barred California movie studios from enforcing contracts longer than a seven-year term. Henley settled his suit out of court but only after making some costly concessions to his record company.

In response to Petty's defiant actions, MCA and Shelter Records both filed lawsuits, charging him with a "breach of contract." During the legal proceedings, Petty cut his ties with Cordell. Although Cordell had given Petty his big break, it was obvious that the terms of Petty's original recording contract were bleeding him dry, no matter how successful he might be in the future. Cordell later defended his business practices at Shelter Records, arguing that he gave many other artists and songwriters the same financial deal Petty received, but most of the others had never managed to earn any profit for the company. Cordell contended that signing Petty and placing him on a salary was a monetary risk and therefore the label was due any financial rewards.

Petty petitioned the court to invalidate his contracts with both ABC and Shelter, arguing that he could more easily pay off his debts by signing with a different record company. As *BAM* magazine reported, "When word got around that Petty was fighting MCA over the contract, numerous other labels swooped down and made lucrative offers to Petty, with some even offering to cover the legal costs that might be incurred from a long battle.... [But] MCA succeeded in getting a court order blocking Petty from negotiating with other labels as long as his contractual situation was unresolved."

Meanwhile, Petty would continue to work on his third album. After spending his mornings and afternoons in court being deposed and grilled by high-priced lawyers, Petty would spend his evenings trying to compose and record music.

But the level of animosity in court was often surpassed by what occurred at the group's nightly recording sessions. Stan Lynch and Jimmy Iovine were constantly at each other's throats, with Lynch frequently threatening to quit and Iovine threatening to bring in another drummer. In fact, Lynch quit on more than one occasion and Iovine occasionally brought in other drummers including Jim Gordon, Phil Seymour from the Dwight Twilley Band, and B.J. Wilson from Procol Harum. But none of the replacements had the right sound for the Heartbreakers. Lynch recalled his reaction to Iovine's decision to bring in outside drummers: "I thought they were idiots for wanting to try someone else. The kindest thing I could say was 'help yourself.'"

Then during one heated moment, an exasperated Petty reached his breaking point and was ready to abandon both the album and his music career. After a verbal confrontation with Lynch – during one of the times he had quit the band – Petty was about to do the same. Petty recalled: "That's when I thought I couldn't take it anymore. I went to the studio one afternoon and I told Iovine, 'I'm going out the back door. You tell everybody I'll call them later.' Iovine stopped me in the hall and said, 'T.P., look what you're doing.... You gotta work this out.'" But Petty was worried about his future: "If I lost, we were trapped. They were never gonna promote the records or even buy ads. So I said, 'What's the point of making the records if no one's gonna hear 'em?'"

Fortunately, the level-headed Iovine helped Petty to put the situation in perspective. Petty then telephoned Lynch, but after a few more choice words, Lynch quit again. Then with Petty and Lynch opening up their souls to each other, the rift was healed and both men returned to the studio. Years later, Lynch would soften his opinion about Iovine's tactics: "In Jimmy's defense, he was under a lot of pressure. He was hired as a hit producer to make hits. He wasn't there to listen to my opinion. In retrospect, I can see that."

But Ron Blair was also unhappy with the pace and structure of the sessions. As he recalled, "When we started doing the third record, some heavy kind of producer guys came in and really tried to professionalize it. And from that point on, it entered the uptight era. It just got uptight from really that moment on."

With MCA claiming ownership of the album's unfinished tracks, Petty had to resort to some fancy footwork to keep the master tapes out of sight. Petty recalled: "We'd be working in the studio and then they'd say 'You gotta look out for the marshals, the marshals are gonna come in tonight and grab the tapes.' It got to the point where poor Bugs (the Heartbreakers' chief roadie) was just carrying all these tapes around in his car, and moving 'em, so on the stand I could honestly say, 'I don't know where the tapes are.' 'Cause these guys would have released the album in whatever condition it was in. It got to where the judge came into the studio and they got out all the tapes and they had to make legal arguments as to what is a record and what isn't a record – is this finished? I was kinda just sittin' there mute, listenin' to these guys discuss whether it was done. It was totally ridiculous."

Needing cash to survive, Petty wanted to schedule a few concerts. He recalled: "Eventually I convinced the judge to let me go on a Californian tour so I could make some money. The MCA lawyers were telling the judge I couldn't do it because I'd incur all these debts and I couldn't show any security. So I said to the judge, 'But judge there is no security in rock 'n' roll,' and he laughed and let me do it." In late July, an exhausted Tom Petty led the Heartbreakers on a short tour across California, which was dubbed the "Why MCA?" or "The Lawsuit Tour." With fans fearing the Heartbreakers might never tour again, all five of the shows were sold out. During the short tour, the group introduced two new tracks – "Here Comes My Girl" and "Even The Losers" – and performed a rock oldie that summed up their legal battle, "I Fought The Law."

Selling most of his possessions to raise money for the mounting legal fees, Petty, who was living in Santa Barbara at the time, had spent half a million dollars defending himself. Oddly enough, attorneys for both sides of the lawsuit worked for the same law firm! With little to show for his effort, Petty had few options left. He then decided to up the ante with a new strategy – declaring insolvency. On May 23, Petty filed for Chapter 11 bankruptcy – a legal plea requesting the reorganization of his debt. When MCA filed a countersuit demanding payment of $576,638, the bankruptcy filing revealed that Petty had a net worth totaling a mere $56,845. In legal documents, Petty provided a list of his assets which included household goods, $6,777; clothing, $113; and cash on hand, just $36. As one music magazine asked at the time, "Have legal hassles and bankruptcy torpedoed this rocker's career?"

Meanwhile, Petty's bankruptcy action forced MCA to offer a quick solution if it wanted him to remain with the label. If the court approved Petty's bankruptcy, then his previous legal agreements with Shelter and ABC would be voided. With MCA realizing Petty was about to break loose from his past contracts, the label was eager to make a deal.

As a compromise, Petty was placed on an MCA subsidiary label, Backstreet Records. The label was administered by 26-year-old Danny

Bramson, the executive director of the MCA-owned music venue, Universal Amphitheatre. Although Petty was not the label's first signing, he was the label's first major act and would be joined by a number of artists including Nils Lofgren, Men Without Hats, Ry Cooder, and Walter Egan. Bramson recalled, "I intended Backstreet to be to MCA what David Geffen's Asylum was to Atlantic – a small, well-attended roster of performers where communication with the artist was more personal than corporate, yet the artist retained the sales, marketing, and distribution expertise of a major label. And Tom is everything I ever wanted Backstreet to represent." With Tom Petty and the Heartbreakers agreeing to the deal, the lawsuits were dropped. (By 1983, Backstreet would be dissolved and absorbed back into MCA Records.)

To nearly everyone's surprise, Tom Petty was now free and clear. A music journalist succinctly summed up Petty's legal triumph: "Tom Petty fought the law and the law lost. That was really something." Although Petty was legally barred from commenting on the details of the agreement, other insiders were free to discuss the matter. With the legal battle finally behind him, an emotionally frayed Petty delivered the completed master tapes for the third Heartbreakers album.

Petty stated at the time: "Something like this builds you in a way, because you don't always realize how much you love something until you're not allowed to do that thing anymore. You realize that you take things for granted. I wanted to play music, yet I was going to court every day."

▶ CHAPTER 15
TORPEDO ROCK & ROLL

The title of Tom Petty and the Heartbreakers' third album, *Damn The Torpedoes*, was taken from a quotation by Admiral David G. Farragut during the Battle of Mobile Bay in 1864, when he disregarded the presence of 67 underwater mines and reached his target, forcing the surrender of Confederate troops. As a result, Tom Petty took "damn the torpedoes" to mean "full speed ahead." Petty said at the time: "We all have torpedoes to look out for. Ours missed by this much."

In one important aspect, the finely-crafted album was far different than the group's previous two releases. To Petty's chagrin, producer Jimmy Iovine had pushed Petty's vocals to the forefront: "I was afraid to put my voice up really loud.... Then, with *Torpedoes*, Jimmy Iovine came in and [said]: 'You gotta get the vocals up, you gotta hear the singing.'" In addition, Iovine also fought to have the lyrics printed on the album's jacket or inner sleeve. As Petty recalled, "Jimmy Iovine told me, 'People'll never know how good your songs are because you sing like you've got a mouth full of food.' I don't like lyric sheets. Not being able to hear the words clearly gives people the incentive to listen more closely."

Meanwhile, the Heartbreakers' newly-hired co-manager Elliot Roberts played a large role in one key aspect of the project's cover art – he wanted only Petty on the front of the album. As Petty recalled, "Elliot came in and said, 'Look, you'll do better if you just focus in on somebody instead of five people. Maybe on this album you should just put Tom on the cover.' Nobody liked that very much, but Elliot was right, I guess."

The cover featured the most iconic and recognized image of Tom Petty: while wearing a simple black jacket and solid red shirt, Petty is holding a vintage 12-string Rickenbacker guitar he borrowed from Mike Campbell. Campbell had found the prized guitar in the classified section of a small newspaper and paid a mere $150 for the rare instrument. Petty later said of the guitar's unique sound: "The Rickenbacker is rich and acoustic-sounding. It's great for rhythm, which is mostly what I do. Rhythm playing is a lost art these days – there aren't a lot of people who do it seriously anymore. But it's really important to our band that I play the rhythm, because the music sounds different if I don't." In an amazing coincidence, the guitar's serial number was just one number away from an identical instrument owned by George Harrison.

Before the album's official release date of October 19, rock stations in Cleveland, Los Angeles, and Philadelphia leaked some of the tracks. Then just two days later, Tom Petty's mother, Kitty, passed away. In poor health for some time, she had been unable to speak for several years. Although Petty was devastated by the loss, he was forced to skip his mother's funeral because of the likely media fray that would have followed him to Gainesville. He explained at the time, "I just didn't want to disgrace the ceremony with a circus."

*   *   *   *   *   *

Initially, the Heartbreakers viewed the five-year-old track, "Don't Do Me Like That," as a throwaway effort and potential outtake, and were surprised when their label released the song as the album's first single. Jimmy Iovine, too, had originally dismissed the track, which languished in what was called "the reject pile." Petty recalled, "I thought it was a little lightweight compared to the rest of the album." The song was originally recorded by Petty's previous group, Mudcrutch, at a session in 1974. (The original Mudcrutch version was later issued on the boxed set, *Playback*.) Petty explained the origin of the song's title: "It was something my dad used to say, 'Don't do me like that.'"

A breakthrough hit on both top-40 and album-rock radio, "Don't Do Me Like That" was the most pop-oriented track on the album. Lyrically, the song explored love gone bad, a very common theme of the group's early output. Meanwhile, with the Heartbreakers on the cusp of stardom, Petty told an interviewer at the time: "We're always hearing that we're the future of rock 'n' roll. I don't want to be the future – I want to be the present."

The followup single – the hard-rocking "Refugee" – was another surprise choice. Mike Campbell had written the song on a four-track recorder at his home after listening to the Albert King track, "Oh Pretty Woman" (which was not related to the similarly titled Roy Orbison song). Released during the second week of January 1980, "Refugee" would climb into the top-20. An extremely difficult song to record, the sessions "almost broke up the band. That one took its toll early in the game. That was a hard record to make for some reason. It was so simple that it was impossible," Stan Lynch explained. Echoing the sentiment, Jimmy Iovine recounted: "It took four weeks to make 'Refugee' work; it just felt stiff. We kept pounding away until we got it. Tom had something going lyrically that I really liked. That's something I got from John Lennon: to get to the musical and lyrical point of a song and stress it." Years later, Petty would lament: "We played 'Refugee' 200 times, 200 takes. If we had known then what we know now it wouldn't have been so difficult to do. But at the time we just didn't know any better."

As a result of "Refugee" – which was the group's most hard-rocking song up to that point – the Heartbreakers were no longer considered a New Wave or punk act. And while "Don't Do Me Like That" was aimed at pop radio, "Refugee" turned Petty into a fixture on album-oriented rock radio. Soon, these same radio stations – many of which had ignored the group in the past – began playing tracks from the first two Heartbreakers albums, with "Breakdown" becoming an AOR staple in the 1980s. But although the Heartbreakers had taken a decidedly mainstream turn, Los Angeles modern-rock pioneer, KROQ, continued to play the group's music, with "Refugee" ranked as the #3 song on the station's annual, year-end chart in 1980.

Meanwhile, a music video for the song was filmed out of necessity. Tom Petty recalled: "We made a video for 'Refugee' because we didn't want to appear on *The Merv Griffin Show*. We thought if we sent a film clip, they'd play it – which they did. We showed up with our guitars, the director said, 'Stand here,' and that was it. It was meant to be shown once.... In those days we were actually cutting film by hand in the editing booth, and I was there right through the cut, through everything. So when MTV came along, I was an old hand at it. But I never dreamed those things would be seen repeatedly."

On November 10, 1979, Tom Petty and the Heartbreakers made their first appearance on *Saturday Night Live*, with Buck Henry as the show's guest host. The group performed two songs, "Refugee" and "Don't Do Me Like That." The next night, the group launched the *Damn The*

Torpedoes tour at the historic 3,000-seat Palladium in New York City; wearing a tight tuxedo jacket and a white, V-neck undershirt, Petty performed to a sold-out room. But just two nights later, Petty was stricken with a serious case of tonsillitis while on stage at the Tower Theater in Philadelphia and quickly lost his singing voice. With his throat problems failing to improve, Petty was forced to postpone a scheduled show in Boston. *Rolling Stone* magazine reported: "During the first week of what should have been his triumphant *Damn The Torpedoes* tour, Petty ruined his voice onstage."

After a painful month of touch-and-go performances and postponements, Petty entered a Los Angeles hospital on January 27 and underwent a tonsillectomy. Petty was "unable to speak after the operation, he lay in bed wondering if he'd sing again." But while Petty rested, anxious tour promoters bombarded his management team for medical updates. But less than a month after the surgery, Petty was back on stage, behind a microphone.

Meanwhile, on February 21, Tom Petty appeared on the cover of *Rolling Stone* magazine for the first time: "Being on the cover of *Rolling Stone* had a certain intangible thing to it – like, 'You've arrived.' Those were pretty exciting days, as I remember. They wanted a red theme for the cover because it was Valentine's Day. We were told to bring red clothing, and the only red clothing I had was this red flannel shirt with bird dogs on it that I wore all the time anyway, so I just wore that. I remember Annie [Leibovitz] painting a heart on my bare chest. The shoot was really pleasant, and I liked Annie a lot. It's my favorite of all the ones I've done. Though when I saw the cover I was in the hospital having my tonsils out, and I just kind of grunted at it." Ironically, Stevie Nicks had appeared on the cover of the magazine the previous week.

"Here Comes My Girl," the third single from the album, was described by notable rock critic Dave Marsh as "a genuine love song in an era without any." Much like the sessions for "Refugee," it took the Heartbreakers weeks to record the track. The song was unusual for Petty in that the verses were spoken, not sung. As Petty recalled: "I got the idea for the narration from Debbie Harry, who we'd been playing with at the time... where she just talked in the song." Although the track failed to reach the top-40, it received heavy airplay on album-rock radio. As Petty's favorite song on the album, he was not happy when it was chosen as the third and final single. He said at the time: "It had nothing to do with me, the company guys take care of that.... I think it's the best song we've ever done."

Another topnotch track on the album, "Even The Losers" was a dramatic rocker. Petty later admitted: "I wanted to write anthems for underdogs, songs like 'Even The Losers' and 'Refugee'... The theme of the album wasn't self-conscious but when I put it together afterwards I could see it was about standing up for your rights."

Reaching the U.S. top-10 in February 1980, *Damn The Torpedoes* was an important commercial breakthrough for the Heartbreakers. Peaking at #2 on the charts and staying there for seven consecutive weeks, the album was blocked from the top spot by Pink Floyd's smash, *The Wall*. Concerned about his sudden mainstream success as well as his integrity as a recording artist, Petty told a reporter at the time: "I was offered the cover of *People* magazine, but I turned it down because it seemed out of character for us. I don't think the kids who are really our fans, who put us here, want to see us there."

In March, the Heartbreakers headed for Europe. Their performance at the Empire Theater in Paris was broadcast on French television. Then following a concert later that month at the Oxford Polytechnic in England – which was broadcast live on the BBC music program, *Rock Goes To College* – the Heartbreakers launched their first-ever tours of Japan, Australia, and New Zealand.

In 1980, Tom Petty and the Heartbreakers spent nine months on the road, during which time the group went from playing theaters to headlining arenas. Despite their increasing fame, the Heartbreakers did not bother with elaborate stage sets, pyrotechnics, smoke machines, or any of the bombastic production tricks that were prevalent in rock music at the time.

Instead, the Heartbreakers preferred a traditional stage configuration, without much glitz. Both Tom Petty and Mike Campbell would tour with an increasingly growing number of guitars – not to show off – but to employ the appropriate instrument for the group's expanding catalog of hit songs. As a skilled rhythm guitarist with an appealing style, Petty had a fan in bandmate Mike Campbell: "His way of playing the guitar against a vocal is just right. He sticks in little rhythm things, and when he's singing, he backs off and comps his guitar to the vocal. It balances itself real good. He's real good at that. He has a good feel for solos, too. He can play a Chuck Berry/John Lennon-style solo. He's not like Eddie Van

Halen, but in his style he has a great touch."

Meanwhile, Benmont Tench would trap himself in the middle of multiple stacks of pianos, organs, and synthesizers of all varieties; at one point, Tench installed a number of rearview mirrors to observe what his bandmates were doing on stage. Conversely, Stan Lynch preferred to use an unadorned, compact drum kit, which he considered better suited for the Heartbreakers' sound. Meanwhile, the unassuming and dependable Ron Blair would stand behind Petty and attract little attention.

▶ CHAPTER 16
HARD PROMISES

After enjoying great success with *Damn The Torpedoes*, Tom Petty and the Heartbreakers followed up with a project that employed a similar formula of catchy melodies, strong hooks, and straightforward guitar-oriented rock and roll. Released in May 1981, the group's fourth album, *Hard Promises*, was another solid seller. Petty recalled: "I think I'll always be a little partial towards *Hard Promises*. It's really the one that meant the most, at the time and now. I got most of the ballads out of my system with that, and it was, you know, well liked by a lot of people."

While recording the album at Cherokee Studios in Los Angeles, Petty was excited about the possibility of meeting John Lennon, who was scheduled to work on a track with Ringo Starr. But the meeting never took place. That week, Lennon was murdered by a crazed attention seeker in New York City. Petty later recounted, "His death hurt real bad, still hurts.... I was in the studio when Lennon died. My producer, Jimmy Iovine, had worked on a few of John's albums, and Ringo was recording just down the hall from me. The day before John died, we heard that he was planning to come out and do something with Ringo, and I thought, Great! He'll be right next door. When he got shot, Jimmy got a call with the news. We went on working for a while, then stopped. The spark was gone." Petty subsequently ordered the tribute "WE LOVE YOU J.L." etched into the closing grooves of the first pressings of *Hard Promises*.

After the completion of the album, trouble struck when Petty became mired in yet another tussle with his record label. MCA had decided to raise its LP list price from $8.98 to $9.98 for some of the label's releases. Predicting that the record buying public would be willing to pay more for a hit record, MCA had instituted a policy called "superstar pricing." The label had already priced Steely Dan's *Goucho* and the *Xanadu* soundtrack at $9.98, and had planned on following suit with

Hard Promises. But when Petty balked at the price hike, he was forced to wage yet another protracted battle. Initially withholding the master tapes, Petty even threatened to re-title the album, *Eight Ninety-Eight*, to make his point. The album's front cover featured Petty in a leather jacket and red plaid shirt, standing next to a crate of LPs that were priced, appropriately, at $8.98. At the time Petty remarked, "I hope we're not remembered as the band that fought the record company." The pricing battle was celebrated by *Rolling Stone* magazine, which put Petty on its cover in July. With the caption, "One man's war against high record prices," Petty was pictured tearing a dollar bill in half. He later explained, "I was fighting the record industry... so *Rolling Stone* wanted me in a suit and tie to reflect some kind of corporate angle. [The photo] looked really silly to me – like my head had been cut off and pasted onto another body. I was not really all that comfortable with it."

But once again, Petty had fought his record company – entirely on his own – and was disappointed by the lack of support from his fellow musicians, even at his own label: "I took a huge stand on that.... I never saw any other artists backing me up or saying, 'Yeah, we're not going to stand for it.'" Years later, Petty would lament, "If they'd have listened to me in 1981, the music business wouldn't be in the shape it is. That's the whole reason it crumbled. You wouldn't have so many downloads if the records were 10 bucks. I [didn't fight] to be noble."

The album's lead-off single, "The Waiting," was recorded on Petty's birthday. Petty recounted: "That was a song that took a long time to write. Roger McGuinn swears he told me the line – about the waiting being the hardest part – but I think I got the idea from something Janis Joplin said on television. I had the chorus very quickly, but I had a very difficult time piecing together the rest of the song. It's about waiting for your dreams and not knowing if they will come true. I've always felt it was an optimistic song."

While recording *Hard Promises*, Tom Petty and the Heartbreakers had an unexpected visitor in the studio – Stevie Nicks. During this period, Nicks was working on her first solo album, despite some initial hostility from her bandmates in Fleetwood Mac: "They were not supportive when I first went to do *Bella Donna*, they questioned my reasons, and once they realized that I was simply looking for an outlet for my songs – because three songs for Fleetwood Mac every two years just wasn't enough – they understood I wasn't trying to leave the band."

But that was not the only reason Nicks wanted to record a solo project. After completing a grueling but very successful world tour to promote the Fleetwood Mac album *Tusk*, Nicks was informed by bandmate Mick Fleetwood – who was also the group's manager at the time – that the 18-month tour had earned no profit due to high production costs, despite 112 sold-out performances.

As an integral part of Fleetwood Mac, Nicks was both a songwriter and one of the group's lead singers. Also the visual focus of the group, "she had a vivid stage 'look' defined by billowing chiffon skirts, shawls, top hats (or, later in her career, feathered berets), layers of lace, and her long curly hair. Only five-feet-one in her stocking feet, she habitually wore six-inch suede platform boots and walked with a confident, erect posture of a beauty queen."

After learning of Nicks' intention to record an album apart from her group, Warner Brothers promised to increase Fleetwood Mac's royalty rate if she remained at the label as a solo artist. Ignoring the offer, Nicks co-founded her own label, Modern Records, and entered into a five-album arrangement with Atlantic Records.

Planning her solo project since the late-1970s, Nicks had originally wanted Tom Petty to produce her record. Eventually, Nicks hired Tom Moncrieff, who was best known for his work with Walter Egan. But the other two co-owners of Modern Records had envisioned someone else behind the knobs in the control room. Although label co-owner Danny Goldberg wanted to hire Jimmy Iovine, Nicks fought to retain Moncrieff. Goldberg recalled: "I got Petty to come with me to the studio to personally tell Stevie about Iovine's process.... He did what was asked of him out of loyalty to Jimmy. Tom swept Stevie off her feet with his shambling rock and roll intensity and understated Florida charm." Then after a congenial meeting with Iovine, Nicks was convinced to replace Moncrieff. But the situation would quickly progress on multiple levels. "A week later Jimmy had moved in and would be her boyfriend as well as her producer for the next year," Goldberg recalled.

The recording sessions were delayed for a month when Nicks was summoned to France to provide some vocal tracks for the next Fleetwood Mac album. But to the surprise of her bandmates, Nicks brought along Jimmy Iovine to the sessions. After fulfilling her responsibilities, Nicks returned to Los Angeles to resume working on her solo project.

Needing more material for her album, Nicks set her sights on one of her favorite songwriters – Tom Petty. Nicks recalled: "I first met Tom in the studio, and he was pretty much what I expected. There's not a fake bone in his body." After repeatedly asking Petty to write a song for her, he finally agreed. As Petty recounted: "Near the end of the sessions [for the album *Hard Promises*], I ran home and wrote ['Insider'] in a day. I came back and played it for the band and it was like, 'Whoa, T.P., you wrote that in a day?' Everybody flipped. So we cut it, sent over a demo of it to Stevie, and she came back in the next day saying how much she loved it."

But something unexpected happened at the recording session. As Petty recalled, "She came into the studio to sing it, and she left my lead vocal on in one earphone so she could learn the melody. But she kept singing harmony instead of the melody, and finally decided that that's the way she wanted to do the song – as a duet. It sounded great. I got really excited about it, because I'd always wanted to record a song like that. I'd always loved duets like Gram Parsons and Emmylou Harris on *Grievous Angel*, or George Jones and Tammy Wynette. Those things kill me. Finally, Stevie just said, '*You* take the song,' and it ended up fitting the album perfectly."

In exchange for "Insider," Petty allowed Nicks to choose a track from his nearly completed album. She selected an unfinished, mid-tempo song written by Petty and Campbell, "Stop Draggin' My Heart Around." Petty recalled, "When Stevie heard it, she lit up like a Christmas tree and said, 'That's what I wanted all along!' She could have written a million songs like 'Insider,' but she wanted a rocker and that's what we ended up giving her." Benmont Tench played a large role on Nicks' solo album, working as the chief arranger, keyboardist, and the co-writer of another track, "Kind Of Woman."

The title of another track, "Edge Of Seventeen," was taken from a conversation Nicks had with Petty's wife, Jane. And despite rumors that the song was written about Nicks' past relationship with Fleetwood Mac bandmate Lindsey Buckingham, it was actually inspired by Nicks' budding romance with Jimmy Iovine.

With Nicks needing legitimacy on rock radio as a solo artist, the two other co-owners of Modern Records decided to release "Stop Draggin' My Heart Around" as the first single from *Bella Donna*. They selected the song because it was the project's most rock-oriented track. Later that year, when Nicks went on the road to promote the album, she performed "Stop Draggin' My Heart Around" as a duet with her guitarist, Waddy Wachtel.

Despite the success of the Petty/Nicks duet, the Heartbreakers were not comfortable with an outsider at their recording sessions. Petty explained the mentality of the group at the time: "We've always kept our group enclosed unto itself and never let anybody else in. I think we even put poor Stevie through some weird stuff because it's so hard to get inside our closed circle."

Meanwhile, during this period, MTV made its debut on cable television. On August 1, 1981, "Stop Draggin' My Heart Around" was the 24th video to air on MTV's first day of broadcasting and was sandwiched between clips by Blondie and Lee Ritenour. Several months later, "Stop Draggin' My Heart Around" would earn a Grammy for Best Rock Performance by a Duo or Group with Vocal.

Petty later recounted his first exposure to MTV: "When I first saw it, I didn't know how long it was going to be on that day so I must have sat there six hours waiting for that show to end and it just kept going, over and over. And I liked it. I thought, this is going to be interesting."

Realizing that MTV was an important promotional tool, the Heartbreakers embraced the music video format in a big way. Petty recalled, "for *Hard Promises*, we did four videos in two days, directed by my high-school buddy [and former bandmate], Jim Lenahan, who did our lighting and staging on tour. 'A Woman In Love' was really good. The Police completely stole that. They stole the cinematographer, Daniel Pearl, the location, everything, for 'Every Breath You Take.'" But Andy Summers of the Police later insisted that his group's video was based on a 1944 film about jazz musicians that was shot by Gjon Mili, and claimed to be unaware of Petty's accusations.

Over the next several years, Stevie Nicks was completely open about her desire to become a part of the Heartbreakers and would often join the group onstage during the 1980s and '90s. But Petty would declare a "no girls" policy in the band. During this period, Nicks would cultivate a close friendship with both Tom Petty and his wife, Jane.

Released as the second single from *Hard Promises*, "A Woman In Love (It's Not Me)" was the most emotionally charged track on the album. A *Rolling Stone* magazine reviewer remarked: "A gray mist of loneliness blows throughout *Hard Promises*.... This taste of loneliness is clearest in the album's masterpiece, "A Woman In Love".... Petty's aching, murmured vocal – leaping for and missing a falsetto in a move that sums up dashed hopes and heartbreak – is the finest thing he's ever done." Appearing on the track, Donald "Duck" Dunn played the prominent bass line. But after the second take, the Heartbreakers were unsure if they had anything special. As Stan Lynch recalled, "Iovine immediately says, 'It's too fast.' Tom says, 'No, it's too slow.' So they get into it, and Duck says, 'Let's just go hear it.' So they push play and... it's going by like a freight train. By the end of the thing nobody says a word, there's this uncomfortable silence. Then Duck says, 'Y'all didn't like that?' All of a sudden, Jimmy goes, 'That's great, that's amazing.' And Tom goes, 'Yeah, I think that'll work.'" A few months later when the Heartbreakers performed the song on *The Tom Snyder Show*, Benmont Tench played a 30-second piano intro that was not included on the recorded version.

However, with the Petty/Nicks duet, "Stop Draggin' My Heart Around," receiving heavy airplay, top-40 radio was unwilling to play a second Petty single at the same time. Consequently, a frustrated Petty watched "A Woman In Love" wither on the charts. Although top-40 radio had ignored the song, that was not the case with rock radio or MTV, where it was already in heavy rotation even before the release of the single. (Even though the song became a fan favorite, it was dropped from the Heartbreakers' live repertoire for many years, until 2013.)

Later, when Nicks released her followup album *The Wild Heart*, the songs were not as strong. As Danny Goldberg recalled: "It had not escaped Tom Petty's notice that Stevie's solo album, buttressed by one of his songs, had sold far more than had the Heartbreakers' [last album], so another Petty song was not an option."

But Nicks did not have to ask Petty for another song. It was Petty who offered to contribute a composition. Backed by the Heartbreakers, Petty and Nicks reunited for the ballad, "I Will Run To You." The song was recorded multiple times at three different studios before Nicks was satisfied with the final version. But the track was not released as a single and would receive only minor airplay. Despite their obvious musical chemistry, Petty and Nicks would never collaborate on an entire album's worth of material.

*   *   *   *   *   *

At his newly purchased home in Encino, Petty began noticing that his rising popularity and fame could be measured by the growing number of female fans who began camping out on his front lawn. Needing security, Petty hired a guard to chase away the squatters. The situation was the impetus for another track on *Hard Promises*, "Nightwatchman." An affluent community, Encino has been home to a number of notable entertainers including John Wayne, Richard Pryor, Annette Funicello, and Johnny Cash.

Meanwhile, the tour to promote *Hard Promises* was struck by a series of minor mishaps. After Petty injured his knee in a trampoline accident, the tour was delayed for several weeks. Finally, in mid-June, the Heartbreakers hit the road with various opening acts including the Fabulous Thunderbirds, Joe Ely, and Split Enz.

With the Heartbreakers enjoying their hard-earned rock star status, the group performed in sold-out arenas around the country. But as a result of overzealous fans, a three-date stint at the 14,000 seat Forum in Los Angeles was nearly cancelled. Petty recalled, "I remember being shut down after the first [show]. The fire marshals were very upset at how out of control the crowd was and wanted to cancel the next two nights. We really had to do a song and dance for the fire department." But even Petty became overly animated during one of the performances when he ran across the stage, directly into a preoccupied Mike Campbell, who was knocked off his feet and onto the floor.

Then in Chicago, one of the city's leading rock stations threatened to boycott Petty's music. After WLUP had bought up all 15,000 tickets to Petty's June 18th concert at the Rosemont Horizon – and gave the tickets away to the station's listeners – rival radio station WMET was not amused. As Petty recalled, "[WLUP] came to me and said they wanna buy all the tickets and you get paid and the kids get in for free. I said, 'I can't argue with that.' I thought it was a great idea and I still do, and if they don't play us on the other station, then they won't." In September, a day before a concert in Tucson, Petty drove two hours north to Tempe and joined one of his early influences, Muddy Waters, on stage for a few songs.

Then on October 7, Tom Petty and the Heartbreakers arrived in Gainesville for a homecoming concert. Earlier that day, the members of the group received the keys to the city. But after the performance, Petty was forced by doctors to cancel the last two shows of the four-month tour due to physical exhaustion.

After a two-month rest, Petty was a surprise guest at a Del Shannon concert at Dooley's nightclub in Tempe. Petty also showed up at Shannon's next gig in Reseda, California. During this period, Petty was producing Shannon's comeback album, *Drop Down And Get Me.*

As Del Shannon's biographer Howard DeWitt recalled, "Petty's backup band, the Heartbreakers, were the perfect studio group to revitalize Del's career. In November 1978, Petty and the Heartbreakers went into Sound City [studio] in Van Nuys to get the feel of playing with Shannon. As [Shannon's manager] remarked, 'it was just to mess around.' There was also a gig at the Santa Monica Civic Auditorium on New Year's Eve where Shannon was going to join Petty and his group to perform 'Runaway.' After the rehearsal at Sound City, Del played a tape of a song called 'Drop Down And Get Me,' which later became the title cut [of the album.]" Although the album was not a strong seller, Shannon's remake of the rock oldie "Sea Of Love" reached the top-40 charts in 1982.

▶ CHAPTER 17
GOODBYE RON, HELLO HOWIE

Although Tom Petty and the Heartbreakers were selling plenty of records and filling large venues, all was not well within the group. While Petty had little trouble adjusting to the physical and mental demands of the band's busy recording and touring schedule, the same could not be said for bassist Ron Blair. One day, Blair suddenly quit after informing Petty that he "couldn't get back on the bus" for another tour.

Blair had gotten married, was now the father of a young child, and felt he was neglecting his responsibilities to his family. Leaving the Heartbreakers after seven years and four albums, Blair had also developed a distaste for the widespread treachery in the music industry. Remaining a fan of the band, Blair attended numerous Heartbreakers concerts over the next two decades and would stay in regular contact with Mike Campbell. Blair parted with the Heartbreakers following their homecoming concert in Gainesville.

After abandoning his music career, Blair purchased a swimwear store in the suburban Los Angeles community of Tarzana. Naming the store Shapes, Blair operated the successful retail outlet for the next 12 years. Blair later recalled with amusement, "The first couple of years we were open, there was a rumor that Tom Petty's wife had opened the shop. We didn't do anything to squelch it." (Remarkably, Blair's mother-in-law later became a nun and was the subject of the book, *Prison Angel*.) After his marriage ended in 1985, Blair continued to operate the swimwear shop.

In 1990, Blair reflected on his departure: "At the time, it was really a gut decision." But as Petty explained: "When he first quit, he didn't quit the band, he quit the whole music thing. He was fed up. But we were all young boys then."

In desperate need of a replacement bass player, Tom Petty would not need to look very far.

*   *   *   *   *   *

Howie Epstein (born Howard Norman Epstein) was raised in the city of Milwaukee. Much like Tom Petty, Epstein was motivated to start his own rock and roll band, at age eight in 1964, after watching the Beatles on *The Ed Sullivan Show*. Epstein grew up in a musical household and had constant access to various instruments. Howie's father, "Sam Epstein, was a top local record producer who worked with various rock 'n' roll and soul groups in the '50s and '60s. Howie got to bang around the studios watching his father work, as well as doing a little recording under his father's watchful eye at a very young age." After mastering the electric guitar in his early teens, Howie began forming his own bands. When Howie was just 13, his group won a battle of the bands competition.

But following the death of his father from a heart attack in 1970, fifteen-year-old Howie found himself with only sporadic supervision at home. Suddenly, "there was little parental restraint as Howie and his two brothers hosted raucous jam sessions that were often shut down by Fox Point police, either because the music was too loud or the brothers were beating the hell out of each other."

In 1973, Epstein managed to graduate from Nicolet High School. One of his classmates was future talk show queen, Oprah Winfrey. Over the next several years, Epstein and fellow Milwaukee musician Jason Klagstad would form a series of local groups including Forearm Crash and the Craze. "The funny thing is... the rock bands I was in were always a little bit like the Heartbreakers. I loved the Byrds, loved Dylan," Epstein later revealed.

Yearning to test the musical waters outside of Milwaukee, Epstein decided to relocate to New York City. But at the last minute, he accepted an offer to join the backing band of singer-songwriter John Hiatt. At 23-years-old in 1978, Epstein headed to the West Coast to meet with Hiatt, who was without a recording contract at the time. Years later, Hiatt recalled his first encounter with Epstein: "I was a terrible drunk at the time, so my memories are vague. All I remember is a sweet little straight-laced Jewish kid from Milwaukee with an afro." Spending two years in Hiatt's band, Epstein performed on a pair of moderately-selling albums, *Slug Line* (1979) and *Two Bit Monsters* (1980).

While on the road, Epstein was more concerned with improving his musicianship than attending parties with the band. As Hiatt explained, "Howie was the sane one. He was the least likely to have wound up the way he wound up. I remember feeling no matter how crazy everybody else got, I could always look to Howie and think, 'Well, Howie's got his shit together.'"

After the completion of a tour in 1980, Epstein parted with Hiatt and remained in Los Angeles to work as a session player. Around this time, Epstein had switched from the rhythm guitar to the bass. That same year, he performed on Dick Clark's *American Bandstand,* which was something his future bandmates in the Heartbreakers would never accomplish. Epstein appeared on the program as a member of singer-songwriter Cindy Bullens' backing band. After the group finished its performance, Bullens introduced her baby-faced bass player as "Howard Epstein."

Meanwhile, Tom Petty first met Epstein later in 1980 during the sessions for Del Shannon's comeback album. Petty was immediately impressed by Epstein's vocal abilities: "He played the bass, and that was really great, but then he sang and just knocked me out."

While touring with Shannon in early 1982, Epstein was invited to fly to Los Angeles and meet with Petty. After auditioning a few other bass players, including Donald "Duck" Dunn, Petty came to realize he wanted Epstein. In a telephone call to Shannon, Petty apologized but held firm about his decision. Petty recalled, "When I asked Howie to join the Heartbreakers in 1982, Del was pissed off with me. Bless Del's soul, he said, 'Wow, you can't take Howie.' I said, 'Del, I love you, but I'm taking Howie.'" Realizing there was nothing he could do about the situation, Shannon was deeply upset but would remain friends with Petty.

Epstein later explained, "I was definitely happy when I joined the band. I really think it was stranger for them. I don't think the guys had been in many other bands. They were so closeknit, where I was used to playing with lots of bands. I think it was a little weird for them to have this new guy in there." In the band, Epstein stood out for another reason. While the other members of the Heartbreakers retained some traces of their Southern accents, Epstein spoke with a strong Midwestern dialect.

After joining the Heartbreakers, Epstein would stay in the background, choosing to avoid the glitz of the music industry. Going out of his way to avoid the press, Epstein gave less than a dozen interviews while with the band.

With the hiring of Epstein, the Heartbreakers cancelled all of their previously-announced summer shows and instead spent the time breaking in their new member. Then after two concerts in early September at the 2,000-seat Civic Auditorium in Santa Cruz, California, Petty and the band prepared for their headlining slot at a large music festival on the West Coast.

The US Festival was financed by millionaire Steve Wozniak and organized by veteran promoter Bill Graham. Wozniak had made his fortune as a co-founder of Apple Computers, but had left the company the previous year after suffering injuries in an airplane crash. Wanting to merge technology, art, and music at one event, Wozniak positioned the festival as the Woodstock of the 1980s.

The US Festival was staged ten miles north of San Bernardino, California, at Glen Helen Regional Park. After bulldozers finished carving out a level field at the edge of a desert, workers constructed a stage and a massive sound system. The vast stage was draped by a natural backdrop of majestic mountains. Taking place over Labor Day weekend in 1982, the concert drew half a million attendees and was broadcast on MTV.

As the headlining act on day two of the three-day event, Tom Petty and the Heartbreakers performed after the sun had gone down, following a half-hour set by Pat Benatar. Earlier in the day, the temperature on the crowded field had reached a dangerous 110 degrees Fahrenheit and it was still in the 90s when the Heartbreakers began playing.

The Heartbreakers opened their set with the then-unreleased track, "A One Story Town." The surprise musical selection of the night came with the frat-rock classic "Louie Louie." As Petty explained, "It really was a spontaneous choice. I saw a videotape of our show there, and you can see us discussing it for a minute – like, '*What* are we playing?'"

Meanwhile, Howie Epstein looked comfortable onstage and was quick to fit into the band. As Benmont Tench remembered: "We're playing in front of 250,000 people. And right in the middle of the set, Howie casually strolls over to Stan, shouts over the music, 'You call that drumming?'" The group performed eight songs in all and finished with

"Even The Losers." Petty would soon learn to rely on Epstein to fill in some of the vocals on more difficult songs such as "Free Fallin'" and "Refugee."

Even though Wozniak lost in excess of $10 million on the event, he staged a second festival the following year, which was remembered for performances by David Bowie, Van Halen, and the Clash.

*   *   *   *   *   *

In the heyday of the AOR format in the 1980s, Tom Petty and the Heartbreakers had reached a solid level of stardom. During this period, working-class rockers like Tom Petty, Bruce Springsteen, Bob Seger, and John Cougar Mellencamp were at the forefront of the Heartland-style rock of Middle America. There was "Born In The U.S.A." There was "R-O-C-K In The U.S.A." There was "Old Time Rock And Roll." And there was "American Girl." When asked to compare himself to these other rockers, Petty insisted: "I think that I'm a little more – dare I say – *eccentric* than those guys. I know all those people quite well and I think they're terrific. We all get along very well, we're all about the same age, we do have the same musical favorites.... [But] I don't know if Bruce would do 'Don't Come Around Here No More.'"

But as the Heartbreakers became more successful, the members of the group began to drift apart. As Stan Lynch commented at the time, "In the old days, when the band would get together we'd do a lot of different things. We'd go drinkin' together, bullshit together, talk about sex together, dream together. Now, the dreams are really separate. This guy's got a wife and kids. This guy is into this other thing. Now what we do together is pretty defined. We get together and do one thing – make Tom Petty and the Heartbreakers music. And that's fine. I really don't want to do anything else."

▶ CHAPTER 18
LONG AFTER DARK

After the highly publicized and expensive legal battle during the recording of *Damn The Torpedoes* and the subsequent fight over the list price of *Hard Promises*, MCA Records decided it was time to punish Tom Petty. Shooting themselves in the foot to make a point, MCA chose not to promote an album by one of the label's best-selling acts. As Petty later recalled, "When it came to my next record, I couldn't even get an ad." But even with all of his success, Petty did not feel confident during this period. He told a reporter: "We've probably been the most successful underdogs in this business. And I still feel we're underdogs. It's not all laid on a plate for us."

The fifth Heartbreakers album was recorded over a one-year period at several studios around Los Angeles. Ron Blair played the bass on one of the tracks, "Between Two Worlds," and his replacement Howie Epstein took over the bass duties on the remainder of the songs. Although the Heartbreakers would again work with producer Jimmy Iovine, the sessions were far less intense than previous outings.

Released in November 1982, *Long After Dark* was a more guitar-oriented album than its predecessors. Of the 19 songs recorded for the project, just 10 were used. During the sessions, Lynch was fired from the band for a few days after yet another heated dispute.

The album's first single, "You Got Lucky," was built around a drum loop created by Mike Campbell. Although some longtime fans were angered by the perceived arrogance of the song's lyrics, Petty explained: "[It's] the most misunderstood song I ever wrote. That's a very insecure person saying that! But it's a very real emotion. I found it amusing, really, to sing that. But some people said, 'God! The audacity!' Insecure people say things like that to protect themselves, to protect the real pain that they know is coming later."

As the first Heartbreakers hit to feature synthesizers, the song was a nod to the New Wave acts that were omnipresent on MTV during this period. But using a synthesizer as the lead rhythm instrument was an exception, not the norm, for the Heartbreakers. As Petty would later proclaim, "I think that those [musicians] who went for the sequencers and the synthesizers at the time really dated themselves by doing that. We always saw them as not timeless instruments. We stay organic; if we want to make a synthesizer sound, we'll find some organic way to do it. Those computer instruments seem to date themselves, and if you look back at a lot of that music from the '80s, you almost kind of laugh at it. It's very much of an era, and I think the best songs are kind of timeless. They last a long time."

Mike Campbell recounted another key aspect of the song: "The solo in the middle of 'You Got Lucky' was Tom's idea. We had the track pretty well finished, and we wanted to put some sort of unique solo on there. He said, 'Why don't you do something like a Clint Eastwood kind of thing with the vibrato?'" As Petty explained, "I've always admired those Clint Eastwood movies, with the music by Ennio Morricone. That's what the song reminded me of, so we made the movie ourselves."

The song's Mad Max-inspired music video received heavy airplay on MTV. "I thought let's just get out of the box here and do something different," Petty explained. "There was a minute-long scene where we walk through the desert, uncover a dusty old boombox, and push play, and that's when the music begins. Michael Jackson called us, saying what an incredible idea that was," Petty recounted. The video also featured a scene in which Petty destroyed an arcade video game, which symbolized the war between the makers of coin-operated video games and the music industry in the early-1980s, with both entities competing for the same entertainment dollar.

A followup single, "Change Of Heart," was another example of Petty's penchant for writing songs about damaged personal relationships. On the track, Epstein provided the prominent, matching harmony vocals. With the single issued shortly before Valentine's Day, the first 100,000 copies were pressed on red vinyl.

Although *Long After Dark* was popular with fans and critics alike, Petty would later reveal, "I didn't even want to make that album. I liked a lot of the songs, but we seemed to be going for the same sound. I was worried that we were beginning to pander to the audience for the first time. I can see now that some of the passion was gone, and I don't think we really got it back until we went on the road with Bob (Dylan)." Petty also felt restless during this period and had considered relocating the band from Los Angeles to London: "L.A. is not nearly as bad a place as it's portrayed, but I don't think it's really the ideal place for us to continue right now. I don't think it would be a bad idea for us to get out of there for a while."

In November, the Heartbreakers began the European leg of the *Long After Dark* tour. In December, the group played three shows in Germany. At a concert in the city of Dortmund, the band got lost in the catacombs of a large entertainment complex. While trying to find their way to the stage, the Heartbreakers inadvertently stepped into an indoor tennis court. A documentary team from MTV captured the embarrassing incident. The mishap was later spoofed in the comedy film, *This Is Spinal Tap*.

Then from January through June 1983, the Heartbreakers would remain on the road for an extended U.S. tour. On February 14th, the group performed on the legendary Grand Ole Opry stage in Nashville. Petty said at the time, "We played a little country set on our last English tour.... I like country music, so the thing is always there, but I'm not sure if people would understand us doing a lot of country licks." (Years later, in 2013, Petty would ignite a controversy when he described modern country music as "bad rock with a fiddle.") Just five days after their Opry performance, the Heartbreakers appeared on *Saturday Night Live*, with guest host Howard Hesseman (better known as Dr. Johnny Fever on *WKRP*).

After the completion of the tour, Tom Petty and his bandmates needed some time apart. Petty explained at the time: "After that last tour, I just wanted to push the chair away from the table for a while. [We] had been recording, then touring, more recording, more touring, for something like seven years, and I just felt burnt." Petty wanted an extended break to wind down from the pressures he faced as the bandleader of a successful rock act: "I just needed time off. I went to England for a while, took trips down South and all of a sudden I was writing things without even thinking about them. It felt natural again." Petty also spent some time in northern Florida, where he stayed at Stan Lynch's home.

Also during this period, Petty would reconnect with his good friend and former labelmate at Shelter Records, Dwight Twilley. At the invitation of his former producer Noah Shark, Petty provided the prominent backing vocal on Twilley's comeback hit, the top-20 single, "Girls." In the song's music video, Tom Petty's vocals were lip synced by Carla Olson, the female lead singer of Textones, who at the time could have passed as Petty's twin. As a result, some viewers assumed it was actually Petty in the video. (Petty also provided the backing vocals on a second Twilley track, "Forget About It Baby," which the label chose not to release at the time but would later appear on a reissue of the album.)

Additionally, Petty began constructing a large recording studio in the basement of his home. But with his neighbors soon complaining about the noise, Petty had to fortify the sound walls. It was rumored at the time that Petty had built the studio with the intention of recording an album apart from the Heartbreakers.

Meanwhile, Petty's bandmates were pursuing their own individual projects. Stan Lynch teamed with rockabilly revivalist T-Bone Burnett for a brief tour. Howie Epstein accepted some session work and also reunited with John Hiatt for a tour. Benmont Tench joined Lone Justice, an alternative-country band, in the studio and on stage. He also began dating the group's lead singer, Maria McKee. Tench was later the subject of McKee's composition, "A Good Heart," which chronicled the couple's unsuccessful relationship; a remake of the song by Feargal Sharkey would top the British charts in 1985. (Benmont Tench would later write another hit for Sharkey, "You Little Thief.") In addition, Lone Justice would score an MTV hit with the track, "Ways Of The Wicked," which featured Benmont Tench on the organ. The song was an outtake from the *Damn The Torpedoes* sessions and, without the permission of Tom Petty, was offered to Lone Justice by producer Jimmy Iovine.

With the individual members of the Heartbreakers engaged in their own separate endeavors, the music press began speculating that the group might be finished as an outfit. Mike Campbell recalled: "It was reaching a point where everyone was getting a bit stale with eachother, inspirationalwise. We just weren't committed as a band."

At one point, Petty called a meeting at his home just to make sure he still had a group. Petty recalled, "It took us all getting together in one place and saying 'Well, do we break up?' and no-one wanted to."

▶ CHAPTER 19
PETTY'S SOUTHERN ROOTS

After a long hiatus, Tom Petty and the Heartbreakers reconvened for their next album. But unlike the group's previous rock-oriented efforts, *Southern Accents* was a radical departure from the classic Heartbreakers formula on many levels.

Tired of the costs and limitations of working in a traditional recording studio, Petty recorded the album at the newly constructed studio in the basement of his home. He explained, "It's always taken us a long time to make records, and sometimes it's hard to let your mind flow freely when you know it's costing $200 an hour, and you have to leave at midnight because somebody else has the studio booked." In an arduous but gratifying process, the 24-track studio was constructed over a four-month period with the aid of Mike Campbell and recording engineer Don Smith, who had previously worked with Petty on "Stop Draggin' My Heart Around." Needing a name for the studio, Petty dubbed the complex Gone Gator One.

Petty had initially wanted to record the album somewhere near his hometown in Florida, but that was not feasible. He told a music writer at the time: "For a while I thought about coming down to the South to make the record, then I thought no, because I need technicians, and I need this and that. And [in Los Angeles] I can pick up the phone and get it. And here, it's not oriented toward recording."

Southern Accents would take longer to record than any previous Heartbreakers album, with Petty spending 18-months on the project. But like the proverbial kid in a candy store, Petty had opened up the recording process to a slew of producers, guest musicians, and outside collaborators. Petty also employed a classical cellist and even used a horn section on a few tracks. But without hiring a full-time producer to establish limits, make schedules, and set goals, there was little discipline during the sessions, which often lasted well into the night. There were other distraction as well. As Petty later admitted, "drugs had entered the picture" and "it was kind of like the best bar in town on Friday night." The studio soon became a playhouse where friends, fellow musicians, and certain undesirable characters would congregate for impromptu parties. Even Stan Lynch was concerned: "Tom was dancing with the devil at that point... Something was going to happen real bad."

Something "real bad" did indeed happen. On October 23, 1984, during a late night recording session, Petty became frustrated while mixing one of the album's tracks, "Rebels." During the intensity of the moment, Petty nearly destroyed his career by violently punching a wall. Wounding his left hand, Petty did not immediately realize the severity of his injuries. At 4 AM, he was driven to Cedars-Sinai Medical Center, a facility in the West Hollywood section of Los Angeles known for its discretion when treating celebrities.

Petty recalled, "My manager and I were just sitting in [the doctor's] office, laughing, thinking I might have to be in a cast for a couple of weeks or something, and all of a sudden the doctor looks at me real seriously. He finally says, 'You're a guitar player, huh.... Well, I think you can have some trouble here'.... But I never really accepted the possibility that I couldn't play again. The band also tried to keep it real light. They'd joke about how I'd have to take less money if I was just the singer." With that single punch, Petty had pulverized several bones in his hand. An emergency operation took four hours. While recuperating in a hospital bed, Petty watched an MTV news segment, which reported he would never be able to play the guitar again.

Petty left the hospital the following day with his hand set in a large cast, which he was ordered to wear for the next four to six months. Surgeons had replaced a number of bones in his hand with metal wires and inserted metal pins into his knuckles. The longterm prognosis for his hand was very poor.

The initial news reports suggested that Petty broke his hand during a celebration in his studio. Petty later struggled to justify the incident, "When I broke my hand, I mean... it was just... it's hard to explain... I don't really know exactly why I broke my hand. I know I was very frustrated at the time with the record. I'd finished recording, and I'd been over to the record company and played 'em some stuff. They weren't pushing me, but they were saying, 'Can we have it by the end of the year?' I said, 'Yeah, all I gotta do is mix it. I'm not gonna do a double – I'm gonna pare it down.' So then, tying up the ends was another six-month job, which I wasn't prepared to accept; I thought it was a six-*week* job to go in and mix it. And the day I broke my hand, I think we'd been in there around the clock for a week with two teams of engineers and I was in the other room playin' the mixes on a ghetto blaster. And I'm sayin', No, this isn't what I pictured, and I was bummed. Walkin' up the stairwell back to the house, I just... hit the wall and broke my hand. I think the record made me so nuts." Stan Lynch agreed that the uneven pace of recording and the preparation for an upcoming tour to promote the record were causing Petty acute stress: "I know he didn't mean to do it, and I sure felt bad for him; but it took the pressure off us. We were in such a big hurry; now we could say to ourselves 'we're just not gonna hurry.'"

Petty's hand injury also affected the fate of the album, which MCA was hoping to issue before Christmas. Ultimately, the record would be delayed for an additional five months. And instead of a double album, Petty would salvage the project as a single disc. With some of the tracks still needing a few tweaks, a frazzled Petty was happy to see Jimmy Iovine make an unplanned appearance to offer his services. And after suffering a serious injury, Petty realized he needed to step away from his unhealthy rock star lifestyle, which had distracted him over the previous year.

Although Petty's cast was removed earlier than expected in mid-February, doctors could not determine the functionality of his hand for another several weeks. Undergoing a daily regimen of physical therapy, Petty had to retrain the muscles in his damaged hand. In the end, Petty would sum up the experience with a levelheaded attitude: "Breaking my hand was unfortunate, but I think that improved the album quite a bit. It made me really sit back and take stock of it a little bit longer. I was too deep into the album [and] my perspective was hurting." But he added, "I hope I don't have to go through a major disaster just to make an album. But it was good. It calmed me down quite a bit; I haven't hit a wall since."

Meanwhile, during the sessions for *Southern Accents*, Mike Campbell had written an instrumental demo of what would become "The Boys Of Summer." But while Tom Petty did not show interest in the song, Jimmy Iovine sensed a hit. Informing Campbell that Don Henley was looking for some quality compositions for his forthcoming solo album, Iovine set up a meeting between the Heartbreakers guitarist and the former Eagles drummer. Drawn to the moody melody, Henley modified the song to fit his vocal range. Henley then added lyrics and titled the song after Roger Kahn's classic book, *The Boys Of Summer*, which chronicled the history of the famed Brooklyn Dodgers. Released in late-1984, the single became Henley's highest-charting solo hit. (Campbell would later co-write another Henley hit, "The Heart Of The Matter.")

*   *   *   *   *   *

After many setbacks, *Southern Accents,* the sixth Heartbreakers album, was finally released in April 1985. Although Petty had written 26 songs for the project, he also wanted to record a number of traditional Southern folk songs; however, Petty's record company balked at the idea. After the album was completed, Petty lamented: "There were three important songs which would have helped it to work conceptually, but they didn't get on. I can only blame myself for not realizing it at the time." In the end, the album featured just nine songs.

The album was intended as Petty's musical tribute to his Southern heritage and was built around the sentimental title track, "Southern Accents." Petty explained the background of the song: "We had lived in California for about 10 years at that point and I started thinking about growing up in northern Florida, which is a lot different from Miami Beach. It's close to Georgia and I came from a real Southern family, and I wanted to address that world. Once I came up with this song, I decided to write an entire album about the theme." Petty added, "Coming back [to the South] after spending time away, I was able to see both sides. I don't think I would've seen the South that way otherwise. It's such a rich place for material."

A *Rolling Stone* reviewer commented, "Here is Petty at his most forthcoming, telling us how it feels to be a born-poor Southerner – an outsider in the glittery East Coast-West Coast music establishment.... As Petty tries to figure out who he is by remembering where he has been, he also gives us Yankees the chance to grow up Southern." Petty recounted: "When I read the reviews to *Southern Accents*, I thought I'd written a book. I remember saying to my wife, 'I didn't mean to write a book.'"

An 1865 painting by artist Winslow Homer titled *Veteran In A New Field* graced the album's front cover. The famous work was completed just after the end of the Civil War and the assassination of President Abraham Lincoln. The painting depicted a Union soldier who had returned to his job as a solitary farmer; off to the side were his discarded military jacket and canteen. Using a traditional symbol of death – an oversized scythe – the farmer harvested a bountiful field of wheat, which at the time was considered a Northern but not Southern crop.

The album opened with the track, "Rebels," which was notable for its generous use of horns. Petty explained the story behind the song: "If you go down to some places in the South, the Civil War is still very present.... When I was in Atlanta I was noticing all that stuff about the Civil War around – rebel flags. They won't lay that down. It's still handed down, father to son, just a little bit."

Another track on the album, "Spike" was inspired by the bullying Petty experienced during his youth and by the roughnecks at a bar in Gainesville called the Cypress Lounge. As Petty recalled, "We recorded it first in a sort of heavy metal version, all electric. I even had a couple different verses. Then one night I was playing it on my acoustic guitar in a different key... and I came up with this whole other feel. I said, 'Whoa – this might be the way to go!'"

But the album's most talked-about track, "Don't Come Around Here No More," had a complicated history. However, the song's inclusion on a project with a Southern theme was perplexing. In contrast to the traditional Southern-tinged country-rock of "Rebels" or "Southern Accents," the experimental "Don't Come Around Here No More" was an example of electronic psychedelia bordering on New Wave.

The song had its origins at the Wiltern Theatre in Los Angeles after a performance by the Eurythmics, a British New Wave duo consisting of Annie Lennox and Dave Stewart. Backstage, when Stevie Nicks approached Stewart, he boldly said to her, "I want to be your boyfriend." The two musical stars had never met before and, coincidentally, Nicks had just broken up with rocker Joe Walsh on the previous day. Invited to her home that evening, Stewart overheard a pleading Walsh trying to speak to Nicks from behind a locked door. Rejecting his pleas, Nicks shouted, "Don't come around here no more!" From an expression of romantic frustration, a song was born. In time, Walsh and Nicks would reconcile before breaking up permanently. Nicks later described Walsh as the greatest love of her life.

Borrowing the phrase he heard Nicks speak to Walsh, Stewart wrote the basic structure of "Don't Come Around Here No More" a few days later, immediately after a Eurythmics concert in San Francisco. But in his autobiography, *The Dave Stewart Songbook*, Stewart claimed he had originated the phrase himself.

Several weeks later, Dave Stewart met Tom Petty for the first time at the Sunset Sound recording studio in Hollywood. After a Eurythmics concert in May 1984, Stewart wanted to discuss some unfinished songs with producer Jimmy Iovine, who at the time was working on Stevie Nicks' third solo album. Out of the blue, Iovine decided he needed Petty's input. Taking a much needed break from the arduous recording sessions in his basement studio, Petty was happy to meet with Iovine. Arriving at Sunset Sound, Petty instantly clicked with Stewart. The feeling was mutual, with Stewart recalling, "Tom Petty came down and he was truly the coolest cat I'd ever met. We hit it off immediately."

While sharing a bottle of aged whiskey, the two men quickly completed Stewart's unfinished composition, "Don't Come Around Here No More." Stewart had intended to give the track to Stevie Nicks. But after Petty contributed some of the lyrics, he came to realize that he wanted the song for himself. Stewart recalled the tense situation: "He said to Jimmy, 'I think I should sing this song,' and then they started having a kind of row amongst themselves – well not a real row, but a strange conversation. Tom and Stevie had done a duet of Tom's song called 'Stop Draggin' My Heart Around,' and Jimmy had put it on Stevie's album. It was a huge success for her, but not for him as it kinda stopped his album in its tracks. I think Tom saw history repeating itself and decided he wanted to put this one on his album." With Stevie Nicks out of the room at the time, Petty managed to convince Iovine to let him have the song. But Nicks later admitted, "Even though I was deeply hurt, I knew it was a great song and that Tom deserved to sing it. He sounded great singing it and I told him so. I said nothing about feeling wounded, I kept those feelings to myself."

Then after a few more drinks, Stewart advised Petty to expand his newly-built home studio from 24 to 48 tracks. But Petty was taken aback when Stewart suggested they compose some songs, right then and there. Over the next hour, Petty and Stewart co-wrote the track, "Make It Better (Forget About Me)," which would appear on *Southern Accents*.

Over the next couple of years, Petty and Stewart became close friends. The two men began frequenting the clubs of Los Angeles and, for a time, were inseparable. For the first time in his career, Petty began indulging in the domain of rock star excess.

Announcing to the less-than-thrilled members of the Heartbreakers that an outsider – Dave Stewart – would be joining them at their sessions, Petty tried to smooth over any suspicions. But shortly after Petty had made the announcement, Stewart entered the studio and, in Petty's words, was "wearin' like a Kentucky general's outfit. He had on about six belts, handcuffs, these great big boots with spurs, and this great big white coat down to here with medals pinned on it – this is in the middle of summer – a hot, burnin' day – and a hat with a big plume comin' out the side. Which I thought was hilarious, you know, and I could see the looks on their faces."

Stewart would also influence Petty's fashion sense, both on and off stage. Petty traded in his simple working-man's uniform for a stylish, modern wardrobe. Several years later when he appeared on the cover of *Spin* magazine, Petty projected an image that was far closer to Jimi Hendrix than fellow Heartland rocker Bruce Springsteen, as he wore a neo-hippie outfit that was accessorized with funky tinted glasses and black suede boots.

Meanwhile, Petty had big plans for "Don't Come Around Here No More." As he explained: "I wanted to make a single that sounded like nothing anybody had ever done, and to this day, I don't know that anybody's ever made a single like that. We worked very hard on that song... and we were doing things like right in the middle, there's a big piano note, a grand piano, and we literally grabbed the tape and pulled it across the heads [of the tape recorder] so it makes this kind of 'whoooooo.'"

But the track kept evolving and underwent countless changes. Petty recalled: "When we wrote that, it was more of an R&B song.... We were trying for almost a Marvin Gaye feel." But the sessions dragged on and on, with no end in sight. As Petty recounted, "I just got carried away with that single, Dave and I worked on that single for months. That song could have come out as ten different records depending on what faders were up. There was one version where it was double time all the way through." Stewart explained, "It was my idea to bring the cellos in. And it was my idea at the very end to get the girl from Talking Heads to sing the 'oh yeah' lick."

When the track was finally completed, Petty received conflicting feedback: "There were two camps when I would play if for people. There were people that would go completely religious about it, just have to hear it all night. And then there the people who just looked at me like I'd lost my mind. Which in a way sort of encouraged me because I'd think, 'Well, if it's gettin' that drastic a reaction, there's definitely something worth putting out there. If it's shaking people up, it's usually pretty good."

As the album's lead-off single, "Don't Come Around Here No More" would also generate Petty's best-known music video. When Stewart suggested an Alice in Wonderland theme, Petty loved the concept. Petty recalled: "The director [Jeff Stein] and I came up with it all, slowly. Dave Stewart had a hand in it too. One night he said he'd like to be sitting on a giant mushroom playing the song, so that's what we did in the video with our demented minds. I just wanted to do something a *little* different than the normal MTV fare.... I wanted something off-the-track. I liked the lunacy of it all, and it's done with a sense of humor."

The video opened with Stewart as a sitar-playing psychedelic guru, sitting atop a giant mushroom with a glowing hookah pipe at his side. Despite Stewart's protests in the press that the experience was strange for him, he had already established a reputation as a creative eccentric whose videos during his Eurythmics period – including "Missionary Man" and "There Must Be An Angel" – were far from the mainstream. (By the early-1990s, Stewart "admitted [to] experiencing 'Paradise Syndrome' – a psychological condition where sufferers become severely depressed because achieving great wealth and fame leaves them feeling there is nothing left to strive for.")

The video's lead character, Alice, was played by Stan Lynch's soon-to-be girlfriend of five years, 21-year-old actress Louise "Wish" Foley. While Petty portrayed the Mad Hatter, the members of the Heartbreakers wore Victorian clothing, sipped cups of tea, and nibbled on donuts. But throughout the video, the smirking Mad Hatter tormented a perplexed Alice.

But it was the infamous cake-cutting scene that sparked the most controversy, as Petty was publically charged with encouraging cruelty towards women, glorifying violence, and even promoting cannibalism! Petty recalled: "[MTV] actually made me edit out a scene of my face when we were cutting her up. They said it was just too lascivious. It was just a shot of me grinning, and they were like, 'Well, you can do it, but you can't enjoy it that much.'"

Criticism of the video also came from an unexpected source, the wife of then-Senator Al Gore. The outspoken Tipper Gore co-founded an organization called the Parents Music Resource Center (PMRC), due in part to her daughter's fearful reaction to Petty's video. Tipper Gore later wrote: "A visual image doesn't have to be on the screen for very long to have an impact. My six-year-old was disturbed by Tom Petty's 'Don't Come Around Here No More' because the last scene showed an Alice... turning into a cake and being sliced up." (Ironically, years later when Tom Petty performed at Al Gore's concession party following his loss in the November 2000 presidential election, Tipper Gore went onstage to play the drums.)

Even Petty's record company and members of his own band had reservations about the video. Petty recalled, "Mike [Campbell] didn't like it, I think. The label hated it, [it] was like, 'What the hell is this?' It was one of the only times that I went, 'OK, we're going to make a single.' So it was a real satisfying thing to see it work. The video played a huge part in making it work, and it is a damn good video." The star of the video, Wish Foley, would later appear in a second Petty clip, "Make It Better (Forget About Me)."

*   *   *   *   *   *

Miraculously, Tom Petty was able to play the guitar again. With a long scar along the back of his hand, he initially struggled with the strings of his instrument. One year after breaking his hand, Petty told a reporter: "It's never going to be normal. It still hurts if I play for too long."

While vacationing in Florida, two months before the start of a summer tour, Tom Petty and the Heartbreakers performed on a rooftop balcony, atop the ritzy Don CeSar Hotel in St. Petersburg. Wearing a black top hat and a light shirt with rolled-up sleeves, Petty led the Heartbreakers though a jam session under the blazing summer sun. According to Petty, the outdoor performance was Stan Lynch's idea.

Not surprisingly, the loud music caused a commotion on the ground as spectators congregated along an outdoor swimming pool and a nearby beach, where they could not see who was performing. Flying overhead in a helicopter, a camera crew from a local television station captured some of the ruckus for the evening news. After starting their set with "American Girl," the Heartbreakers continued to play for nearly two hours. Eventually, a member of the hotel's security team barged onto the balcony and put an end to the open-air concert, just as the band had finished playing "Dogs On The Run." Footage from the rooftop show was included in the 1986 MTV documentary *Southern Accents*, in which Petty discussed both the album and his devotion to his Southern roots.

With Petty's hand sufficiently healed, the long-delayed tour finally commenced on June 6 at the Kiel Opera House in St. Louis. For the tour, Petty added a pair of female R&B vocalists, who were nicknamed the Rebeletts, and a three-piece horn section, the Soul Lip Horns, who had just finished a two-year stint with Rod Stewart. It would be the largest group that Petty would ever take on the road: "I remember hiring all those people and not even rehearsing them – you know, 'Just play along.'" Dave Stewart made a few surprise appearances on the tour, joining Petty on "Don't Come Around Here No More" and a cover of the 1960's garage-rock nugget, "Little Bit O' Soul."

Not surprisingly, Petty adopted an extravagant look for the tour. As a music critic in Miami noted, Petty "now sports 1965 Byrds' granny glasses, a Nudie suit [designed by flamboyant tailor Nudie Cohn] like the one Gram Parsons wore for *The Gilded Palace Of Sin* LP and monstrous muttonchop sideburns a-la Buffalo Springfield in 1966." But all was not well on the tour. After spending nearly a decade together as a group, the members of the Heartbreakers began bickering among themselves. But there was another more pressing concern – ticket sales for the tour were lagging.

Petty also had to deal with an unexpected controversy when a large Confederate battle flag was used as the backdrop during the performance of the track, "Rebels." As the traditional symbol of the American South, the Stars-and-Bars flag was embraced by Southern rock bands like Molly Hatchet and Lynyrd Skynyrd, on stage and on their album art. Decades later, even rap-rocker Kid Rock would display the flag at his concerts.

In the less politically-charged environment of the mid-1980s, the display of the Confederate flag resulted in only spotty complaints, with one *Billboard* magazine columnist accusing Petty of "insensitivity." Within the rock community, Petty was criticized by Mike Mills of

R.E.M., a group formed in the Deep South town of Athens, Georgia. Petty later responded to the attack: "One of those guys in R.E.M. criticized me for using the Confederate flag; he said it was stupid. I didn't mean it in any racist sense at all; I just used it to represent the character of the song." Not wanting to offend a portion of his fanbase, Petty eventually had a change of heart about displaying the flag on stage.

Meanwhile, at the 2nd annual MTV Video Music Awards on September 13, Tom Petty's video for "Don't Come Around Here No More" won an award in the category for Best Special Effects. Although the clip was nominated in *five* different categories – including Best Video of the Year – somehow, Petty earned just a single Moonman trophy.

Also that year, Petty scored an unexpected hit when Rosanne Cash recorded the track, "Never Be You." The song was written by Tom Petty and Benmont Tench – their first-ever collaboration – and was originally recorded two years earlier by Maria McKee.

Cash recounted how she came to record the song: "I had received a call from Tom Petty's management asking me to come to Los Angeles and sing for a potential [movie] soundtrack, on a song called 'Never Be You,' which Tom had written with my friend Benmont Tench. The sessions were a little tough. Jimmy Iovine was producing, and I did not find him to be the most gracious person in the world. However, Hal Blaine was playing drums on the tracks.... Tom and Benmont were lovely, and I did my best, but I didn't feel I could deliver what Iovine wanted. Months later it became clear that 'Never Be You' was not going to appear on the intended soundtrack, so I asked Tom and Belmont if I could record it myself, and they agreed." A few months later, "Never Be You" became Rosanne Cash's fifth number-one hit on the country charts.

Meanwhile, in 1985 Tom Petty and the Heartbreakers shocked music industry insiders by signing a new contract with MCA. Petty explained, "When I re-signed there wasn't anyone left from the time I was fighting them. The company had been turned over to Irving Azoff, who I'd known for years, and he brought in a new staff. Otherwise I never would have done it. Now I'm treated very well, but people are gonna treat me well, because they see money in it."

▶ CHAPTER 20
LIVE AID & FARM AID

In 1985, Tom Petty and the Heartbreakers would perform at two historic charity concerts. The first event, Live Aid, was staged in two cities – London and Philadelphia – and was viewed by an estimated 1.9 billion people around the globe. The Heartbreakers were in the middle of a tour and flew in from Florida to perform at JFK Stadium in Philadelphia. (Surprisingly, Dave Stewart turned down an invitation to perform at the event. Also, George Harrison declined the opportunity to join Paul McCartney for a duet of "Let It Be," and remarked, "Paul didn't ask me to sing on [the song] ten years ago, why does he want me now?")

Before taking the stage, an upbeat Petty spent some time chatting with Robert Plant and other rock luminaries. Then following a bouncy performance by Madonna, Tom Petty and the Heartbreakers were introduced to the stadium crowd by a very tanned Don Johnson. Petty, who looked surprisingly comfortable in the blistering 95-degree heat, had not decided which songs to play until just before hitting the stage. After launching into "American Girl," the Heartbreakers followed up with "The Waiting," "Rebels," and "Refugee." In the British television feed of the concert, the Heartbreakers were described as "one of the greatest American rock and roll bands."

Bob Dylan, the headliner at the Philadelphia portion of Live Aid, would soon play an important role in Petty's career. Event organizer Bob Geldof recalled the difficulty in bringing aboard the legendary folk-rocker: "I had called Dylan through everybody: personal friends, lawyers, [his] record company. He never said no, he'd also never said yes. Usually he spends the summer with his children on the West Coast, but we needed the person who articulated the conscience of an earlier generation." A week before the concert, Dylan's participation was confirmed by his manager.

But Dylan would create a storm of controversy during an unscripted moment between songs when he suggested that a small portion of the funds should go to struggling American farmers: "I'd like to say I hope some of the money that's raised for the people in Africa, maybe they could take a little bit of it – maybe one or two million, maybe – and use it to pay the mortgages on some of the farms.... the farmers here owe to the banks." Upon hearing the short monologue, Bob Geldof was incensed. He later called Dylan's actions, "crass, stupid and nationalistic." (Years later in 2005, Dylan would skip a similar event organized by Geldof, which was dubbed Live 8.)

But Dylan's public plea to help American farmers directly led to the creation of an annual fundraising concert. Just one month after Dylan made his comments at Live Aid, singer Willie Nelson – who spent several summers picking cotton and corn during his youth in Texas – began planning Farm Aid. Naturally, Nelson asked Dylan to be a part of the event. Taking place a mere ten weeks after the Live Aid concert, Farm Aid was staged on September 22 at the University of Illinois Memorial Stadium in the town of Champagne.

When Bob Dylan mentioned to Neil Young, one of the performers and organizers of Farm Aid, that he wanted an established rock act as his backing band, Young suggested Tom Petty and the Heartbreakers, who were also on the bill. Dylan had previously worked with most of the Heartbreakers: Benmont Tench had performed on Dylan's 1981 album *Shot Of Love*, and Tench was joined by Mike Campbell and Howie Epstein on 1985's *Empire Burlesque*. Petty had first met "the Voice of a Generation" in 1978 when he was given free tickets to a Dylan concert, after which he was invited backstage.

To prepare for Farm Aid, Dylan joined the Heartbreakers for some practice sessions at the Universal Sound Stage in Los Angeles. Petty recalled: "We spent a week rehearsing... and we would play a lot every night. Hours and hours and hours. We did Hank Williams songs, Motown songs.... We even played 'Louie Louie' one night. And 'Then He Kissed Me,' the old Crystals song."

But despite the many hours spent practicing, Dylan and Petty were perfectionists who decided to visit the site of the event on the night before their scheduled performance. As Buddy Lee, the promoter of the first Farm Aid concert, recalled: "There was nobody in the stadium, just a very small crew.... Everybody else had gone to bed, but we were doing the final checks before calling it a night. Bob Dylan had requested a sound check. We weren't giving sound checks to anybody because we were still painting the stage at the time – that's how quick everything had to fall into place. But he wanted a sound check. The only time he could have a sound check was at midnight. He came in a van with Tom Petty.... Dylan, Petty, and the Heartbreakers played their whole set to about ten of us. That was a magic moment."

On the following morning, Farm Aid opened at 10 AM with 78,000 spectators packed into the massive 62-year-old football stadium. The 14-hour musical marathon aired on the Nashville Network, which billed the event as "A Concert for America." After Tom Petty and the Heartbreakers performed four songs – including a spirited rendition of the Animals' classic "Don't Bring Me Down" – Dylan joined the group for an additional set, which was highlighted by the protest song, "Maggie's Farm." The Dylan/Petty collaboration was well received by the large crowd. Petty recalled: "When we went to the gig, we only did twenty minutes, so everyone was saying, 'Boy, it's a shame we can't really play for a while.'" Also on the bill at Farm Aid was another legendary rocker who would also play a role in Petty's future, Roy Orbison. Dressed in black and wearing his trademark dark Ray Ban sunglasses, Orbison gave a convincing performance.

With the Farm Aid concert raising $9 million for American family-owned farms, the organizers decided to stage the event on an annual basis. Bob Dylan would later comment: "Live Aid and Farm Aid are fantastic things, but then musicians have always done things like that. When people want a benefit, you don't see them calling dancers or architects or lawyers or even politicians – the power of music is that it has always drawn people together."

Meanwhile, near the end of 1985, MCA issued the double-album, *Pack Up The Plantation: Live!* Not counting the limited-edition promotional release *Official Live 'Leg*, this was the Heartbreakers' first live album. The record was primarily recorded at the intimate 1,850-seat Wiltern Theatre in Los Angeles during the group's 1985 tour, but also featured several tracks from other shows, including a nine-and-a-half minute rendition of the Isley Brothers classic, "Shout," which was recorded at the since-demolished Richfield Coliseum near Cleveland. The Wiltern Theatre concert was also filmed for a possible theatrical release but was instead issued on home video. A single from the album, a remake of the 1960s pop standard "Needles And Pins" featuring Stevie Nicks, reached the lower portion of the top-40. Remarkably, it was the first time Petty and Nicks had performed the song together. Meanwhile, rock radio and MTV instead jumped on another track from the album, a remake of the Byrds' "So You Wanna Be A Rock 'n' Roll Star."

▶ CHAPTER 21
DYLAN & PETTY

When Tom Petty received a telephone call in July 1985, asking if he would like to team with Bob Dylan for a five-week tour, an excited Petty replied, "Are you kidding? Put me down. Send me the itinerary!" Suddenly, Petty found himself preparing to tour with a musical icon. Petty admitted, "I was a little nervous at first. I didn't know Bob very well, and he's a hard person to know. He turned out to be a good friend. Some of our best times were on the plane rides."

In December, Bob Dylan joined Tom Petty and the Heartbreakers for a few weeks of rehearsals. Howie Epstein described the unorthodox daily sessions: "[Dylan would say], 'Here's the song, here's the chords, let's do it.' There are no arrangements, we just play."

Dubbed the True Confessions Tour, the Far East jaunt began in New Zealand and continued with fourteen shows across Australia and then four in Japan. The tour's first date in Wellington, New Zealand, was nearly cancelled by angry city officials "after the under-rehearsed band whipped up the ire of local residents by turning an outdoor sound check at Athletic Park into a lengthy, full-volume practice session. Tempers eventually calmed, however, and the show went on."

But the concert did not go smoothly. *Rolling Stone* reported: "According to some reviews, the tour got off to a shaky start in New Zealand, where the opening-night audiences responded more fervently to Petty's set than Dylan's. But within a few shows, Dylan was storming into such songs as 'Clean Cut Kid,' 'Positively 4th Street,' 'Rainy Day Women' and 'Like A Rolling Stone,' often facing off with Campbell and Petty in fierce three-way guitar exchanges and launching suddenly into songs that nobody had rehearsed, and that some band members hardly knew."

Having three guitarists on stage at the same time resulted in some unusual musical interaction. As Petty recalled, "It was an interesting thing to be playing and not know who's going to take a solo. Someone'll start and you just look for your hole. If Bob or I are starting to disintegrate, Mike'll jump in. Sometimes we all play a solo at once which sounds *really* interesting. There's an unspoken thing, 'If you're blowing it get out of the way.'" While in New Zealand, Bob Dylan secretly became a father for the sixth time, with a woman he would marry – also in secret – later that year.

During the tour, Dylan and Petty were occasionally joined by guitarist Mark Knopfler of Dire Straits. Additionally, Petty invited Stevie Nicks to join the Australian leg of the tour as a surprise guest. Nicks later recalled, "I got to sing 'Knockin' On Heaven's Door' with Bob and Tom! I'll never forget... walking out to perform and having Bob Dylan turn and do a little bow. It made everything all right – all the pain, all the trouble, all the hassles that come along with this kind of a life in rock and roll. They all went away that moment." But for legal reasons, she was able to perform with the Heartbreakers just twice. Nicks was in Australia for a three-week vacation but was nearly deported by government authorities who insisted she needed a work permit – not a mere visitor's visa – if she continued to appear on stage with Petty and Dylan. (Nicks would return to Australia later that year for several solo concerts – this time after formally acquiring a work permit.)

While in Australia, Petty and Dylan recorded the politically-incendiary blues-rock track, "Band Of The Hand," for the film of the same name, which was directed by Paul Michael Glaser. Produced by Petty, the song featured Dylan on lead vocal with Stevie Nicks providing the harmonies. Despite the massive amount of media coverage surrounding the Dylan/Petty tour, the song was not embraced by radio.

Meanwhile, a documentary culled from two concerts in Sydney was broadcast on HBO and also issued on home video as *Hard To Handle.* The concert film captured Dylan and Petty hitting their stride, particularly on the track, "Knockin' On Heaven's Door." But for whatever reasons, the film's producers focused on Dylan and nearly ignored Petty's contributions. During this period, Petty was continually quizzed about his touring partner: "Everyone's always saying to me, 'What's Bob Dylan like?' It's funny, but people still attach a lot of mystery to Bob... I think they figure that, since we've spent time around him, we can *explain* him, as if he's somebody who needs to be explained. I mean, Dylan's just a guy like anybody else – except he's a guy who has something to say. And he has a personality that makes it his own. There's not many people that can walk into a room of 20,000, stare at them and get their attention."

Performing with Dylan on a daily basis, Petty appreciated the structured routine: "With the rehearsals and the soundchecks, we've been playing four or five hours a night. We've just been playing, playing, and playing. We've done it so much together recently, we kind of feel funny now if we don't play." While on stage, Petty and the members of the Heartbreakers had to learn the non-verbal cues Dylan used for communicating with his backing singers and musicians. As Petty explained: "With singers, he used little hand gestures, but with us, it was a glance of the eyes – he had a certain look that meant 'Something's about to happen,' or 'You're not doin' this right,' or 'You *are* doing it right.' It was all in his eyes.... You really had to pay attention, though – all the time." During the tour, Petty was also very careful not to mimic Dylan's vocal style: "As a matter of fact, I try to avoid singing like Dylan, just because I don't want to seem like I'm imitating him. I have been conscious of that."

In April, Petty and Dylan announced an extension of their tour, with 22 U.S. dates scheduled for the months of June and July. One music critic observed at the time: "It's a sure bet that Petty and the Heartbreakers, far more of a star attraction on the concert circuit these days, have helped business."

Taking a three-month break from the road, Tom Petty and the Heartbreakers entered a recording studio to back Dylan on his 24th studio album, *Knocked Out Loaded*. The group was joined on the sessions by a litany of guest musicians including Al Kooper, Dave Stewart, Ronnie Wood, and T-Bone Burnett. Not one of Dylan's better albums, the project included a composition Petty composed with Dylan, "Got My Mind Made Up," which Dylan historian Howard Sounes called "one of the most forgettable songs of Bob's career." In exchange for helping to produce the album, Petty was given a work of art – a Dylan self-portrait. The painting later found a home on the wall of Petty's basement recording studio.

Going back on the road, the Dylan/Petty rock ensemble began the U.S. portion of the tour on June 9th, with a stop at the San Diego Sports Arena. A reviewer said of the performance: "If the audience wanted a chance to hear more of Petty's material, he seemed to revel in not having to be in the spotlight. He joined Dylan at the microphone to share vocals several times, but, more often, he simply looked like an artist who was thrilled to be playing with one of his major influences."

But the tour was not free of problems. At the Greek Theater in Berkeley, Dylan escaped serious injury when he tripped and came crashing down on the darkened stage. But that mishap was overshadowed by another incident which occurred later in the evening, when a simmering conflict between Tom Petty and Stan Lynch came to the surface. At one point during the concert, Petty glanced at Lynch and according to Petty, "he somehow thought it was a dirty look. He gave me the finger on-stage, I just snapped. I went... [and] put my guitar down and walked off in the middle of the tune. They just kept playing, solo after solo, waiting for me to come back, but I didn't. I went to the dressing room and asked to be taken home." Eventually, Al Kooper took over on guitar while an enraged Petty remained backstage. It took some pleading by Dylan to convince Petty to finish the show. When Petty returned to the stage, he was joined by blues legend John Lee Hooker. But when all was said and done, a rumor was floated that Petty and Lynch had traded punches and during the scuffle, Dylan had been struck and knocked down.

Beginning with a performance in Minneapolis on June 26th, Dylan and Petty teamed with the legendary Grateful Dead for a handful of stadium shows. Dylan and Grateful Dead leader Jerry Garcia were longtime friends and decided to schedule five summer concerts. According to Garcia biographer Blair Jackson, "Garcia had attended a Dylan-Petty show... that spring and had spent considerable time chatting with Dylan backstage.... They were mutual admirers who shared similar roots in American folk and blues. And they had both carried heavy loads since the '60s – Dylan as the defacto poet laureate of American music; Garcia as the embodiment of the libertine Haight-Ashbury ethos – and had attracted more than their share of fanatics and devoted followers who placed them on uncomfortable pedestals. Garcia had more Dylan tunes in his repertoire than did any other major American singer."

Petty recalled, "I gotta say, when we did that first show I looked out at the crowd and I still haven't gotten over it. Those Deadheads gave me a whole new respect for that band... I had no idea. I mean, it's easy to laugh at, but that audience is a whole social phenomenon. It is like the '60s in a way, but I found it very healthy. Those people were so charged up, they listened – really listened – to every little lick we played from the first note of the show." Curiously, the Heartbreakers received *third* billing on these dates. The concert posters read: "Bob Dylan and the Grateful Dead, with special guest Tom Petty and the Heartbreakers." Admission to these shows was a mere $20.

A portion of the Dylan-Dead-Petty concert at Rich Stadium in Buffalo was aired, live by satellite, at the second Farm Aid benefit in Austin, Texas. Petty told the audience: "We wish we could be there with you. This is our own kind of party this afternoon. But we want to tell all the farmers there that we're with you a hundred-percent." During the mini-tour, tragedy struck when Grateful Dead leader Jerry Garcia lapsed into a life-threatening diabetic coma for five days.

Meanwhile, on October 13th, Tom Petty and Benmont Tench performed at the initial Bridge School Benefit at the Shoreline Amphitheatre in Mountain View, California. It was the first time in Petty's career as a Heartbreaker that he played an all-acoustic show – and it clearly showed. Petty was followed by comedian Robin Williams. (For the second Bridge School Benefit, Petty wisely brought his entire band.)

Also in 1986, Petty managed to score a number-one hit, but not on the pop or rock charts. Petty sang a full verse of Hank Williams, Jr.'s updated rendition of "Mind Your Own Business," a song originally recorded by Williams' father, nearly four-decades earlier. The single topped the country charts for two weeks.

*   *   *   *   *   *

In early January 1987, Tom Petty asked Jeff Lynne for his help on a solo album. Although Lynne was in a rush to return to England, he was persuaded to remain in Los Angeles for another week. Petty recounted: "We started playing around at home. I'd written this song called 'Yer So Bad.' I played it for Jeff; he suggested a couple of chords, which made it so much better. I couldn't believe how good it sounded. So we wrote another one, 'Free Fallin'.' Being immensely pleased with them, I wanted to get them on tape somehow. The only place I knew to go was [Mike Campbell's small home studio]. The Heartbreakers weren't even in town, so we called up Phil Jones, this brilliant drummer we'd known for years, and went in and cut these two songs. When they were done, they were like records. They weren't demos, by any stretch of the imagination."

Thrilled with the sessions, Petty recalled, "I remember coming home with those two songs on a cassette and playing them over and over, just saying, 'Wow, this is really good.' I had to talk Jeff into finishing the album with me." Although Petty was steadfast about Lynne taking over the production duties, Lynne was apprehensive about accepting the job. Petty recalled: "He was very nervous about overtaking the record. He didn't want it to sound like Jeff Lynne. He wanted it to sound like me. I had no qualms whatsoever with having Jeff produce me, especially after the job he did on George's *Cloud Nine*. That's an incredible sounding record. It's just so much louder and sounds more exciting than other records. Whatever you think of ELO, you have to admit those records were very well produced."

Soon after, Petty experienced another spark of musical creativity: "While they were mixing [the two tracks], we went into a little soundproof booth at this studio and wrote 'I Won't Back Down.' By the time those [two] songs were mixed, we were sitting on another song that we went in the next day and recorded." During the sessions for "I Won't Back Down," George Harrison stopped by and provided some guitarwork and harmony vocals. Those three soon-to-be rock classics were written and recorded in just three days. Petty later explained: "All the songs were written on 12-string or 6-string acoustic guitars. I wanted to experiment with the art of rhythm guitar. Jeff and I feel that acoustic guitars can be rock 'n' roll instruments, not just folk instruments."

Meanwhile, Stan Lynch discovered that Tom Petty had started working on a new album, but no one bothered to inform him it was a solo project. Flying in from Florida, Lynch was unhappy to learn from a close friend that Petty would not be needing his services. For whatever reason, Petty had not personally notified Lynch of the situation. Lynch, who was initially angry, recounted the predicament: "About a year later I realized they were embarrassed. We're old friends. How do you call an old friend and say you don't want him at the wedding?" It would not be the first or last time Petty and Lynch would alienate each other. Lynch flew back to Florida to renovate a beach house he had just purchased.

During this period, Petty would complete most of the album's tracks. But putting aside his solo project, he was soon immersed in another musical venture.

*   *   *   *   *   *

Tom Petty found himself in yet another legal tussle, this time over the unauthorized use of his music in a television commercial. But the merchandising of rock music is as old as rock and roll itself. Elvis Presley's manager Col. Tom Parker marketed a slew of Elvis products aimed at teenagers, from bracelets to sneakers; during Elvis' early concerts, the cigar-chomping manager personally hawked cheap souvenirs to audiences during extended intermissions. When the Beatles made their first flight to the United States in February 1964, their fellow passengers were not tourists on vacation. The Beatles' manager "Brian Epstein got a chuckle out of the discovery that most of the gray-haired businessmen who shared the cabin were actually merchandisers, keen on gaining the Beatles' endorsement for their products. Every half-hour a stewardess would deliver to Brian a fresh item for consideration. Taking a sheet of monogrammed notepaper out of his briefcase, [Epstein] would write a polite note of rejection. Meantime, the plastic guitar or mop-headed doll would be passed about among the Beatles, each [member] breaking off a piece until the sample was destroyed."

But numerous rock acts have appeared in radio and television ads. In 1964, the Rolling Stones sang the praises of Rice Krispies cereal in a television commercial. Then in 1967, Jefferson Airplane recorded a psychedelic-tinged, minute-long radio spot for Levi's jeans. And many rock artists including the Who and the Moody Blues have recorded jingles for Coca-Cola.

Decades later in 1988, MTV banned Neil Young's video, "This Note's For You," because the clip satirized the relationship between MTV, record companies, and large corporations. Young's video parodied a number of his fellow musicians including Eric Clapton who had performed his classic hit "After Midnight" in a beer commercial earlier that year. Eventually, MTV relented and the clip would win the network's award for Best Video of the Year.

Just like Neil Young, Tom Petty has been adamant about not allowing his music to appear in radio or television ads. Although Petty accepted corporate sponsorship from Levi's and Tecate Beer during his early tours, he later regretted his actions. Petty explained, "I really have turned down – and sometimes I wonder if I'm stupid – many millions of dollars. And that's no exaggeration. I still turn down that kind of stuff all the time... because I don't feel right about it. I think it hurts everything. It helped kill rock 'n' roll in a big way. [Musicians] trivialize themselves to the point where they're just trivial. I just don't want to see myself as a jingle writer. I take this stuff pretty seriously."

Taking a similar stand, John Mellencamp spent years attacking the corporate sponsorship of rock music until 2006, when he gave in and allowed his track "My Country" to be used in an ad campaign by Chevrolet. Mellencamp even appeared in a commercial, strumming an acoustic guitar while sitting next to a classic Chevy pickup truck. Mellencamp attributed his change of heart to the realization that the music industry was ignoring older, veteran rockers. As *The New York Times* reported at the time: "[Mellencamp] said a turning point for him came last year, after he heard *Highway Companion*, the latest album by his contemporary Tom Petty. He liked it and thought the single "Saving Grace" would be a hit, but then never heard the song on the radio or saw it on the video channels. Fearing a similar fate for his own music, Mr. Mellencamp said he decided to accept Chevrolet's offer."

Unlike Mellencamp, Petty continued to stand firm. In early 1986, B.F. Goodrich's advertising agency tried to secure permission to use the Heartbreakers song, "Mary's New Car," in a television commercial for the company's tires. As expected, Petty declined the request.

Despite Petty's refusal, a B.F. Goodrich tire ad employed background music that sounded suspiciously similar to the song in question: "They called me and asked me if they could use it in their tire ad. I told them no. I don't allow anyone to use my songs in commercials. I don't think they should be used that way. So then they turned around and did it anyway. They got a soundalike singer, changed it a little bit, but not really very much, and my friend saw it on TV. I asked [them] nicely... to stop and of course they wouldn't."

On March 4, 1987, Petty obtained a restraining order against the Akron-based tire company. Not surprisingly, U.S. District Judge J. Spencer Letts agreed with Petty's position and ruled from the bench: "They are very, very much alike... in a number of ways. The words are alike. The music is alike. The tempo is alike." In the end, Petty would win his case.

Years later, Petty would come to the defense of John Densmore, the drummer of the Doors, in a dispute that involved the licensing of the group's music. In 1968, Doors singer Jim Morrison had threatened to smash a Buick on live television after learning that his bandmates had signed a contract, without his knowledge, allowing the group's iconic theme "Light My Fire" to be featured in a Buick commercial. Wisely, Buick backed down and did not air the ad.

In the decades that followed, the surviving three members of the Doors continued to reject offers from advertising agencies to license the group's music. But in 2000, Densmore was the only holdout when Cadillac dangled an astounding $15 million for the use of the Doors song, "Break On Through (To The Other Side)" in a television campaign. As anticipated, Densmore's former bandmates Ray Manzarek and Robby Krieger were not happy. But Densmore continued to maintain the position that artistic integrity was more important than monetary gain. As Tom Petty wrote on the back cover of Densmore's book, *Unhinged*, "We have seen so many great artists succumb to the theory that any dollar that's my dollar, is a good dollar." Densmore echoed the sentiment: "I remember reading about Petty having the same reaction as I did when I heard 'Good Vibrations' (a metaphoric song for the sixties by the Beach Boys) selling Orange Crush soda pop. I was crushed. Whatever 'gift' I felt I received about the message of love in the counterculture was doused with yellow dye #5. My flower power was wilting and almost dead from the onslaught of inorganic commerce and pesticides."

Then later when Manzarek and Krieger had appropriated the Doors' name and logo, and began touring with a new lead singer as "the Doors of the 21st Century," Densmore filed an injunction and took his former bandmates to court. In 2004, Petty would testify on Densmore's behalf to defend the Doors' legacy in a battle that would again pit commerce against art. After a lengthy trial, Densmore was victorious and his former bandmates were legally barred from calling themselves the Doors.

▶ CHAPTER 22
REFUGEE: THE HOUSE FIRE

Recorded mostly at Sound City during a five-week break in the Dylan-Petty tour, Tom Petty and the Heartbreakers' seventh studio album, *Let Me Up (I've Had Enough)*, would mark the group's new approach to recording. After spending a great deal of time with Dylan in the studio and observing his informal recording style, the Heartbreakers decided to change course and abandon the intense Jimmy Iovine method of making records. Instead, the sessions were straightforward, uncomplicated, and noticeably stress-free.

But the Heartbreakers had not planned on recording the album. As Mike Campbell explained at the time, "It started out that Bob Dylan had some studio time. We were going to go in together, but then he got busy with other projects. So we took the time to just go in and fool around, and before we knew it we had a bunch of tracks. We liked the way it was going, so we went ahead and finished it ourselves. We didn't feel like bringing in someone else. The next album we may feel like bringing in eight producers, but this one we did on our own." As Petty recalled, "We didn't tinker with this record as much. Most of the overdubs we put on we later took off."

During this period, the Heartbreakers were in the middle of a creative whirlwind. Petty recounted: "Our engineer, Don Smith, would say, 'You've got twenty tunes, maybe you should go back and finish some of them.' But we wanted to break ground every day. And some days nothing happened until maybe the last hour of the session; I'd get an idea, and here came a song. It was really fun.... We recorded up to the day we had to leave for the tour." In a very brief period, the Heartbreakers had managed to record thirty songs. But instead of issuing a double-album, Petty selected eleven of the tracks for a single disc. And as he said at the time, "there's two or three songs I'll use on future albums."

In April 1987, *Let Me Up (I've Had Enough)* was released to mixed reviews and was the group's first studio album that failed to crack the top-10 in nearly a decade. The album's inner sleeve featured a news photo of "a small plane that actually went nose-down into a woman's backyard swimming pool, near the studio where the Heartbreakers were recording. Petty wrote a verse in 'My Life/Your World' about it."

The first single, "Jammin' Me," was one of two tracks on the album co-written by the team of Dylan, Petty, and Campbell. After Campbell composed the melody, Petty and Dylan worked on the lyrics in a hotel room. Although the song appeared to include a personal attack against a trio of Hollywood stars – including actor Eddie Murphy – Petty joked to a reporter: "We were just taking names from the entertainment section [of a newspaper]. I hope no one is offended by it. I'm a big fan of Eddie Murphy's."

But Murphy was, indeed, offended. During a press conference to promote his film *Beverly Hills Cop II*, Murphy was apprised of the song's lyrics by one of the journalists in attendance. Caught off guard by the situation, Murphy hurled an expletive at Petty. A day after Murphy's angry outburst, Petty admitted that he "deserved" the reaction, but insisted, "we weren't puttin' him down; I wonder if he'll understand that – I guess he will.... In rehearsal I sing different names every time I sing it." In concert, Petty would alter the song's lyrics and substitute actress "Tallulah Bankhead and [televangelist] Jerry Falwell for Vanessa Redgrave and Joe Piscopo, as if to drive home the point that he did not mean those celebrities in particular but the idea of 'a celebrity.'"

The music video for "Jammin' Me" featured a montage of newsmakers from the 1980s, including Pope John Paul II, Ronald and Nancy Reagan, Muammar Gaddafi, and Ayatollah Khomeini. In the video, Petty was dressed in a conservative black suit and plain white dress shirt – all while bucking conformity with a dangling, gold earring.

Another highlight of the album was the mid-tempo track, "All Mixed Up." As Petty explained, "On 'All Mixed Up,' we were all knocked out by Benmont's magic fingers. Benmont had this thing that sampled horns on his keyboard. It's like *so cool!* Benmont played five things at once. He'd have everything on – his organ, his piano, just a circle of stuff.... He's got this hotel key that he can stick in the organ and hold a note down, turn around and play somethin' else. The engineer'd be going',

'Where's all this shit *comin'* from?!'"

Then in an odd chain of events, one of the album's songs was nearly stolen – accidentally. During a visit to Petty's home, Stevie Nicks was given a number of tapes, one of which contained an unfinished, instrumental demo written by Mike Campbell. After adding some lyrics and recording the track with Fleetwood Mac, Nicks played the finished song over the phone for Petty. But an angry Petty would not allow Fleetwood Mac to issue the track, which the Heartbreakers had included on *Let Me Up (I've Had Enough)* as "Runaway Trains."

*   *   *   *   *   *

On May 17, 1987, an intruder torched the hillside Encino home of Tom Petty. Shortly before 9 AM on a Sunday morning, Petty and his wife smelled smoke while seated at their breakfast table. The couple grabbed their five-year-old daughter, located their housekeeper, and then rushed outside. Petty's other daughter was staying overnight at a friend's house.

Running around in his bare feet, Petty grabbed a garden hose in a futile attempt to extinguish the shooting flames. But the fire quickly engulfed the back of the house before spreading to the wood shingle roof.

Not surprisingly, the paparazzi of Los Angeles began swarming the grounds even before the arrival of the first fire truck. With firefighters fearing the blaze might spread to the surrounding ground brush, ten fire companies rushed to the scene. Even though the fire was extinguished in less than one hour, the damage was immense. News footage showed complete devastation: while a car was being driven away from a smoke-filled garage, just fifty feet away an undamaged child's bicycle was resting against a concrete wall. Although the first floor and attic were total losses, the basement was left relatively unscathed. Petty's housekeeper, who suffered minor burns on her hands, was the only one injured.

After barely escaping with his life, Petty was devastated by the tragedy. Aided by dozens of friends who had arrived for a planned afternoon birthday party for Petty's wife, Jane, Petty was able to retrieve some items from his newly-built basement recording studio, including a collection of guitars and the master tapes of all his albums.

With his family's personal belongings destroyed by the fire, Petty was a father first and doted over his two young daughters. "I was really glad to be alive. I was like someone who had survived a plane crash. You are just really glad that they didn't get you. If you've ever had anybody try to kill you, it really makes you re-evaluate everything," Petty explained.

Mike Campbell told the press at the time, "The band is pretty weirded out by the whole thing. Tom is safe, his family's safe.... Tom really wanted to make sure this didn't affect the tour. He showed up the next day at rehearsal, and I said, 'Well, do you want to call it off?' He said, 'No, no, I'd rather work, I want to make sure this comes off.' In a twisted sort of way, it probably is better that he's going on the road."

Later, firefighters discovered residue from a flammable liquid on a rear, outdoor staircase of Petty's two-story home. But authorities were unable to identify any suspects or determine any motives, and no one was ever prosecuted for the crime. Amazingly, the arsonist managed to commit his crime in broad daylight without attracting attention. Petty later explained, "The funny thing was I kept insisting it was an accident, telling the investigators, 'Who'd want to kill me?' And then 10 people confessed to the police. None of them did it. But they wanted to confess."

Although the torching of Petty's home remained a mystery, the criminal act might have been motivated by the lyrics of his hit at the time, "Jammin' Me," in which three Hollywood celebrities were seemingly attacked. Although Petty repeatedly defended the lyrics as a commentary on the culture of fame, an overzealous fan of one of the three entertainers might have thought otherwise. A few weeks after his home was set on fire, Petty mentioned in an interview that it was actually Bob Dylan who came up with the three celebrity names. Then coincidentally, a suspicious fire erupted at Dylan's home. Fortunately for Dylan, the blaze was quickly extinguished. But on more than one occasion, Petty has hinted that he might know the identity of the arsonist.

On May 30th, Tom Petty headed out on the Rock 'N' Roll Caravan tour, which featured a pair of opening acts, the Georgia Satellites and the Del Fuegos. Realizing he was spending far too much time away from his family, Petty brought along his wife and two young daughters, who traveled in their own tour bus. Playing 44 dates in nine weeks, the tour was an emotionally cathartic experience for Petty. Throughout the tour,

Petty triumphantly announced to audiences, "They burned my house down – but they didn't get my guitar!"

During the tour, Petty performed a pair of cover songs, including a rendition of the 1960s protest song by Buffalo Springfield, "For What It's Worth." And belatedly, Petty acknowledged the "punk" label he was saddled with early in his career, and tackled the punk standard, "Should I Stay Or Should I Go?" by the Clash.

▶ CHAPTER 23
HANDLE WITH CARE

In late August 1987, Tom Petty and the Heartbreakers reunited with Bob Dylan and began rehearsing for the next leg of their extended tour. At one point, Dylan and Stan Lynch missed a night of practice so they could attend a concert in Los Angeles. As Lynch recalled, "I took Dylan to see Sammy [Davis, Jr.] and Frank [Sinatra] at the Greek Theater.... That's a true story. The first week of rehearsals for the Dylan tour, Dylan hadn't spoken to us all week. We were all playing and I said, 'Look, I gotta bug out early tonight.' And they go, 'Lynch, what's your crisis?' I go, 'I got tickets for Sammy and Frank at the Greek.' The whole band covers their eyes going, 'Oh geez, I can't believe he really said that.' And Dylan looked up at me in all seriousness and said, 'Sammy and Frank? I love those guys.' So Dylan and I went to the Greek.... I don't mind saying I was a little starstruck by the whole concept that I came from Gainesville to L.A., and now I'm sitting with Bob Dylan watching Sammy Davis and Frank Sinatra."

The Temples in Flames tour began with two dates in Israel before heading to Europe for nearly thirty shows over the next six weeks. Dylan recalled, "In these first four shows I sang eighty different songs, never repeating one, just to see if I could do it. It seemed easy." Near the end of the highly successful tour, the rock and roll troupe performed for three nights at the National Exhibition Centre in Birmingham, England. Present at the shows were George Harrison and Jeff Lynne. It was here that the seeds for a future collaboration were planted.

Then backstage the following week in London, Mike Campbell experienced a heart-stopping moment when he stood, face to face, with a former Beatle: "We were pretty worn out. George and Jeff came by backstage. George walked up to me and I said 'hi,' and he did one of those things where instead of shaking hands he took my hand in both of his hands, looked me right in the eye and goes, 'Bless you.' I remember thinking, 'Wow, this is a heavy cat.' It was a sweet gesture and I felt a connection." Harrison would subsequently join Dylan and Petty onstage for an encore performance of "Rainy Day Women #12 & 35."

Although he deeply cherished his two-year collaboration with Dylan, Petty knew the tour had to come to an end. Petty needed to rebuild his home and tend to his wife and young daughters, and informed Dylan of his decision. Petty came to the realization after the London concert: "I just thought, okay, it's time to get off this bus now and get back to being us. I think he thought we could do both, but we couldn't [because] it was wearing me out." Though disappointed by the news, Dylan – himself a strong family man who fawned over his children – did not try to change Petty's mind.

Touring with Dylan had been a psychologically-cleansing experience for Petty: "By the time we got out on the tour with him in Australia, I just felt really free for some reason. Everything was clear again. I was so busy focusing on playing well that I forgot about all my problems. I was enjoying music again. I realized that I was worrying too much about pleasing other people or being accepted."

Although the tour had been a career high for Petty, the same could not be said for Dylan. He later revealed in his autobiography: "I'd been on an eighteen month tour with Tom Petty and the Heartbreakers.... I had no connection to any kind of inspiration. Whatever was there to begin with had vanished and shrunk. Tom was at the top of his game and I was at the bottom of mine. I couldn't overcome the odds. Everything was smashed. I didn't have the skill to touch their raw nerves. Couldn't penetrate the surfaces. It wasn't my moment of history anymore. There was a hollow singing in my heart and I couldn't wait to retire and fold the tent."

But shortly after the completion of the tour in December, Dylan had a change of heart and went back on the road. But after hauling around a large entourage of musicians and backing vocalists for years, Dylan embarked on a low-key tour with a stripped-down rhythm section.

*   *   *   *   *   *

Tom Petty had first crossed paths with George Harrison a number of years earlier: "I first met him in 1974 when I came out to Los Angeles.

I hadn't been out here very long. I was working at Leon Russell's [home studio], and there were a few nights [of] sessions with George and Ringo. It's a scary thing meeting Beatles, but George was so nice to me and included me in everything." Then during the European leg of the tour with Bob Dylan, Petty had a few opportunities to speak with Harrison: "I reminded him that we'd met, and there was some kind of weird click. It felt like we had known each other all our lives, and in a very personal way."

Upon Petty's return to California, destiny seemed to take over: "I went back to L.A., and almost by fate I went into a restaurant, spur of the moment. I hadn't planned to go, and the waiter came over and said, 'Oh, your friend is in the next room, he wants to see you.' I didn't know who he meant. I walked in, and it was George. He said, 'God, it's so weird, I was just asking Jeff Lynne for your number.' He said, 'Where are you going?' I said, 'I'm just going home.' He said, 'Do you mind if I go with you?' He came to my house and stayed for days. George came to L.A. fairly often, and I went to England and visited him a lot."

A lifelong Beatles fanatic, Petty would soon find himself in an unimaginable position as a member of a group that included one of his early musical idols. Petty recounted, "We weren't even thinking about being in a band together, but we loved having a few beers and just talking, just visiting. Kind of like when you see people and feel like you've known them for a long time. That's how I related to George and Jeff. Then I came home and I was at a red light Thanksgiving Day, going to buy some baseball gloves, 'cause I wanted to play baseball real bad and the only place open was Thrifty Drugs. Now George had given me his *Cloud Nine* album just before it was released. I loved it and I'd been playing it all day before I went to get these mitts. So when I get to this light, and there's Jeff, the next car over.... He was going to produce Brian Wilson at the time. And he said, 'Do you want to come to the studio with me.' I said, 'Nah, I'm going to play baseball.' But we agreed to stay in touch and it turned out he lived in my neighborhood, just up the street."

Meanwhile, George Harrison and Roy Orbison had first met in May 1963 when the Beatles were scheduled as *the opening act* for Orbison during a three-week tour across Britain. (The Fab Four's second British single, "Please Please Me," had been written by John Lennon in an attempt to emulate Orbison.) But when Lennon and the group's manager

Brian Epstein demanded a reversal in the billing – with the Beatles closing the shows as the headliners – Orbison graciously consented. As Orbison remembered: "I agreed because I was singing ballads and they were singing songs like 'Twist And Shout,' so it all made sense. Anyway, I was making four or five times as much money as they were, so I gave them a break. As you can see, it was the right move."

On the opening night of the tour at the Adelphi Theatre near London, Orbison was a smash hit with the audience, which kept screaming for an encore. But "when Roy started to go back on stage, Lennon and McCartney could restrain themselves no longer, grabbing him by the arms and refusing to let him take his curtain call. Roy struggled, but John said, '*Yankee, go home!*'"

Eventually, Orbison and the members of the Beatles would establish a warm relationship. With both Orbison and Harrison regularly sleeping in late and missing their ride to the next stop on the tour, the two men shared a number of amicable conversations during long car rides. Surprisingly, Orbison was also friends with Bob Dylan during this period and had attended the folk singer's 21st birthday party. (Conversely, Dylan was a fan of Orbison's music, and once said, "His songs had songs within songs.... There wasn't anything else on the radio like him.")

Then on August 28, 1964, several months after Beatlemania hit the U.S. shores, 21-year-old George Harrison first met Bob Dylan, who was just two years his senior. With the Beatles preparing for a concert in New York City, Dylan visited the group at the Delmonico Hotel. Although John Lennon was absorbed with the young American folk singer and had invited him to the group's hotel room, the other members of the Beatles treated Dylan with the utmost admiration and were in awe of his second album, *The Freewheelin' Bob Dylan*. A hipster who was wise to the ways of the world, Dylan rolled a joint for each member of the group during his visit. (Although the members of the Fab Four had experienced their own share of vice while playing in the seedy bars of Hamburg, they had just briefly experimented with marijuana in the past.)

Later, in an attempt to keep up with the shifting tastes in popular music, Bob Dylan went electric in 1965. When folk purists viciously attacked Dylan, Harrison publically came to his defense: "The people who walked out [of his concerts] must have been idiots.... It was all still pure Dylan, and he has to find out his own directions. If he felt he wanted electrification, that's the way he had to do it. Who's laying down the rules?"

Four years after their initial meeting, Dylan and Harrison decided to collaborate on some songs. Their first creation, "I'd Have You Anytime," later appeared on Harrison's first post-Beatles solo album. As author Marc Shapiro observed in *All Things Must Pass: The Life of George Harrison*: "George, in his late twenties and showing a marked sense of maturity when it came to music, went back to the United States for a visit with Bob Dylan. During this visit, all barriers came down and the two musicians were able to deal with each other as people. During this visit, Dylan was generous and forthcoming in inviting George into his latest musical vision, sitting together for hours, swapping lyrics, chords and ideas. George came away from his visit with Bob Dylan renewed, inspired and anxious to make new and personal music away from the glare of the Beatles spotlight." In the wake of his sojourn with Dylan, Harrison composed "Old Brown Shoe," which the Beatles would record in 1969. The following year, Harrison recorded the Dylan original "If Not For You," which later became the debut hit for Aussie singer Olivia Newton-John. Then in 1971, Dylan made an appearance at Harrison's charity benefit, the Concert for Bangladesh.

Years later, George Harrison hired former ELO frontman-turned-producer Jeff Lynne to oversee his 1987 comeback album, *Cloud Nine*. Lynne later explained: "We were three-quarters of the way through *Cloud Nine*, and every night, as we were relaxing with a few drinks after mixing a big epic or whatever, George and I had the same conversation, 'We could have a group, you know?' George didn't like the idea of being a solo guy – that's what he told me. He was never comfortable with it. He wanted a group, and, of course, he could do whatever he wanted." Remarkably, during this period Lynne was producing solo albums for Harrison as well as *both* Tom Petty and Roy Orbison.

Petty recalled, "So [Jeff Lynne] had Roy over one day and wondered if I wanted to write some songs with him. I didn't really know him. That's sort of when we first got to know each other and wrote a couple songs, 'You Got It' and 'California Blue.'" But the Orbison record was taking much longer than expected and Lynne had to ask him for a break in the sessions in order to complete Harrison's album.

After moving from Nashville to Southern California in 1985, Orbison had experienced a major career revival. His dramatic ballad, "In Dreams," enjoyed renewed attention after it was prominently featured in

David Lynch's 1986 film, *Blue Velvet*. The following year, Orbison was inducted into the Rock and Roll Hall of Fame, with Bruce Springsteen telling the audience, "In 1975, when I went into the studio to make *Born To Run*, I wanted to make a record with words like Bob Dylan that sounded like Phil Spector – but most of all, I wanted to sing like Roy Orbison." Just months later, Springsteen performed at the star-studded tribute, *Roy Orbison And Friends: A Black & White Night*.

Then in a pivotal moment in rock history, George Harrison wanted to record a B-side track for a 12-inch single he was releasing in Europe, "This Is Love." On the evening of the recording session, he dined with Jeff Lynne, who had brought along Roy Orbison. With the three legends sitting together at one table, Harrison asked Orbison and Lynne to help him with the song. For the sake of convenience, Lynne suggested they record the track at Bob Dylan's home studio. Dylan's estate was located nearby on a coastal bluff in a rural section of Malibu. Enroute to the session, Harrison picked up a guitar he had left at Tom Petty's house. Sensing a creative opportunity, Harrison invited Petty to join the musical festivities.

Harrison quickly realized the good fortune at his disposal when he arrived at Dylan's finely furnished home. With all five musicians playing acoustic guitars, the core musical track was written and then recorded. After dining on some barbecued chicken in Dylan's backyard garden, the men worked out the song's lyrics. After Harrison provided the opening line, the rest of the lyrics quickly fell into place. Staring at a box of Ampex recording tape, Harrison came up with a title for the song: "Handle With Care."

Returning to the cluttered studio in Dylan's garage, the men added their vocals to the song. Lynne would also provide the bass guitar and drum tracks. The following day, the 24-track tape was taken to a nearby recording studio. Mike Campbell, who was asked to play on the song, recalled: "Tom called me down to the studio and they wanted to put a solo on it. So I went down there with a little Marshall amp and a Stratocaster, and Jeff (Lynne) and George (Harrison) were there. I knew them a little bit, but was pretty intimidated, coming down to play a solo with George Harrison sitting there, but I tried to put my blinders on and just do the job, so I went down there and got a sound. They played the track, and Jeff was real supportive when I played a few things, he said, 'That's the right direction,' and I played something that was a little like something Clapton might play. So I played a few things and I wasn't really thinking that it was helping the song, and George was sitting there and I said, 'Why don't you play a slide on this, because I think if you played it would be really better than what I'm doing,' and he said (nonchalantly) 'Well, OK,' he picked up the guitar with the sound that I had, and he played that amazing, beautiful solo. I was really happy that the heat was off of me."

Recording engineer Don Smith explained the song's final touches: "'Handle With Care' was finished at Westlake Audio [in Hollywood]. I had worked with Tom a lot, so he called me to come on by and just oversee what was going on. I recorded Roy's vocal 'cos he hadn't done it yet, and Tom overdubbed the harmonica because Bob didn't want to come down to the mix. And then George overdubbed his vocals. This whole thing was for a B-side. So it wasn't a big deal, and we were in there just having fun. And then all of a sudden, it's six o'clock the next morning, and they're like, 'Whoa – this is really good. You know what? This isn't just a B-side, guys.'"

When Harrison played the finished track for his record label, Warner Brothers executives Mo Ostin and Lenny Waronker were excited about what they were hearing and sensed a far bigger opportunity. With the label bosses suggesting that Harrison and the other four rock legends regroup to record an entire album, it seemed as if everything was falling into place. But Harrison was enjoying a significant comeback with the release of his solo album, *Cloud Nine*, and was apprehensive about taking on a major side project. Harrison was persuaded after Ostin argued that an all-star album would provide the former Beatle with another creative outlet and could potentially become a sizable career boost. Harrison recalled, "The record company said, 'Oh, we can't put that out, it's too good!' So I thought, 'Well, we'll just have to do another nine songs and make an album.'" Almost in the same boat, Petty had to contend with his day job as the leader of his own group.

A week after "Handle With Care" was recorded, Harrison asked the other four musicians who played on the track if they would be interested in forming a band. Jeff Lynne, who had been encouraging Harrison to start a new group, was the first to join. Next up, Petty and then Dylan both agreed to participate. Petty recalled how the group's lineup was finalized: "We all jumped in a car to go see Roy play [at the Celebrity Theatre] in Anaheim. We ran into Roy's dressing room, threw everybody out and said, 'We want you to be in our band, Roy.' He said, 'That'd be great,' then gave this unbelievable show.''

Despite the fact that Orbison was in the middle of a tour, he made time for the project. Petty was also forced to put aside his solo album for the moment. After all, he was now a member of a band that included an actual Beatle!

George Harrison's wife, Olivia, recounted the origin of the band's quirky name: "[George] and Jeff used to call gadgets in the studio 'wilburys,' like, 'Let's give that sound a trembling wilbury.'" But while Harrison had originally wanted to call the group the Trembling Wilburys, Lynne intervened and the two men settled on the Traveling Wilburys.

Although all five members of the group were individually signed to various labels, the project went forward as planned without any legal glitches. As Orbison explained at the time, "We didn't ask any of the record companies or [any] manager or attorneys or anybody. We just went ahead and did it and no one knew about it. It was right in the middle of my album with five songs recorded and five to go. We just kept it a secret until the writing and singing was done and then we mentioned it to all the record companies, to CBS, Warner, Virgin and MCA, who all said no problem, which was great. I think if we had tried to get together and told everyone that we were forming a little group they would have told us that there were too many problems. I remember one executive said, 'Well, I'm not going to stand in the way of history,' and just hung up the phone.''

Petty and his new bandmates crafted the bulk of the album at Dave Stewart's estate, atop Coldwater Canyon in the Encino Hills section of Los Angeles. The recording studio was set up in Stewart's guest house – an unassuming Spanish-style, wood-framed cottage – which was situated in a relaxed, wooded yard. As Stewart later recalled, "It was kind of weird to look out my back window and see Bob Dylan, Roy Orbison, Tom Petty, George Harrison and Jeff Lynne strumming their guitars sitting on the grass under a tree." Stewart, who had prior commitments in England, left shortly after the start of the recording sessions.

Needing a drummer, the group brought in Jim Keltner, who was later given the nickname, Buster Sidebury. Petty had first worked with Keltner in the mid-1970s, after Mudcrutch had disbanded. (Keltner had previously recorded or toured with three of the four Beatles and performed at George Harrison's charity event, the Concert for Bangladesh.)

Surprisingly, it was not a challenge for the five individual rock stars to put aside their personal egos for the sake of the album. Of the five Wilburys, Petty at age 38 was by far the youngest member of the group, while Orbison, at 52, was the oldest. Petty later recalled, "Well, they treated me equally, which was nice. But I always felt like I was the kid in the band. I was the one who was really lucky to be there. But they never treated me that way."

Harrison emerged as the chief Wilbury, pushing and prodding his bandmates during the entire creative process. "We got everyone to agree and did the other nine [songs] the same way, writing them like we had to be done tomorrow," Harrison recalled. With Dylan scheduled to begin a solo tour, it was imperative that the sessions were completed on time.

The album was recorded over a short period in early May, with most of the tracks written in an informal atmosphere inside Stewart's kitchen or living room. Petty explained the daily routine: "We'd start out every day in the living room of the main house, tossing lines out." When the writing was done, the five men would head to the guest house and record multiple takes of the track to determine whose lead vocal best suited the particular song.

The group used a basic 24-track mixing board, with Lynne usually at the controls. With a slew of wires leading to the control room, the five men sat in a circle as they played their guitars. Petty and Orbison – both heavy smokers – would usually sit next to each other and share an ashtray on the floor. With the two men becoming close friends, Orbison would soon begin calling Petty by his nickname, "Tommy." At one point, Jim Keltner tapped his drumsticks on a refrigerator to get the right sound.

As for settling disagreements, Petty recalled, "We usually went by a group decision. We were pretty honest with each other. In recording or writing, when somebody gets the right part, everybody knows." Although the entire group was credited with writing the songs, some of the individual members played bigger roles in the process by bringing in their own partially-completed compositions. Petty contributed two songs, "Last Night" and "Margarita."

Remarkably, the tracks were written and recorded in just ten days.

Then after taking a one-week break, Harrison and Lynne headed to London – with master tapes in hand – to clean up and tweak the songs. Working in Harrison's personal studio at his Friar Park residence, the two men were later joined in the control room by Petty and Orbison. A mere six weeks from the start of the sessions, the album was completed. Through it all, Petty somehow managed to keep news of the project from most of his friends and his bandmates in the Heartbreakers.

*   *   *   *   *   *

After the completed Traveling Wilburys album was delivered to Warner Brothers, the label did not have high hopes for a project that was recorded by five older musicians, quickly and cheaply. With some members of the group refusing to consider a tour to publicize and promote the album, Warner Brothers initially neglected to spend any real money on trade ads, radio spots, or record store promotions.

In addition to the Traveling Wilburys, the 1980s saw the formation of several other notable rock supergroups such as Bad English, the Damn Yankees, the Power Station, and Asia. But as one rock critic wrote at the time, "Supergroups are almost always a disaster.... The reason supergroups are routinely tumultuous is that they're rooted in an awkward balance of egos. Where a band typically learns to blend its individual personalities while struggling toward success, the supergroup is composed of performers already accustomed to the perks and prerogatives of stardom. Where a hungry band might argue about who ate the last slice of pizza, supergroups tussle over more substantive issues. Like the spotlight." As George Harrison conceded, "Just getting some famous people together doesn't guarantee success. More often than not it's just a clash of personalities and a big ego detour."

Wanting to avoid the classic trapfalls, Tom Petty argued at the time: "We definitely didn't want to treat this like a supergroup. I don't even like the term all that much. But we were aware that it would be viewed as such. We look at the Wilburys as a completely other persona." Consequently, all five members of the group decided to use aliases. While Petty took the name Charlie T. Wilbury, Jr., the other members emerged as Otis (Jeff Lynne), Lucky (Bob Dylan), Nelson (George Harrison), and Lefty (Roy Orbison). Their real names did not appear anywhere on the album. According to the group's official biography, "each of the five mythical Wilburys was born to a different wife of the same father, Charles Truscott Wilbury, Sr., a notorious drinker and womanizer."

Released in October 1988, *The Traveling Wilburys, Vol. 1* was met by positive reviews in the rock press. Almost immediately, the album exploded on the charts. What Warner Brothers failed to grasp was that each of the group's five members had their own loyal following. And it also helped that the album contained a number of well-written, hook-filled songs. The album's first release, "Handle With Care," enjoyed heavy airplay on AOR stations and was a turntable hit on top-40 radio, with the single stalling out at #45 on the charts. Selling more than two-million copies in the U.S. during its first year of release, the album was also a strong seller around the world, particularly in Australia and Canada.

The album's second single, "End Of The Line" – which was primarily written by George Harrison – combined elements of the British skiffle movement of Harrison's teen years and the folk-rock stylings of 1960s-era Dylan. The video for the track was filmed shortly after the sudden death of Roy Orbison and just three weeks after the album's release. During Orbison's vocal solos, the camera focused in on his framed portrait, which was perched near a rocking chair. In the video, Petty wore a menacing outlaw-style hat.

Three members of the Wilburys – Petty, Harrison, and Lynne – promoted the album with an appearance on MTV. But Harrison dominated the interview with the announcement that he was retiring. During the 19-minute segment, an overly-relaxed Petty was happy to sit quietly off to the side, where he eventually began snacking on an apple.

Over the next year, the album would continue to garner heavy radio airplay with tracks such as "Last Night" and "Tweeter And The Monkey Man." With the group's unforeseen success, Harrison began contemplating the possibility of a Wilburys "adventure film." The project would have been handled by Harrison's production company, Handmade Films, which he established in 1978 with his business manager, Denis O'Brien, to produce the comedy spoof *Monty Python's Life Of Brian*. In order to finance the film, Harrison had mortgaged his 120-room mansion. Over the next ten years, the company produced nearly two-dozen films, including the 1986 Madonna box-office bomb *Shanghai Surprise*. (In 1994, Harrison would sell his stake in the business for $8.5 million.)

Meanwhile, with both Bob Dylan and the Beatles inducted into the Rock and Roll Hall of Fame on January 20, 1988, Harrison was able to reconnect with Dylan. That evening, Dylan and Harrison stood side-by-side on stage, sharing a microphone for an all-star rendition of the Dylan gem made by popular by Jimi Hendrix, "All Along The Watchtower." Joining the pair on stage were Mick Jagger, Bruce Springsteen, Little Richard, John Fogerty, and many others.

*   *   *   *   *   *

Several years after joining the Heartbreakers, Howie Epstein emerged as a successful producer. In 1988, he began working with Carlene Carter, the stepdaughter of Johnny Cash and the granddaughter of country pioneer Maybelle Carter. It was Maybelle who taught a young Carlene how to play the guitar.

With high aspirations, Carlene Carter once told a writer, "I wanna be a mega-star. I wanna be enormous! I wanna be in everything!" Talented and attractive, Carter was married to British rocker Nick Lowe when she first met Epstein. Lowe's music video for his 1979 hit, "Cruel To Be Kind," included a reenactment of his wedding to Carter. But Carter's marriage to Lowe would not last. As Lowe later admitted, his addiction to alcohol caused their breakup: "My domestic life was in tatters. My first marriage to Carlene Carter had not broken up, but sort of disappeared, just sort of vanished. I let everything go and didn't have control over anything. I was an alcoholic, really, to all intents and purposes, I certainly was drinking all the time.... I got a divorce, tried to make it [as] amicable as possible, I didn't want to have a fight, and she was fantastic. She is really great." But like the lyrics of a jaded country song, Carter had been married and divorced three times by the age of 35.

With Epstein determined to return Carter to the music charts, the pair would spend long hours at Epstein's 24-track home studio in Los Angeles. Released in 1990, Carter's comeback album, *I Fell In Love*, was well received by both Nashville and country radio, and spawned four hit singles. Epstein and Carter collaborated with Benmont Tench and Epstein's longtime songwriting partner from Milwaukee, Perry Lamek, to compose the album's top-10 title track, "I Fell In Love," which was later nominated for a Grammy. (Both Epstein and Tench would also appear in the song's music video.) The following year, Epstein brought singer-songwriter John Prine into his home studio, with the resulting album, *The Missing Years*, earning a Grammy.

By 1993, Epstein's relationship with Carter had grown from professional to romantic. Although the two musicians were soon inseparable, very little about their romance was revealed to the press. In fact, their engagement in 1995 received little attention. Ironically, Carlene Carter had told an interviewer in the mid-1980s, that if her marriage to Nick Lowe would end in a divorce, "I definitely won't get married again. No way!"

*   *   *   *   *   *

In 1989, Petty had finished rebuilding his fire-gutted home in Encino. The significantly enlarged structure was made fireproof with poured-concrete walls and a reinforced steel frame. The home was constructed in a Frank Lloyd Wright style and looked much like a traditional Western lodge. Before moving into their rebuilt home, Petty and his family had been renting a large house that was previously owned by both bandleader Xavier Cugat and actress Charo.

Looking like a home fit for a rock star, Petty's unconventional residence was described by a *Newsweek* writer as "kind of a cross between a mansion and a garage. The living room is an airy two-story foyer with a curving staircase, balcony and enormous free-standing fireplace and chimney. There's lots of polished wood, spotless carpeting and a German shepherd guard dog named Enzo to greet you. But hidden behind the vast chimney is a platform where Petty has his band gear set up, rec-room style."

▶ CHAPTER 24
SONGS FROM THE GARAGE

Prior to forming the Traveling Wilburys, Tom Petty had been working on a solo album, which was tentatively titled *Songs From The Garage*. Explaining the upbeat nature of the album, Petty admitted that losing his home and nearly perishing in a fire were transforming experiences: "My life changed, the whole tone of my music changed. That anger went away. You hear *Full Moon Fever* – it's a very happy, pleasant and positive album and was meant to be so. And that was a result of just being so glad to be alive." Additionally, *Full Moon Fever* veered from the traditional Heartbreakers sound with its subdued drums, scarcity of keyboards, and prominent use of acoustic guitars. Although *Full Moon Fever* was considered a solo work, all of the Heartbreakers except for Stan Lynch performed on the album.

Not surprisingly, Petty's two side projects were causing some tensions inside the Heartbreakers camp: "I think there was some confusion about it. They didn't know what I was doing, especially after I joined the Wilburys. They were probably ticked off for a while. I don't know because they're not really the kind of people who will call you up and tell you how they're feeling. They just kind of disappeared." But Petty was also disheartened by the lack of positive feedback or support for his solo album from his bandmates. As Petty recalled, "[Benmont Tench] used to say, 'Oh, I liked that song, 'Free Fallin'.' I think that's really good.' [But] none of them ever came up and said, 'Hey, great album!'"

But Petty's bandmates were not alone in failing to grasp the album's potential. After playing the completed tracks for the label bosses at MCA, Petty was shocked when the project was panned and passed over for release. Petty later recalled: "It's the only time in my life that a record's been rejected. And I was stunned. And I was so high on the record, and I tried to think, 'What did I do wrong?' They said they didn't hear any hits, and there turned out to be, like, four or five hits on the record, some of the biggest ones I ever had." Remaining optimistic, Petty recounted, "I carried a tape around and played it for everyone. And everybody liked it except the record company. They were quizzical. They were the last ones I was able to convert." Convinced that the record executives at MCA were dead wrong, Petty simply waited them out. In the interim, he decided to add a few more tracks to the album.

On January 6, 1989, at the Ventura Theatre near Los Angeles, Petty was a surprise guest at a concert by a new lineup of the Byrds, which featured Roger McGuinn, David Crosby, and Chris Hillman. Petty joined the three rock legends for a performance of "So You Wanna Be A Rock 'n' Roll Star." Hillman recalled: "We had Tom Petty on rhythm guitar that night! He based his whole musical career on the Byrds, and took it to another level." Just days after the concert, Petty was inspired to record a rendition of the Byrds' classic "Feel A Whole Lot Better" for inclusion on his solo album. Petty recalled, "My daughter thought I wrote it. And I played it for [Roger] McGuinn and he said, 'Is that us?'"

Finally, when the old regime at MCA had been replaced, Petty returned with his solo album. This time the new management team loved the songs and Petty was vindicated.

Released in April 1989, *Full Moon Fever* was a huge smash. Remarkably, eight of the album's twelve tracks received airplay on AOR radio. But the initial reviews were not entirely positive. A *Rolling Stone* critic said of the album, "*Full Moon Fever* isn't Petty's best record."

In terms of subject matter, the project was a dramatic change of pace for Petty. As one critic observed, "The album seemed [to be] a turning point as far as *lyrics* go. Instead of the semi-autobiographical angst-ridden, heartbroken romance-type person singing, Petty started inventing *characters* – odd but ordinary folk, kind of like the ones in Randy Newman songs." Petty explained his songwriting process at the time: "It was sort of deliberate, when I realized I could do it. It was kind of like a bolt of lightning to my head, that it didn't have to be me, that I *could* assume characters. I really enjoy doing that a lot."

The first single, "I Won't Back Down," was a multi-format hit. The track featured what Petty described as an "acoustic wall of sound.... There were four of us – myself, Mike, Jeff and George – playing acoustic [guitars] live in the studio. One guitar was a 12-string, two were probably six strings and one was Nashville strung. Then we doubled the parts so we had eight acoustics playing the rhythm parts, which created this huge sound." But there was an unexpected issue with Campbell's performance. He played "a deeply inspired, very Harrison-esque slide solo on this tune. In fact, the solo was almost left on the mixing room floor for sounding too much like Harrison."

But Petty had regrets about openly exposing his vulnerable side on the track: "'I Won't Back Down' is purely me. That song frightened me when I wrote it. I didn't embrace it at all. It's so obvious. I thought it wasn't that good because it was so naked. So I had a lot of second thoughts about recording that song. But everyone around me liked the song and said it was really good and it turns out everyone was right – more people connect to that song than anything I ever wrote." Additionally, Petty's Southern accent comes through on the track, more so than on any other song on the album.

Meanwhile, Petty scored a major coup when he wrangled half of the Beatles to appear in the song's music video. Flying to England to film the clip, Petty was joined by George Harrison, Ringo Starr, Jeff Lynne, and Mike Campbell. When Harrison arrived at the video shoot, he came bearing gifts and handed everyone in the band a vintage Beatles watch from the 1960s. Petty recalled, "It was George's idea to get Ringo. What am I going to say – No? I knew Ringo. He would hang around with us. But I still can't believe that happened. We had amps on the set, and we'd be jamming between takes. I remember playing and looking at Mike, like, 'How about this?'" (In the video, Campbell played a vintage Fender Stratocaster guitar that George Harrison had used in the 1967 Beatles film, *Magical Mystery Tour*.)

The followup single, "Running Down A Dream," was a fast-paced, behind the wheel, driving song. Petty later said: "To me American music was all about listening to music in the car. The old records, we used to do a mix and then run them out and play it in the car, and if it didn't sound right we'd do it again." That same philosophy provided Motown Records with a string of hits in the 1960s, as label owner Berry Gordy used a cheap car speaker during the mixing process to simulate what the typical listener would actually hear.

But the album's biggest and most enduring hit was "Free Fallin'." The track would set a longevity record on *Billboard* magazine's album-rock survey, spending nearly seven months on the chart. In the past,

Petty had been disappointed by his label's refusal to issue ballads as singles. Petty recalled, "I don't think we had a hit ballad ever until 'Free Fallin'.' And I remember with that, there was some question. I went on *Saturday Night Live*, and the single at the time was 'I Won't Back Down,' and I played 'Free Fallin',' and MCA was just furious at me. But my thinking was, "I Won't Back Down' is already a hit, let's play something they don't expect.' I'm sure it helped the record later. Sometimes you gotta do what you think is right." The performance on *SNL* was the group's first in two-and-a-half-years. But the mood on the set was somber due to the death earlier that day of former cast member, Gilder Radner.

The song's music video – the first of several Tom Petty clips directed by Julien Temple – was mostly filmed on Ventura Boulevard. Set in the 1960s, the video featured a series of iconic American images including muscle cars, record stores, and skateboarders, and starred professional surfer Devon Jenkin. In addition to "Free Fallin'," Temple would oversee some of the most inventive videos of the classic MTV era, including "Come Dancing" by the Kinks, "Blue Jean" by David Bowie, and "Undercover Of The Night" by the Rolling Stones. Later, "Free Fallin'" enjoyed a revival after its inclusion in the blockbuster film *Jerry Maguire*, with Tom Cruise's character singing along to the song in his car.

Full Moon Fever would continue to generate additional radio hits including "Love Is A Long Road," "A Face In The Crowd," and a song inspired by a group of young punks Petty had encountered in a Los Angeles diner, "Zombie Zoo." The latter track featured backing vocals by Roy Orbison.

But the album's standout track was "Yer So Bad." The humorous but dark song attacked the yuppie culture of the 1980s. Surprisingly, the track was not released as a commercial single. The song's music video was nearly banned by MTV over the allegation it depicted a woman snorting cocaine.

Remarkably, *Full Moon Fever* was the first Tom Petty album to reach the top-10 charts in Britain. Although the U.K. had given Petty and the Heartbreakers their first taste of stardom in 1977, the group would fare poorly in terms of British record sales and airplay for most of the 1980s.

*   *   *   *   *   *

Having been apart from some of the Heartbreakers for a full two years, Petty had to reacquaint himself with some of his longtime confederates. Missing from the once close-knit outfit was the daily social interaction among the members, who were immersed in their own separate ventures.

Because *Full Moon Fever* was a solo Petty project, the members of the Heartbreakers had to learn how to play the songs after the album was released. Stan Lynch complained at the time: "That was the first time a tour ever felt like work to me – I never want to feel like I'm in a cover band."

The group launched the Strange Behavior tour in Miami on July 5th, with Petty again bringing along his wife and daughters. On the second stop of the tour, Roger McGuinn joined the Heartbreakers on stage to perform four Byrds classics. For the tour, Petty splurged on a number of elaborate stage props, including "cattle horns, a suit of armor, a 15-foot totem pole, a stuffed bear and Egyptian hieroglyphics – all emblems that, one way or another, suggest classic." Petty would later install the giant totem pole on the grounds of his home.

At this point in his career, Petty was at the top of his game. In addition to nearly 15 years worth of Heartbreakers standards, he possessed a potent musical catalog that included hit songs from both the Traveling Wilburys and his very successful solo album. But at a time when Petty should have been basking in glory, he was forced to battle an unexpected problem. Petty explained: "For the first time in my career, I developed stage fright. After a whole career in which I was very happy to take the stage, all of a sudden I went through a period of being terrified, puking, the whole thing."

Tom Petty and the Heartbreakers took a detour in September and appeared at the 6th annual MTV Video Music Awards, where they performed a pair of songs with Axl Rose and Izzy Stradlin of Guns N' Roses. Rose had contacted Petty a few months earlier to suggest they perform a duet of "Free Fallin'." As Petty recalled, "Axl said, 'I know this girl, man, and that is her song, that's her story. And I'd really like to sing the song.'" With Rose monopolizing most of the vocal duties, a bemused Petty was comfortable stepping aside. Petty and Rose also performed a metal-tinged rendition of "Heartbreak Hotel."

But Petty's performance was overshadowed by a violent assault that occurred moments later. As guitarist Izzy Stradlin was leaving the stage, he was punched by singer Vince Neil of Motley Crue. The bad blood between Stradlin and Neil was the result of an incident that occurred at a Los Angeles nightclub, involving Stradlin and Neil's wife. Writing in the Motley Crue autobiography *The Dirt*, Neil recounted: "All my blood rushed into my fist. And I decked him. I decked him good, and right in the face. He fell to the ground like a tipped cow." Petty later recalled, "Well, you know us. We manage to get into shit somehow. I don't dig blindsiding somebody, if that's what happened I didn't see it. I just saw Vince Neil go storming by and a guy running behind him with a walkie talkie going, 'Vince? Vince!' I heard a commotion but I didn't know what it was. I just kept going."

With the Strange Behavior tour scheduled to end in mid-September, the members of the Heartbreakers pressured Petty to add more dates. But Petty had other plans. As music writer Bill Flanagan reported at the time: "The Heartbreakers want to stay on the road, strike while the iron is hot, but Petty has decided not to extend the tour. Tom wants to take a break to write. The original plan was for the band to record a new album from late '89 to early '90.... But no one expected *Full Moon Fever* to be such a smash. Now the Heartbreakers want to keep working, but Tom sees no reason to push it.... The underlying fear among the Heartbreakers is that if they quit touring now, Tom will get caught up with the Wilburys again, which will lead God-knows where for God-knows how long, and another year will be lost."

Meanwhile, Petty continued to remain evasive about a possible, second Traveling Wilburys album: "We don't have any plans at the moment to do anything. We're not ruling out that we might do another one. At the moment, we're all catching up with everything else that we put on hold to do the Wilburys. So if we get time one day, I wouldn't rule it out, but at the moment, there's no telling if it'll ever happen again. And, of course, Roy's death was a wrench in the works. There was something in that particular chemistry of people, those five guys, that was real magical. So for the time being, we'll just remain friends and stay in touch and we'll see one day where it goes."

In press interviews, the members of the Wilburys also remained noncommittal about whether or not the group would tour. Petty recalled, "A lot of money was offered to us, but at the end of the meeting, we'd decided not to do it. And I kept getting down on my knees in front of George, saying, 'Please! It's so much money.' And everybody would just start laughing. It was that kind of meeting; we'd look at each other and start giggling nervously, going, 'Nah, we can't.' Like George says, I can't see waking up in a hotel in Philadelphia and having to do a Wilburys sound check." Alternatively, Petty offered the musical services of the Heartbreakers for a solo George Harrison tour. But nothing came of that, either.

Years after Harrison's death, Petty explained, "I wish we had played live. George would talk about it all of the time. But the next day the spirit would have worn off. It became too real. I think if George had lived we would have played some shows." In time, Petty would occasionally perform "Handle With Care" and "Tweeter And The Monkey Man" on stage with the Heartbreakers.

At the beginning of 1990, Petty wanted to start working on a new Heartbreakers album, but was forced to delay his plans after learning Jeff Lynne was in the middle of his own solo project. Instead, Petty asked the Heartbreakers to go back on the road. With *Full Moon Fever* continuing to rack up massive sales, Petty recalled, "promoters kept calling and calling."

Tom Petty and the Heartbreakers began the second leg of their tour on January 26th at the USF Sun Dome in Miami. Although the Byrds had originally signed on as the opening act, they bowed out and were replaced by Lenny Kravitz. The following week, when Petty played a hometown show in Gainesville, he requested 300 tickets for friends and family and was greeted with "Welcome Home Tom Petty" signs all over town.

▶ CHAPTER 25
THE RETURN OF THE WILBURYS

By 1990, Tom Petty had firmly staked his claim as one of America's most successful rock performers. As a *New York Times* music critic observed in a review of fellow Heartland rocker John Mellencamp, "along with songwriters like Tom Petty, he is becoming the establishment of American rock-and-roll, the standard that older generations must live up to and younger bands must reinvent."

Meanwhile, the sudden death of Roy Orbison the previous December had hit Tom Petty hard. Petty stated at the time, "The way Roy saw life and just enjoyed it so much, it just brought home to me that you're only given so many heartbeats and you'd better use every one." But Petty would later reveal, "I always felt like he was very prepared to go, spiritually and mentally. He was in a very good place, spiritually, and I don't think death would've freaked him at all. So I always felt comforted by that, and by the fact that he got a lot of attention, at least in the Wilburys – everyone was always hugging him and telling him how much they loved him. And I'm glad we did."

But Orbison's personal life had been marred by tragedy. His first wife Claudette – who was the inspiration for his 1964 hit "Pretty Woman" – died in a motorcycle accident. Two years later, his house was destroyed in a fire that also took the lives of two of his young sons. From that point forward, Orbison promised himself he would never attend another funeral.

A chain smoker who underwent triple-bypass surgery after collapsing in 1978, Orbison was not blessed with good health. But in a profession where drug and alcohol use were practically mandatory, tobacco was Orbison's only vice. Although he tried giving up cigarettes for a brief period after his surgery, Orbison was not successful.

In the press, Del Shannon and Roger McGuinn were both mentioned as possible replacements for Orbison in the Wilburys. Although Petty would deny the rumors, George Harrison was more open-minded about adding another member to the group: "You can't replace Roy Orbison.... It's not every day you form a group with all these legends. That's not to say there aren't other Wilburys floating around out there. But the four of us need to talk, really, and keep an openness about it."

But the death of Del Shannon on February 9th put an end to the speculation. Shannon, who had been battling a severe bout of depression, shot himself with a rifle. However, with Shannon failing to leave behind a suicide note, his widow initially thought the shooting was accidental. Later, she blamed his actions on the side effects of the medication he was taking, Prozac, and filed a highly-publicized lawsuit against the drug's maker. The double tragedy of losing both Orbison and Shannon in such a short period affected Petty far more than he would admit in public.

In February 1990, the first Traveling Wilburys album won a Grammy for Best Rock Performance by a Duo or Group with Vocal, but would lose to Bonnie Raitt in the category for Album of the Year. Petty had also earned two solo nominations: *Full Moon Fever* for Album of the Year and the single, "Free Fallin'," in the category for Best Rock Vocal Performance, Male. Meanwhile, the following month, Benmont Tench married Canadian actress Courtney Taylor; the marriage would end six years later.

*   *   *   *   *   *

The sessions for the second Traveling Wilburys album began in the spring of 1990, before Petty was able to reunite with the Heartbreakers for their next record. For the second Wilburys venture, the members of the group renamed themselves: while Petty was now Muddy Wilbury, the others took the monikers Boo, Clayton, and Spike. Although Harrison was in charge during the making of the first album, this time around Dylan took the reigns. As a gag, the second album was titled, *The Traveling Wilburys, Vol. 3*. Jeff Lynne recalled, "That was George's idea.... He said, 'Let's confuse the buggers.'"

The surviving four Wilburys decided to splurge on the sessions by renting a 1920s Spanish-style, hilltop mansion in Beverly Hills. At one point, a towering Wilbury flag was hoisted above the compound. But not all was well on the homefront for two of the Wilburys: while Petty had just reconciled with his wife after a painful separation, Dylan would soon be served with dissolution papers from his wife of four years.

The second Traveling Wilburys album was recorded in the mansion's library using borrowed equipment. Preferring to record in an informal setting, Petty explained: "People don't listen to records in a room that's all soundproofed and baffled up and set up for stereo dynamics. So if you can make one in a house, it's a luxury. And you don't have to walk past a receptionist."

Petty and Dylan provided the lead vocals on most of the tracks. As such, Roy Orbison's absence was apparent. Dylan pondered, "There's no telling what kind of record we could have made with Roy. Everyone missed him, but it wasn't like anyone sat around and talked about it." But drummer Jim Keltner noticed a difference in the tone of the sessions: "It was Roy's presence [that] made them rise to the occasion. The second album was really deflated... it was just sad and the enthusiasm wasn't there. So the writing suffered."

However, an optimistic Dylan told an interviewer, "Last time, it was a pretty rushed affair. A lot of stuff was just scraped up from jam tapes. This time, there was a whole lot left over. The songs are more developed. If people liked the first one, they'll love this one." And just like the first album, the second set was written, recorded, and mixed in less than six weeks.

The Traveling Wilburys, Vol. 3 was released on October 6th – just two weeks before Petty would turn 40. Rock critic Jon Pareles of *The New York Times* said of the album: "[it] stays close to 1950's and early 1960's rock roots, drawing on blues, doo-wop, rockabilly and Buddy Holly. But it is faster, jokier, lighter and meaner than the first album, as the band indulges its bile and paranoia along with humor."

Not as successful as the initial Wilburys release, the followup album did not contain any breakout radio hits. The project's most enduring tracks were "She's My Baby" and "Inside Out." But the album's fan favorite, "Wilbury Twist," featured the guitarwork of former Thin Lizzy member Gary Moore. In the opening scene of the song's music video, comedian John Candy attempted to demonstrate the dance.

When Harrison's distribution deal with Warner Brothers expired in 1995 without being renewed, both of the Traveling Wilburys albums remained out-of-print for more than a decade.

*   *   *   *   *   *

Remaining very active during the autumn of 1990, Petty was enjoying the fruits of his creative labor. At his 40th birthday party in October, Petty was joined by the likes of Bruce Springsteen, Jeff Lynne, Roger McGuinn, and Elvis Costello. Then on December 5th, Petty attended the *Billboard* Music Awards in Las Vegas, where he hobnobbed with George Harrison and Brian Setzer.

Then in January 1991, Roger McGuinn released his solo album, *Back From Rio*. Tom Petty and the Heartbreakers played a big part in the project, with Petty co-writing and providing the co-lead vocals on the album's first single, "King Of The Hill," which had a decidedly Heartbreakers sound to it. The song was embraced by AOR radio and became McGuinn's biggest hit in years. Petty also co-wrote the followup single, "Someone To Love."

That same year, Petty launched his own MCA-distributed imprint, Gone Gator Records. The label's first releases were the reissues of Tom Petty and Heartbreakers' first two albums. Petty had purchased the rights to the original master recordings – at a very high cost – and was eager to issue them on CD. But there were problems. As Petty recalled: "We had to switch them over to digital and everything. The old tapes were so worn out, and the oxide was falling off. So I had to go in and do the transfers of literally all the stuff from the '70s. I really enjoyed hearing them, and I was tempted to almost re-mix them. But I thought better of that. At the last minute, I thought, 'Well, it's probably best to put them out the way they were released and not fool around with them.'"

Unhappy with how MCA Records had handled the CD versions of his albums from the 1980s, Petty was determined to oversee the reissue process of his first two albums: "The others were all released – without even a phone call – when the CD boom came. I don't really ever listen to them very much, although I heard *Southern Accents* the other day, and some of the tracks sounded real good to me and some sounded like they were EQed all wrong – really tinny and bright."

Gone Gator Records also issued Del Shannon's album, *Rock On!* As a favor to Shannon, Petty and Lynne had written one of the tracks, "Walk Away." But tragically, Shannon would not live to finish the project. The posthumously released album was completed by Petty, Lynne, and Mike Campbell.

▶ CHAPTER 26
THE TIMES THEY ARE A-CHANGING

After wrapping up the recording sessions for his final studio album at MCA Records, Petty took his family to the quaint coastal town of St. Augustine, Florida, for the summer. The next Heartbreakers tour would not begin until the last week of August. Staying at a beach house overlooking the Atlantic Ocean, Petty felt relaxed for the first time in years. Riding a Honda mini-bike across the beaches and on the city's narrow residential streets, Petty usually went unrecognized by the locals.

Released in July 1991, *Into The Great Wide Open* displayed a mature sound. The group's first album in four years, the project was mostly produced by Jeff Lynne. But Lynne's production style was foreign to most of the Heartbreakers. Unlike previous recording sessions in which the entire group would be present in the studio, Lynne preferred to individually record each musician, one track at a time. Petty defended Lynne's production technique: "I think it was probably the only time he worked with a band... Dealing with the politics of a band just drives him nuts. It can drive anyone nuts – and especially [the Heartbreakers]. I think they were a little indignant I'd done a solo album." But as seasoned professionals, the members of the Heartbreakers eventually adjusted to Lynne's recording method. Petty recalled: "They dug Jeff. It was a good vibe, you know, having a new person in the room. We all tended to listen to him more than we would each other. He's very cheerful at sessions.... And he has a real good sense of organization, so he gets a lot done each day."

However, music writer Bill Flanagan argued that the album was radically different from the group's previous efforts: "Maybe it was a case of too many cooks, maybe it was the awkwardness of the Heartbreakers trying to fit Lynne's blueprint but the spontaneity that had marked all of Petty's projects since *Let Me Up* was missing. *Into The*

Great Wide Open had some terrific individual tracks, and produced some hit singles, but overall the album felt labored-over in a way Petty's other recent work had not." Another critic was far less charitable, describing the album as "full of hazy references, half-baked concepts, unresolved tales, cliched metaphors and strained poetic meaning."

The subdued track, "Learning To Fly," was an unusual choice as the album's debut single. Composed by Petty and Lynne, the song was based on a military pilot's interview during the Gulf War and typified Petty's knack for ambiguous imagery. The song's music video was directed by Julien Temple and filmed at Bob's Airpark, a surreal airplane graveyard in Tucson.

The followup single, "Into The Great Wide Open," provided a cynical look at the state of the music industry. Julien Temple's video for the song chronicled the tragic rise and fall of a fictional rocker named Eddie Rebel. A big budget offering, the clip starred Johnny Depp and featured singers Chynna Phillips and Terence Trent D'Arby. In addition, Petty's real-life manager Tony Dimitriades portrayed Depp's agent. Temple explained: "We just wanted to capture the song's depiction of the perils of rock stardom." As the longest Heartbreakers music video to date – clocking in at almost seven minutes – Petty was surprised when it received heavy airplay on MTV.

With the Heartbreakers launching an autumn tour in support of the album, Petty was forced to deal with a recurring problem. Howie Epstein's growing drug use was beginning to affect the entire group. With Epstein becoming more unreliable, newly-hired session musician Scott Thurston was forced to assume more duties on stage. During the tour, Stan Lynch surprised audiences by singing the lead vocal on a faithful rendition of the 1960s garage-rock classic, "Psychotic Reaction," with Petty providing the harmonica accompaniment.

In March 1992, the Heartbreakers began the European leg of their tour with a stop in Oslo, Norway. At a news conference in London, George Harrison jumped into the middle of the press corps and asked Petty about his future career plans after "the bubble burst." Petty responded, "We're going to move into your guest house." While Petty was in Europe, a pair of previously-recorded hour-long segments from the U.S. portion of the tour were broadcast over two episodes of *ABC In Concert*. The performances were hosted by Johnny Depp.

During this time, the music industry was abuzz over the leaked news that Tom Petty had secretly signed a deal with Warner Brothers. According to reports, the contract had been signed three years earlier. Petty had made the decision to leave MCA in late-1988 at a dinner party hosted by Warner Brothers chief Mo Ostin. After the meal, Petty was joined by George Harrison and Jeff Lynne for an informal performance of the then-unreleased solo track, "Free Fallin'." After Petty explained that MCA had rejected his solo album, Warner Brothers executive Lenny Waronker offered to sign Petty, right there on the spot. Waronker was astounded that MCA had failed to recognize the commercial potential of Petty's solo material.

According to unconfirmed reports, Petty signed an "estimated $20-million, six-album pact" with Warner Brothers and had switched labels "because he was disappointed with MCA's promotion of his music in the mid-80s." Petty also trusted Ostin and Waronker, something that could not be said of the majority of record company executives he had worked with in the past. Music industry veteran Danny Goldberg would describe Ostin in majestic terms: "Although short in stature, Mo was a larger-than-life personality, with an unusually loud, deep voice and commanding presence akin to that of a king of a small but wealthy nation."

Meanwhile, on October 16, 1992, Petty was a featured performer at the 30th anniversary tribute to Bob Dylan, which was informally dubbed "Bobfest." Petty was joined at Madison Square Garden by fellow Wilburys members George Harrison and Jeff Lynne, along with a host of rock dignitaries, including Roger McGuinn, Eric Clapton, and Neil Young. One of the evening's musical highlights was Tom Petty and the Heartbreakers' upbeat rendition of the Dylan standard "Rainy Day Women #12 & 35." Afterward, the Heartbreakers remained on stage as Petty introduced Roger McGuinn, who performed an extended version of the Dylan composition, "Mr. Tambourine Man," which was a huge hit in 1965 for the Byrds. But the night's most talked-about moment came when eccentric Irish singer Sinead O'Connor was booed off the stage. The audience was responding to her actions two weeks earlier during an appearance on *Saturday Night Live*, when she ripped a photograph of the pope and shouted, "fight the real enemy."

The event would mark the last paid concert appearance by George Harrison. Not a fan of the stage, Harrison rarely toured in the last two decades of his life.

$$* \quad * \quad * \quad * \quad * \quad *$$

As a favor to his friend Johnny Depp, Tom Petty volunteered the Heartbreakers to play a charity event at the August 14, 1993, opening of Depp's nightclub, the Viper Room, on Sunset Boulevard in Hollywood. But not everyone in the Heartbreakers was pleased with Petty's decision. An unhappy Stan Lynch flew in from Florida to play the show only after Petty mentioned Ringo Starr as a possible replacement for the performance. The audience was full of celebrities on opening night, including Julien Temple, Quentin Tarantino, and Tim Burton. The nightclub was co-owned by Chuck E. Weiss, who was the subject of Rickie Lee Jones' 1979 hit, "Chuck E.'s In Love."

Unfortunately, the Viper Room would be best remembered as the scene of a fatal tragedy that occurred later that year. Actor River Phoenix overdosed and went into convulsions on the sidewalk in front of the nightclub, at the same time that Johnny Depp was performing with his band on the club's stage.

Meanwhile, Petty still owed a greatest hits album to MCA Records. Not one to dwell on the past or to be pigeonholed as an oldies artist, Petty explained, "I avoid being on those compilations of greatest hits of the '70s and things like that. It took us 18 years to do a greatest hits album."

Although Petty was initially reluctant to record new tracks for inclusion on the album, he had a change of heart. Petty joined the Heartbreakers at Mike Campbell's house in July for some brief sessions. The group recorded a variety of rock standards as well as one new composition, "Mary Jane's Last Dance." ("Mary Jane" was the name of Petty's paternal grandfather's first wife, before the elder Petty would marry for a second time to Tom Petty's grandmother.) Petty had written the song a few years earlier – without a chorus – during the *Full Moon Fever* period.

This would be the final Heartbreakers track to feature Stan Lynch on drums. Lynch later recalled, "I was actually listening to a little hip-hop back then, and I think it rubbed off on that groove. I cut the track really quickly – second take, I think – and it felt really good. Then I just put my sticks down and that was that." The track also featured some bluesy harmonica riffs by Petty, which resulted in Campbell giving Petty a new nickname: Harmonicat. This was the first time Petty had played the

instrument on a Heartbreakers album since *Damn The Torpedoes*.
When "Mary Jane's Last Dance" was released in 1993, the radio
industry in the U.S. was in a state of flux. The steep decline in the
number of traditional album-rock stations coincided with the rise of the
alternative rock format, mostly due to the arrival of grunge rock. As one
of Petty's finest songs, musically it was far more similar in style to
modern-rock bands like Sugar Ray or Smash Mouth than anything the
Byrds had ever recorded. Nonetheless, alternative rock stations ignored
the track. During this period, Petty had publically come out in support
of grunge bands like Nirvana, arguing that the genre had reinvigorated
rock music.

But controversy would strike Tom Petty yet again with the release of
the music video for "Mary Jane's Last Dance." In the unusually morbid
clip, Petty portrayed a morgue employee who took home a female
corpse, portrayed by the lovely Kim Basinger. After dressing "the
corpse" in a wedding dress, Petty wined and dined his date. A shocked
Billboard magazine reviewer called the video, "one of the most revolting
pieces of tape" she had ever viewed. But in the end, the humorous clip
would earn Petty an MTV award for Best Male Video.

The second new song on the 18-track greatest hits compilation was
a straightforward remake of Thunderclap Newman's 1969 rock classic,
"Something In The Air." Rick Rubin produced both of the tracks, which
were recorded during the middle of the *Wildflowers* sessions.

Two weeks before the release of their greatest hits album, Tom Petty
and the Heartbreakers went on the road in November for just two
concerts, both in Florida. Opening both shows was Howie Epstein's
girlfriend, Carlene Carter. At one of the concerts, Petty would meet his
future wife, Dana York.

To Petty's astonishment, *Greatest Hits* sold more than ten-million
copies in the U.S. alone. (The British version of the album featured the
track "Anything That's Rock 'n' Roll" instead of "Listen To Her
Heart.") With both "Mary Jane's Last Dance" and "Something In The
Air" receiving strong airplay, MCA later issued a third single,
"American Girl." But just like the situation seventeen-years earlier in
1977, the single failed to break into the top-40.

▶ CHAPTER 27
RICK RUBIN & WILDFLOWERS

After leaving MCA for Warner Brothers, Tom Petty began working on his second solo project, *Wildflowers*. In homage to the Everly Brothers, who recorded for Warner Brothers in the 1960s, Petty used the label's old-style logo on the album.

In a dramatic change of pace, Rick Rubin – primarily known for his work with rap and metal acts – co-produced the album. While growing up in Long Island, Rubin was a big fan of the Beatles, but not the Rolling Stones. By 1983, Rubin had launched Def Jam Records out of his dorm room at New York University. In 1987, he moved to Los Angeles.

Petty recalled, "Mike had met Rick and suggested he'd be good to work with. All that I knew by him was a Chili Peppers single that I loved, so I called him up and got [to] talking. He came over with a bag of CDs.... I never did hire him – he just kept coming over!" Petty was surprised by Rubin's strong work ethic: "He did drive me a little harder than I've been used to, which was a shock at first. Like: 'Whaddayamean you want me to play that part again?'" Later, when Rubin was asked which production he was most proud of, he told *Uncut* magazine: "Tom Petty's *Wildflowers* would be in there. I tend to use that as a yardstick when I need to remember how good a record should sound."

Most of the album was recorded at the Heartbreakers' favorite studio, Sound City. Working on the album was an emotionally cleansing experience for Petty: "*Wildflowers* covered really everything that had come into my brain and came out again. We drove the engineers so hard on that record, one or two snapped like twigs, and then there were some that couldn't make it. And I remember telling them at some really late hour, 'Stick with me, kid, and I'll see you at the Grammys,' and they did. Both [engineers] won a Grammy, and I was so proud of them." But the relentless sessions were time-consuming. As Petty later recalled, "*Wildflowers* took a massively long time, almost two years of writing and recording, mostly writing."

Petty brought in all of the Heartbreakers to play on the sessions – except for Stan Lynch. Petty later explained, "I wasn't getting along with Stan and I didn't want to play with him on that record. I think that's what instigated doing it as a solo album to be honest – I didn't want to deal with the politics of the group." Instead, Petty used guest drummers such as Carl Wilson and Ringo Starr, before hiring Steve Ferrone.

A British-born drummer, Ferrone was invited to audition for a "major" unnamed rock band. At the front door of the studio, he was met by Mike Campbell and Tom Petty, both of whom he immediately recognized. Ferrone had previously worked with Campbell at a pair of George Harrison concerts. The album also featured some orchestration by conductor Michael Kamen, who had previously worked with a number of rock acts, including Pink Floyd and Metallica.

The album was unexpectedly delayed for three months due to the Northridge earthquake that struck greater Los Angeles on January 17, 1994. The powerful quake was centered just six-miles north of Petty's home in Encino, and would ultimately result in 57 deaths and 8,700 injuries. Petty explained, "The studios were screwed up for months. The aftershocks were nerve rattling, and we spent hours discussing whether we should leave L.A. You take the ground you walk on for granted, and to not even have that as a given really enraged me."

Finally released in November 1994, *Wildflowers* was stylistically similar to the Heartbreakers' previous effort, *Into The Great Wide Open*. A music reviewer summed up the album in one sentence: "[Petty] ruminates about love, loneliness and the pressures of celebrity." But on introspective songs like "Only A Broken Heart" and "Don't Fade On Me," it was obvious that Petty was experiencing some personal problems at the time.

The album's first single, "You Don't Know How It Feels," was Petty's last top-40 hit of the decade. Although Petty refused to address the matter in the press, the song was allegedly based on his relationship with a former girlfriend. With the song stirring up some controversy for its pro-drug lyrics, Warner Brothers issued a radio-only edit, without the drug references. Even MTV banned the music video until the offending lyrics were removed. In response, Petty's press agent said in a statement: "Tom is aware of this – and he's not pleased with this." In defending the song, Petty insisted: "I don't want to be seen as some advocate for dope.... It just seemed like something the character in that song would say." A regular pot smoker for years, Petty began to avoid the drug when he hit his 40s. As Petty explained, "I enjoy a good joint. But I don't take drugs when I play.... I don't want to be prudish about it. It just doesn't work for me, that's all." Not surprisingly, whenever Petty performed song in concert, he was showered with rolled joints from the audience.

A thematically similar track from the sessions, "Girl On LSD" was a humorous novelty-style song that Petty had written in the studio to entertain producer George Drakoulias, while waiting for a piece of equipment to be fixed. Eventually, Rubin convinced a skeptical Petty to record the song. But when Warner Brothers refused to include the track on *Wildflowers*, "Girl On LSD" was placed on the B-side of "You Don't Know How It Feels."

Soon, "Girl On LSD" became a surprise hit that received strong airplay in a number of cities, and even topped the charts in Cleveland. As a result, Petty was forced to add the song to the setlist of his next tour. Although Petty had a long history of releasing quirky B-sides – including "Gator On The Lawn" and "Heartbreakers Beach Party" – this was the first time he scored a B-side hit. The album would spawn three more album-rock hits with "It's Good To Be King," "A Higher Place," and one of *Wildflowers'* few upbeat tracks, "You Wreck Me."

*   *   *   *   *   *

After Tom Petty finished recording his second solo album without Stan Lynch, the longtime Heartbreakers drummer made "no bones about his displeasure. Words were passed. When he refused to tour in support of the album, everyone agreed it was time for a parting of the ways." The animosity between Petty and Lynch had grown to a new level and something had to give.

In many ways, Lynch began to feel like an outsider in his own band. A perfectionist who always showed up on time, he was no longer permitted to join in the day-to-day process of crafting the group's music. Even a decade earlier in 1983, Lynch had complained, "It's gotten to the point now where I won't ante up an opinion on a topic unless I'm asked. If they ask me, they *know* I've got an opinion." But with Petty remaining the group's chief songwriter, Lynch was limited to offering only minor suggestions. "He wanted to do a lot of other things. He wanted more control, more input," Petty said at the time. And in a reversal from the group's earlier days when the members of the Heartbreakers worked together in the studio, Lynch was now summoned to a session only when Petty wanted to lay down the drum tracks.

Unlike his bandmates, Lynch was more rooted in hard rock and metal, and enjoyed playing the group's more muscular, hard-hitting songs like "Refugee" and "Even The Losers." On more than one occasion, he lamented the fact that the Heartbreakers were playing an increasing amount of what he disdainfully called "pop music." When he left the group, Lynch commented: "Over time, people have such different desires, musically, and mine are becoming more apparent to me. I've moved away from them as a person as well as a musician." Lynch performed with the Heartbreakers for the final time at the 1994 Bridge School Benefit.

Petty later explained: "Stan and I always had a turbulent relationship, but it was part of the magic. But there came to be real tension in the music. We honestly couldn't function with each other. I did get mad at one point and sort of pushed him, but I didn't fire him. Stan needed a little shove to make that decision, and I only shoved because of the pain I could see him in, which eventually was causing me pain and problems. In a way, Stan left the room without saying goodbye. I said to him, 'Hey, listen, man, a 20-year run is pretty good.'" Lynch, however, would recall their final meeting in less than positive terms.

After leaving the group, Lynch had some trouble adjusting to his place in the world. He recalled, "I introduced myself as Stan Lynch-from-Tom-Petty-and-the-Heartbreakers because I thought I had to impress people." But that would quickly change as Lynch became better known as a successful songwriter and producer.

Lynch's first foray into songwriting came in the 1980s when he met legendary musician and producer Danny Kortchmar. During the sessions for Don Henley's debut solo album *I Can't Stand Still*, Kortchmar invited Lynch to participate in the project. This would mark the start of a longterm, creative partnership between Lynch and Henley. It helped that both men were drummers and that Henley had experienced an ugly breakup of his own band, the Eagles.

The first fruit of the Lynch and Henley partnership came with the hit ballad, "The Last Worthless Evening." The track was released as the second single from Henley's multi-platinum album, *The End Of The*

Innocence. Allegedly, the song's lyrics were based on Henley's failed attempt at meeting actress Michelle Pfeiffer at a Hollywood party.

As a songwriter, Lynch's biggest success came in 2004 when he teamed with Stephony Smith and Jeff Stevens to compose the smash hit "Back When," which Tim McGraw took to the top of the country charts. Lynch would also collaborate with a number of other songwriters including Eddie Money, Ringo Starr, and members of the Mavericks.

Turning to production work in 1997, Lynch oversaw a few tracks on the Elvis Presley tribute album, *All The King's Men*, which featured a number of rock luminaries, including Levon Helm and Keith Richards, as well as a pair of early Presley sidemen, Scotty Moore and D.J. Fontana. Later, Lynch co-produced an album for Sister Hazel, a notable alternative-rock group from Gainesville.

A year after leaving the Heartbreakers, Lynch – who had turned 40 – was quizzed about his departure: "Am I a fool to let it go? Maybe. But look what I get. I have this whole life that now is my own. I can do whatever I want with it." But in 2008, Lynch would admit: "I'm pissed at myself for not having done a more graceful exit with the fans. I really felt so much love and energy from them."

In November 1994, the Heartbreakers needed a replacement drummer for their guest appearance on *Saturday Night Live*. The group hired Dave Grohl, formerly of Nirvana. On the program, the band played "You Don't Know How It Feels" and a potent rendition of the bluesy track, "Honey Bee." Satisfied with Grohl's performance, Petty asked the 25-year-old drummer to join the Heartbreakers on a full-time basis. Grohl, who was in the process of forming his own group, Foo Fighters, declined the offer. Petty later recounted, "He came very close to joining the band – and we would have been glad to have him."

Two days after appearing on *Saturday Night Live*, the Heartbreakers performed "You Wreck Me" on *The Late Show with David Letterman*. This time, Steve Ferrone was the guest drummer. During a short conversation with Petty after the group's performance, Letterman joked that it was his lifetime dream "to be a Heartbreaker." Surprisingly, longtime Heartbreakers percussionist Phil Jones – who played on Petty's smash solo album *Full Moon Fever* – was not selected as the group's replacement drummer for either of the two performances.

*   *   *   *   *   *

A veteran drummer, Steve Ferrone (born Stephen A. Ferrone) was raised in a small city, sixty-miles south of London. Reared in a musical family, he broke into the entertainment field as a child performer: "Growing up in Brighton, I tap danced professionally. That is how I started playing drums. When I was 12 my parents took me down to audition for the summer show and I got a top-place ranking. I was a pretty good tap dancer! I was onstage dancing professionally at the Brighton Hippodrome. I looked down in the pit at the drummer and I went up to my dressing room and practiced what he was playing.... Tap dancing helped me understand syncopation. We danced to standards. That really helped me understand the construction and dynamics of songs."

At the age of 14 in 1964, Ferrone took up the drums and joined his first band. A few years later, he first heard the drumming of American session player Bernard Purdie and was instantly captivated: "I used to be with a local band that would play American military bases and clubs in France. We'd eat at the bases, and I was in the canteen one day, sitting next to the juke box. This really lanky black guy in fatigues came over, popped in a quarter, and started playing 'What Is Soul' by Ben E. King. It starts off with that drum thing, and I went, 'What the hell is this?' I'd never heard anyone play drums like that. So that was it for me. I listened to all his stuff, all of the James Brown stuff, and any of the Motown stuff." Ferrone would spend the rest of his teenage years jumping from band to band, and was not taking his drumming too seriously. But that would soon change.

Ferrone recalled, "I really just screwed around until I was 21 and then I had to make a decision about what I was going to do. I had to decide if I was going to be a professional musician.... [Then] this French band asked me to go and work with them in France. They were totally schooled musicians who knew their stuff; they could play and knew how to read [music]. So I asked them if they could get me into the local [music] Conservatory and they said, 'Sure that shouldn't be a problem,' so my decision was made for me. The Conservatory was a very classically structured school with a lot of theory, but I also learned drum/percussion technique and how to read properly. The good thing was that I had this residency, so I had a band to play with every night."

Soon after, Ferrone joined the famed 1970s jazz-fusion outfit, Brian Auger's Oblivion Express, and toured across the U.S. for the first time.

Then for an eight-year stretch, Ferrone was a member of the Scottish soul-rock act, Average White Band. Ferrone had replaced Robbie McIntosh and appeared on the classic album *Cut The Cake*. After the group disbanded in 1982, Ferrone worked with Chaka Khan, Peter Frampton, Duran Duran, and many others. For a short period, Ferrone found the time to join the house band on *Saturday Night Live*.

In December 1991, Ferrone backed George Harrison on his final tour when the former Beatle teamed with Eric Clapton for thirteen shows across Japan. The following year, Ferrone backed Clapton on an episode of *MTV Unplugged*. The all-acoustic set would generate a pair of radio hits, "Tears In Heaven" and a new version of "Layla." Ferrone parted with Clapton in September 1992, after five years on the road. "That was one of the greatest bands I've ever played with, a real high point in my life," Ferrone would later recount.

In 1994, Ferrone was invited by Tom Petty to play on *Wildflowers*. At the sessions, Ferrone was surprised by Petty's recording method: "It was all very straightforward – no click tracks, no synthesizers, very few overdubs – just real playing. It was almost like making a live record. We would play one song over and over, almost playing it into the ground. Then Tom would say, 'Let's try something else.' Then we'd move on to another song and do the same thing. The next day we'd go in, play the two songs from the day before, and then add another. By the end of the week we had a set. It was more of a fun situation, and we didn't have the pressure on us of 'Time to record this song' or 'Let's make this a hit.' It was just 'Let's play this song until it's happening.'"

With the departure of Stan Lynch, Ferrone began touring with the Heartbreakers in February 1995. However, Ferrone was a far different drummer than his predecessor: while Lynch was a powerful and passionate force behind the drum kit, Ferrone was a more relaxed and nuanced, finesse-style player.

*   *   *   *   *   *

Meanwhile, Scott Thurston was initially hired by the Heartbreakers as an all-around utility man for the group's live performances. But with Howie Epstein becoming increasingly undependable, Thurston quickly became an integral part of the band. After a few years, Thurston was given a nickname within the band: "Duckhead."

Born Scott Troy Thurston in 1952, he was raised in Medford, Oregon. After graduating from high school in 1970, the quiet and bushy-haired musician relocated to Los Angeles. Overnight, he became a popular session player and performed on numerous projects.

Joining the proto-punk outfit Iggy and the Stooges in 1973, Thurston was a witness to the wild excesses of lead singer Iggy Pop. James Williamson, the group's guitarist, had invited Thurston to join the Stooges after watching him play the piano at a session for Capitol Records. Thurston was briefly tutored by Williamson and then given a copy of the group's album, *Raw Power*, as a study guide. Then just "a few days later, Thurston was on a plane with road manager John Meyers for a show at the Ice Arena... just north of Detroit. Scott's first meeting with the band was the ride to the arena; that night he shared a stage for the first time with Iggy, who was dressed only in knee-boots and bikini briefs. He was stunned. He remained stunned for some time." As Iggy Pop biographer Paul Trynka recalled, "Eventually, Thurston got used to the doomed glamour of his new outlaw life: arriving at venues without any equipment. Borrowing amplifiers from the support band, leaving hired Marshall backlines at venues to avoid paying rental fees, and skipping out of hotels through the back door."

The Stooges disbanded in 1974 after a final concert at Detroit's Michigan Palace for an audience full of hostile bikers. Part of the performance was issued on the album *Metallic K.O.*, which featured Thurston on the piano. Later, Thurston would appear on a number of solo Iggy Pop albums, including *New Values*.

In 1982, Thurston joined the Los Angeles-based group the Motels in time for their hit album *Little Robbers*, which included the hits, "Suddenly Last Summer" and "Remember The Nights." Thurston would remain with the group until 1987. Later reuniting with the Motels, Thurston was joined in the band by early Heartbreakers member Jeff Jourard.

Beginning in 1986, Thurston was also a member of Jackson Browne's backing band and would appear on several albums beginning with 1989's *World In Motion*. In 1990, Thurston was the only musician to accompany Browne for what was billed as a "solo acoustic tour." After parting with Browne, Thurston would work with New Order, the Cult, Glenn Frey, and others.

Tom Petty first tapped Thurston in 1989, initially as a touring session player. Thurston was skilled on a wide variety of instruments including the bass, rhythm guitar, keyboards, and harmonica; he also provided backing harmony vocals. Remaining in the background and never seeking attention on stage, Thurston, according to Petty, "always saw himself as a sideman." But by the mid-1990s, Thurston became a full-fledged member of the Heartbreakers.

*   *   *   *   *   *

The Dogs With Wings tour began in February 1995. Attempting to thwart scalpers, the Heartbreakers announced the sale of 400 "choice" tickets per show, which were offered during an hour-long Tom Petty special on VH1 in January. Although originally planned for 40 cities, the tour was expanded to 56 dates. After taking a brief summer break, the Heartbreakers returned to the road in August and toured for another three months.

During the tour, a bronze-toned fiberglass dog with extended wings was hoisted over the audiences. On stage, the group was joined by a real life canine: Howie Epstein had brought along his massive German Shepherd named Dingo. Benmont Tench recalled, "It was the best look in the world. There's Howie, playing his bass and singing better harmonies than you ever heard in your life, and there's this giant dog at his feet, looking up at him with all the love in the world. I think Howie and Dingo were literally best friends."

Speaking to *Rolling Stone* magazine, Tom Petty explained his pre-concert ritual at the time. After posting a "Do Not Disturb" sign outside the dressing room door and munching on some snacks, "I look over the set list and decide what we're going to play. And then I'll warm up my voice for a while with my acoustic guitar, go into the shower where the echo is nice and warm up for maybe 20 minutes, just get confident that my voice is working well. Then I'll get dressed for the show; I always get down [to the stage] for the last 10 or 15 minutes before we go on and hang with the band – try to catch a group vibe before we go up. At least it's *collective* nervousness at that point."

After taking the stage, Petty would be greeted with a barrage of cheers and applause. As the leader of the Heartbreakers for nearly two decades, Petty was now attracting a new generation of fans. A music critic at a sold-out concert in New Haven, Connecticut, noted that "young people at the show who were singing along to the new songs weren't as familiar with such workhorses as 'Refugee,' but appeared to like them all the same. It was a strange and wonderful thing to behold, renewing one's confidence in the universal appeal of the music." Petty recounted one surprising incident: "We actually had two teenage girls tackle me midshow, which amused us all." During the tour, Petty performed an unreleased track, "Drivin' Down To Georgia," which would later appear on *The Live Anthology*.

Meanwhile, much of Petty's finest recorded output was collected on the boxed set, *Playback: 1973-1994*. Issued in November 1995, the six-CD set was compiled by George Drakoulias, who had scrutinized hundreds of the group's tapes. A treasure trove of classic recordings, the project included the expected hits as well as B-sides, album outtakes, and long-forgotten Mudcrutch tracks. Among the surprises: the original Mudcrutch version of "Don't Do Me Like That," the demo version of "Stop Draggin' My Heart Around" without Stevie Nicks, a pair of Elvis Presley covers, and an outtake from *Full Moon Fever* which featured the Bangles on backing vocals, "Waiting For Tonight."

Then on February 28, Tom Petty won a Grammy Award for "You Don't Know How It Feels" in the category for Best Male Rock Vocal Performance. But Petty later admitted, "I've never even gone to the Grammys. I've won a few, but I've never shown up. I just can't see myself sitting through that. I was actually really honored when I won one – you feel good about that sort of thing – but I still couldn't make it down there." Also that year, he received ASCAP's prestigious Golden Note Award.

*   *   *   *   *   *

On February 22, 1995, Denny Cordell passed away at the age of 51 after a short illness. Following the sale of Shelter Records, Cordell left the music business in 1980. Marrying brewery heiress Marina Guinness and moving to Ireland, Cordell began breeding and training race horses. He had the most success in 1986 with the colt, Baba Karam.

Returning to the record industry in 1991, Cordell was hired by Island Records as a Creative Director. One of his first discoveries was an Irish quartet, the Cranberries. At the label, he also helped produce Melissa Etheridge's hit album, *Yes I Am*.

▶ CHAPTER 28
OUT IN THE COLD

On September 9, 1996, Tom Petty's wife of twenty-two years, Jane, filed for legal separation, citing irreconcilable differences. The petition was filed with the Los Angeles Superior Court after Tom had already moved out of the couple's Encino home, which they shared with their youngest daughter.

Rock and roll marriages have always been notoriously difficult to maintain and Petty was not immune to the curse. While some rock wives like Jerry Hall, Sharon Osbourne, and Yoko Ono enjoyed the media spotlight and shared in their husbands' fame, Jane Petty was an intensely private person who was rarely photographed with her rocker husband.

Tom Petty once admitted to an interviewer: "For a long time, I never told anyone I was married, because I figured discussing it made us a public couple.... When you're gone nine months out of the year, you're not really married. I used to be gone so much that it was hard to feel I had anything going. Telephone romances don't work. I'd take Jane on the road with me, but it's awful to be on a tour and not have a job to do."

Additionally, the constant adulation and praise from fans was another cause of marital strife. As country singer June Carter told her musician daughter, Carlene: "You've got to always remember that when you're out on the road, everyone is telling you you're fantastic. Then you go home and you've got to be normal again. It's really hard to adjust, and you get the blues real bad. You get depressed because you come home after all this adrenaline's been going and the one you love isn't going, 'yeah' ... all the time. And they shouldn't, because you have to come back to normal."

After moving out of his large home, an emotionally bruised Tom Petty landed in an unusual environment. Escaping to a dilapidated cabin on the northwest edge of Los Angeles near the coast, he would spend his days in a habitat more suited to a hobo than an international rock star. "I was living in a pretty rundown shack. I didn't mind it. It was in a part of the Pacific Palisades, in the woods. And I was living back there and had chickens and all kinds of shit. In some places, you could actually see the daylight coming through the walls of the cabin. But it was my bachelor pad, you know. I had a big adjustment to make.... It wasn't the best period in my life," Petty admitted.

With Petty pulling away from the world and becoming a semi-recluse, friends became concerned that he might be abusing hard drugs. But that was not the case. Wanting to be left alone, he was forced to deal with the disintegration of his marriage. Petty recounted: "After the long tour we did for *Wildflowers*, I spent a whole year not doing anything. I kind of came down to earth. You know, that awful period where you have to assess your life. What went wrong and right." But facing the absence of a daily routine caused other problems: "It was a challenge – how to fill my days? I reflected on how orderly my life had been. You know every day where you're going to be at 4 o'clock. Suddenly that's gone." A slow stream of friends would occasionally visit Petty at his temporary home, in which he had set up a basic 8-track recording studio in a small back bedroom.

*   *   *   *   *   *

Earlier in 2006, Petty had agreed to oversee the musical score of the feature film, *She's The One*. After the film was completed, Petty was given just one month to write and record the music. Many of the songs were outtakes from the *Wildflowers* sessions. The romantic comedy, *She's The One,* was written and directed by Edward Burns and starred Jennifer Aniston and Cameron Diaz.

A *Rolling Stone* reviewer noted that the songs displayed "an affection for California and its rich pop heritage, and the uneasy sense that both are in trouble." But as Petty's least successful album, only a few of the songs received airplay – "Climb That Hill," "Walls," and a remake of Lucinda Williams' "Change The Locks." The album also included two different versions of "Angel Dream," a song inspired by Petty's growing friendship with Dana York. Only ten of the album's fifteen tracks were featured in the film. In August, Tom Petty and the Heartbreakers made their first-ever appearance on *The Tonight Show*, where they performed "Walls."

▶ CHAPTER 29
HELLO, MY NAME IS JOHNNY CASH

During the period when Tom Petty and the Heartbreakers were recording *Wildflowers*, their producer Rick Rubin found the time to sign Johnny Cash. Rubin had contacted Cash's manager and was invited to a concert at the Rhythm Cafe in Santa Ana. After the performance, Rubin and Cash had a frank discussion about the music business. Later, following another concert, Cash admitted to Rubin that, for many years, he wanted to record a stripped-down album without the traditional Nashville glitz. Petty recalled, "[Rubin] came in one day and said to me, 'Hey, I've got a shot at signing Johnny Cash, what do you think?' I said, 'God, sign him! Sign him tonight!'"

A musical legend who had a presence that was larger than life, Johnny Cash – nicknamed the Man in Black – was in the waning days of his long and prolific life. Straddling the country and rock genres throughout his career, Cash got his start at Sun Records, the same label that spawned Elvis Presley, Jerry Lee Lewis, and Roy Orbison. In the 1960s, Cash signed a lucrative contract with Columbia Records, where he scored crossover hits with "Ring Of Fire" and "A Boy Named Sue." During this time, Cash was a big Dylan fan: "I took note of Bob Dylan as soon as the *Bob Dylan* album came out in early '62 and listened almost constantly to *The Freewheelin' Bob Dylan* in '63. I had a portable record player I'd take along on the road, and I'd put on *Freewheelin'* backstage, then go out and do my show, then listen again as soon as I came off." In 1965, Cash scored a hit with the Dylan composition, "It Ain't Me Babe." Then in 1969, Cash finally joined Dylan in the studio. Although the two men recorded 12 songs together, just one of the tracks was issued, and appeared on the Dylan album, *Nashville Skyline*.

Embracing a rocker's lifestyle, Cash had experienced drug addictions, arrests, brushes with death, and both fame and failure. By the

1990s, Cash's body was ravaged by years of constant touring and hard living, and the damage was clear to see on his weathered face. During this period, he was also battling a form of Parkinson's called Shy-Drager Syndrome, a degenerative nerve disease.

In the spring of 1993, Cash was taken aback by Rubin's offer to sign him to a recording contract. After Rubin informed the aging icon he could record anything he wanted, the deal was sealed. Cash would later describe Rubin as "the ultimate hippie, bald on top but with hair down over his shoulders, a beard that looked as if it had never been trimmed... and clothes that would have done a wino proud."

Much of Cash's acoustic album, *American Recordings*, was recorded in the comfortable living room of Rubin's home in Laurel Canyon. In all, Cash recorded 80 songs. Rubin personally supervised Cash's comeback with a series of shows at a number of exclusive nightclubs such as the Viper Room in Los Angeles and Fez Under Time Café in New York City. In fact, two of the album's tracks were taken from Cash's brilliant performance at the Viper Room. With the album a critical success, Cash enjoyed renewed interest from various sectors. He later revealed: "According to the media at the time, [the album] caused an overnight change in my status from 'Nashville has-been' to 'hip icon.' Whatever they called me, I was grateful."

Encouraged by the success of *American Recordings*, Cash wanted to record another album. Retaining Rubin as the producer, Cash began working on his followup in late-1995. But instead of another acoustic project, Cash wanted to record an album with a full rock band. When Rubin recommended Tom Petty, Cash instructed Rubin to ask Petty to bring along his entire band. When Howie Epstein did not initially join his bandmates at the sessions, Cash personally invited the Heartbreakers' bass player to perform on the album. Petty, who deeply respected Cash, voluntarily worked without pay. At the sessions, the members of the Heartbreakers were frequently asked to play instruments they were not accustomed to playing. On February 25, 1996, Petty, Campbell, and Epstein joined Cash on stage for a few songs at a sold-out show at the House of Blues in Los Angeles.

Rockabilly pioneer Carl Perkins visited the recording sessions on several occasions and would join Johnny Cash and his wife, June, in reminiscing about Sam Phillips and Sun Records. Petty recalled: "There'd be June telling me stories about Elvis Presley, about when he had a crush on her and he sent her a letter every day. I said, 'God, those letters must be worth a fortune!' And she goes, 'Oh, John threw all those in the lake.'" Also during this time, the Heartbreakers appeared on several tracks of the tribute album, *Go Cat Go!*, which featured duets by Carl Perkins and a number of rock greats such as Paul McCartney and George Harrison. Mike Campbell recalled the atmosphere at the sessions: "It was like being in the presence of God, basically. [Carl Perkins] would sit there with an electric guitar without an amp and start playing; it would sound so good with just his hand on the guitar. We were hypnotized by his presence."

Throughout this period, Petty was a witness to the deep religious faith of Johnny and June Cash. During times of difficulty in the sessions, the pair would take a break and sing old gospel songs. At other times, Cash would lead a prayer and ask God for blessings. None of this was lost on Petty who at the time was battling a number of personal demons.

Issued in late-1996, *Unchained* earned a Grammy Award for Best Country Album. The project was highlighted by cover versions of Soundgarden's "Rusty Cage" and Tom Petty's "Southern Accents." It was Rubin who convinced Cash to record the Petty track as well as a number of other contemporary rock songs. Not surprisingly, one of the songs that did not make the final cut was a rendition of Robert Palmer's "Addicted To Love." While country radio ignored the album, it found a home on alternative-rock and college radio. Although he was just 62 at the time, Cash looked much older on the front cover of the album. Finding it increasingly difficult to perform, the ailing musical legend would soon retire from touring.

Later, Petty worked on two tracks of Cash's followup album, *Solitary Man*, which included a somber and plaintive remake of Petty's 1989 solo hit, "I Won't Back Down." After he heard Cash's rendition, Petty declared: "It felt like God was singing my song." The album also featured a powerful and emotionally-draining version of the Nine Inch Nails track, "Hurt." After Cash filmed a music video for the song, which pictured him in a declining physical state, June tried to stop its release. But in an act of personal faith, Cash overruled his wife.

Realizing that Cash was not long for this world, Petty would spend a great deal of time at Rubin's home studio. A divergent legion of Cash's admirers also came to visit, including Nick Cave, Billy Preston, Don Henley, and Joe Strummer of the Clash. Following Cash's death in 2003,

Rubin assembled a studio band – which included Mike Campbell and Benmont Tench – to finish a number of uncompleted Cash tracks, some of which were just a few lines of lyrics. The songs were issued on two albums, *A Hundred Highways* and *Ain't No Grave*.

*　　*　　*　　*　　*　　*

Wanting to remain active, but not in the mood to go on a full cross-country tour, Tom Petty decided to return to his roots and play a series of nightclub shows. Beginning on January 10, 1997, Tom Petty and the Heartbreakers embarked on an unprecedented run of 20 performances over 30 days at the legendary Fillmore Auditorium in San Francisco. The 1,100 seat venue was sold out for each of the shows. Petty commented at the time: "I just want to play and get away from the land of videos and records for a while. We want to get back to what we understand. We're musicians and it's a life we understand. If we went out on an arena tour right now, I don't think we'd be real inspired." The rejuvenated group would arrive early at the venue each night, just to practice a few new songs.

At the first show, the 95-minute set included everything from "Buddy Holly to John Mayall and the Rolling Stones; Bo Diddley to the Zombies to Ray Charles." With a nod to his mentor Bob Dylan, Petty selected the Wallflowers – a group headed by Bob's son, Jakob – as the opening act. But on the second night, a prankster unleashed a can of pepper spray in the middle of the audience. The stunt caused a 45-minute delay as paramedics treated dozens of concertgoers for breathing problems. Petty recalled, "The second night was maybe one of my best nights... ever. In fact, it was going so good I kind of thought the fuse was going to blow."

Also in 1997, Petty received news that his close friend George Harrison had been diagnosed with throat cancer. But while battling the disease, Harrison suffered a setback to his health when he was stabbed numerous times by an intruder at his Friar Park estate. Although Harrison would eventually recover from the stab wounds, the added strain to his system would ultimately be too much for him to overcome.

During this period, Petty started to work on another album. Struggling to avoid writing songs about divorce and personal loss, he desperately tried to concentrate on his future. Petty recalled, "I started writing the album without even realizing I'd written much. I'd sit and write and put stuff on tape but I'd always think, 'That's not really a song.'"

The album was primarily recorded at Mike Campbell's small home studio. Benmont Tench recounted the unconventional recording schedule: "It was a long process in terms of calendar time, but not in actual studio time. We'd go over to the studio at Mike's house to play, whether Tom was there or not. Tom would bring in songs, Mike would engineer, and we recorded about 30 songs. But we'd work for three or four days at a time, then Tom would go write more songs. It was like 'These are great. You got any more?' It was a good record to make."

Petty explained the group's mindset during the sessions: "We thought on this one, 'Well, maybe we won't play acoustic guitars too much, and maybe we won't really try to go after ballad-type songs too much.' And those were really the only rules we had when we started." Additionally, Petty tried to replicate the production style of one of his favorite 1960s bands: "Musically, this record is an experiment in space. I had the idea from listening to the Doors, of all people. I got fascinated by how much space there is in the records, and how well arranged the records were with very few instruments playing."

*   *   *   *   *   *

Enjoying their extended run of nightclub shows in 1997, Tom Petty and the Heartbreakers returned to the Fillmore in March 1999 for a second string of shows, which were a warm-up for an upcoming summer tour. Scheduling seven shows over a two-week period, Petty lined up a series of prominent opening acts including Taj Mahal and Bo Diddley. The Heartbreakers then played three more nightclub shows at the Irving Plaza ballroom in New York City. Some of the Fillmore performances were later released on home video, *High Grass Dogs – Live At The Fillmore*. Later that spring, Petty maintained his high profile by filming an episode of *VH1's Storytellers*.

*   *   *   *   *   *

Nicknamed "Petty's divorce album," *Echo* was quietly released in April 1999. A *Rolling Stone* reviewer said of the album, "Petty and the Heartbreakers define classic guitar rock better than just about any working band." But for the album, Petty did little promotion, filmed no videos at the time and, for over a decade, refused to play any of the tracks in concert. "That *Echo* album was one of the dark times. I can't even play it. It scares me because I was so down when I made it. It was the toughest period of my life," Petty later admitted. Similarly, Campbell recalled, "It was hard for him to focus for a while, understandably. There were times when he'd say 'I can't work today; I have too many things that I'm dealing with right now.' And we'd go 'OK' and just wait. I think actually, in a way, working on that record probably helped him at that point, just to sort of get back into focus as to what he wanted to do. But it did slow us down."

However, Petty was not the only Heartbreaker in turmoil at the time. Howie Epstein was conspicuously absent from the front cover of *Echo*. After waiting two full days, a frustrated Petty went ahead with a scheduled photo shoot without Epstein. Petty had hoped that the humiliating experience would teach his bandmate a lesson. Meanwhile, Steve Ferrone and Scott Thurston – both of whom performed on *Echo* – were listed as "guest artists" on the album's promotional materials.

A month before the album's official release date, Petty gave away an MP3 of the track, "Free Girl Now." This was during the early days of Napster and the move was considered daring at the time. But Warner Brothers ordered Petty to remove the online track after just two days – and nearly 157,000 free downloads. When asked if the song was written about anyone in his life, Petty initially evaded the question. Eventually, he admitted the song was based on an incident involving his girlfriend – and soon-to-be wife. He explained: "She had a boss who couldn't keep his hands off her. I had heard about this sort of thing but had never experienced it first-hand. At first, I found it amusing. But as it went on I could see that it wasn't amusing at all. She didn't have the power to fight. I finally said to her, 'You should quit.' One day, she did."

The album's opening track, "Room At The Top," was described by Petty as "one of the most depressing songs in rock history." A similar song on the album, "Rhino Skin" expressed Petty's desire to shield himself, emotionally, from the chaos in his life.

Another track, "Swingin'," should have been a bigger hit. Written on the spot by Petty, he recounted the fruitful session: "I just started making up something. Then this song 'Swingin'' appears. We did it in one go, ad-libbed all the way through. When we get to the end, Rick [Rubin] says, 'That's a good song. Let's do that one once more.' So I had to listen to that one, learn it. And do it again, and it was on the record." Another track on *Echo*, "I Don't Wanna Fight," was the first-ever Heartbreakers song that did not feature Petty on lead vocals. Instead, Mike Campbell provided both the lead guitar and the lead vocal. Touring in support of the album, Tom Petty and the Heartbreakers hired 1950s rocker Bo Diddley (who lived near Gainesville at the time) as the opening act for some of the shows.

As Petty continued to fight his own personal battles, he also tried to help Howie Epstein. Still abusing hard drugs, Epstein was unable to break free of his addiction. But Stan Lynch, who had left the band five years earlier, argued that the tour should have been scrapped for the sake of Epstein's well-being: "I'm really pissed that Howie was allowed to die while in the employ of a multimillion-dollar corporation. There were only four or five principals in that corporation, only four or five people who mattered, and Howie was at the top of that list. So why were they on the road at all when Howie was so sick? What was more important? Apparently, not Howie."

Tom Petty suffered another personal tragedy on December 10, 1999, when his father, Earl, passed away at the age of 75. The elder Petty suffered from a variety of chronic ailments including emphysema and diabetes. Putting aside a lifetime of hostility and anger, Tom Petty had some warm words for his father at a memorial service in Gainesville.

Also that month, Petty's divorce was finalized. Petty would never criticize his former wife in the press and appeared to take all the blame for their split. He later explained: "Going through with that was hard, you know, and I'm sort of pledged legally not to talk about it, and I don't really want to talk about it.... I don't regret my marriage. I lived it up. We had a lot of good times. And we just moved on in other directions. But the kids, you know, they had to deal with the shuffle and find what suited them best. You know someone so well, so long, you carry a part of them. So it will always be a bit painful, but you overcome that and you go on with your life." Petty's wife, Jane, would receive possession of the couple's rebuilt home in Encino. In 2013, she would place the property up for sale.

▶ CHAPTER 30
HAVE LOVE, WILL TRAVEL

Moving out of his dilapidated "chicken shack," Tom Petty purchased a heavily-wooded estate in Malibu for $3.75 million. The 10,000 square-foot, 1940s-era dwelling overlooked the Pacific Ocean and was located near the home of Bob Dylan. The affluent community was home to many celebrities and was famous for its pristine beaches.

Petty was eventually joined at his new residence by girlfriend Dana York, a Texas-born blond beauty. After a six-month engagement, Petty, then 50, married York, 37, in Las Vegas on June 3, 2001. Petty was in Sin City at the time for two sold-out performances at the Hard Rock Hotel. With little fanfare and no press in attendance, the wedding vows were exchanged with only family and close friends present. The low-key ceremony was followed by dinner at a steak house.

A few months later, *People* magazine reported that the couple repeated their vows at a private ceremony at Petty's home in Malibu. With forty guests in attendance – including a few celebrities but no paparazzi – the second set of vows was officiated by Little Richard, an ordained minister who had also conducted the weddings of other musicians including Bruce Springsteen, Steven Van Zandt, and Cyndi Lauper. Petty recounted: "[Little Richard] was really nervous, but so was I. He gave a long talk about love and its characteristics, and what it shouldn't do. He was pretty inspirational." While the bride was dressed in a traditional white gown, Petty was gussied up in a lavender tux with Nashville-style ornamental stitching. For the reception, Petty hired a mariachi band.

Over the next few years, Petty bonded with Dana's close-knit family and also adopted her young son. Petty soon purchased a second, smaller home, also located in Malibu. A rustic pine-sided house that was situated on the beach, it served as a peaceful respite for Petty and his new family.

Building a home studio in a small guest house, he would dub the room Loose Moose Studios.

While Petty was enjoying his new family, trouble soon surfaced in the Heartbreakers fold. On June 26, 2001, Howie Epstein and Carlene Carter were arrested by police in Albuquerque, New Mexico. While enroute to the airport, the couple was stopped for speeding, clocked at 78 mph in a 55 mph zone. To make matters worse, their Jeep Cherokee was an overdue rental and Carter was charged with driving a stolen vehicle. When police searched the vehicle, they discovered nearly three grams of black-tar heroin – the cheapest and most addictive form of the narcotic – as well as various drug paraphernalia. A panicked Epstein feared he was unlikely to make it to Scranton, Pennsylvania, for the start of a Heartbreakers tour.

In their police mug shots, both Epstein and Carter looked sickly and disheveled, with Carter looking particularly haggard. Carter claimed the drugs were hers and insisted she was a user, not a dealer. Consequently, Epstein was not charged. After spending the night in jail, Epstein and Carter each paid a bond and were released the following morning. Nearly breaking a cardinal rule of rock and roll, Epstein barely made it to the scheduled Heartbreakers concert on time.

At that point, Epstein's bandmates recognized the severity of the situation. During the tour, Epstein tried to break his addiction to heroin – in an abrupt, cold turkey approach – and experienced severe withdrawal pains. Petty explained at the time: "It's been an ongoing issue with him, and this has popped the balloon. I talked with him last night, and he definitely wants out of this (addiction). He stopped using dope, and he's going through a lot of pain everyday. His rap to me is that the stolen-car incident is blown out of proportion, that he had nothing to do with stealing a car. The most important thing for him right now is to get clean, and he agrees." At the completion of the tour, Petty convinced Epstein to enter a rehab program in Miami. Carter would later plead no contest to a drug possession charge and was sentenced to 18 months of probation.

A few months later in September 2001, America was attacked by an organized group of Islamic terrorists. In the aftermath, Tom Petty and the Heartbreakers appeared on a television benefit for the families of the victims, in what was billed as *America: A Tribute To Heroes*. Stoically dressed in a simple black jacket and white shirt, a visibly shaken Petty performed a poignant, heartfelt rendition of "I Won't Back Down." With hundreds of glowing candles framing the sides of the stage, Petty had some difficulty singing the lyrics, which were mostly spoken as if to emphasize the song's underlining message. The evening's other memorable performances included Willie Nelson's rendition of "America, The Beautiful" and David Bowie's passionate rendering of "Heroes."

Meanwhile, Tom Petty continued to receive bad news; George Harrison had succumbed to cancer and passed away at a friend's home in Los Angeles. Jeff Lynne had spent much time with Harrison in his final days. The death of his close friend hit Petty hard and was yet another wound to his battered psyche. Petty later said of Harrison, "I was mostly just amazed that he would take the time to sit down and play guitar with me. The first time we played together.... it struck me that here's this guy who is a hero of mine, but he's also just a guy who loves the guitar as much as I do. George was a very gracious person, and he always brought little gifts – like hats and Beatles watches – when he came to visit. I loved his humor. I remember telling him once how much I admired his sound with the Beatles, and he said, 'Oh, we had those Gretsches. If only we'd had Strats, we could have been really good!'"

But Petty was also hoping to record a third Traveling Wilburys album: "We never thought we were gonna run out of time." Petty would later reveal, "It's such a shame that everyone's not still here, because I still feel like I'm in that band."

Petty later recalled: "My daughter Adria used to visit him a lot in England when she was over there. She would go and stay at [his estate] Friar Park. She was telling me the other [day] that one night they were out walking in the garden and he goes, 'Oh, Adria, I just wish I could turn into a light beam and go away.'" Meanwhile, over the course of the next few years, Petty began to heal his relationships with his friends and family.

*   *   *   *   *   *

On March 18, 2002, Tom Petty and the Heartbreakers received one of the top honors in their field when they were inducted into the Rock and Roll Hall of Fame. The induction also meant that former members Ron Blair and Stan Lynch would be reuniting with the band. However,

Blair was unaware at the time that he would soon be rejoining the Heartbreakers.

Lynch, who looked healthy and relaxed, was happy to reunite with his old bandmates and had put aside any simmering, unresolved disputes with Petty for the sake of the ceremony. Petty and Lynch had not spoken for almost a decade before that night and would not speak for another decade afterwards.

Petty recalled the practice session for the band's Hall of Fame performance: "We only had to work up two numbers. But we jammed for a good, long day." But when Lynch laid eyes on Epstein, he was shocked by his friend's appearance: "A little bag of dust walked in. The Howie I remembered would beat my ass at arm wrestling. He was a tough kid. But when I saw him at the rehearsals, he was almost emaciated. He didn't look 100 pounds soaking wet." Sadly, this would be the final time Epstein would perform with the band.

The 2002 class of inductees also included Brenda Lee, Gene Pitney, Isaac Hayes, Talking Heads, and the Ramones. Tom Petty and the Heartbreakers were inducted by Jakob Dylan, who admitted to modeling his own band after the Heartbreakers. In his speech, Dylan said: "Tom Petty and the Heartbreakers made it clear that while rock and roll will have its trends and fads, it's really about the opposite. It's about being timeless.... What is rare with Petty is that after twenty-five years, his next song may be his best one yet." As Dylan spoke, the members of the Heartbreakers listened intently at the side of the stage. Epstein – who was wearing a ruffled white shirt, black vest, and black leather pants – appeared to be in pain.

Finally, each member of the Heartbreakers gave a speech at the podium, with Mike Campbell going first. Campbell joked: "I always thought if I hadn't made it in this band, I was going to try to audition for the Ramones." Meanwhile, Benmont Tench thanked his parents for letting the band practice in their living room.

Tom Petty gave a long, heartfelt acceptance speech. Wearing a funky, 1960s-inspired, form-fitting dark tux, he stated: "A rock and roll star is probably the purest, absolute, mainstream manifestation of the American dream.... I thank this rock and roll for the freedom it's given me, and I thank the fans for such a wonderful life, and I thank God for all of it." Sporting a well-manicured graying beard, Petty projected an air of tranquility throughout the evening. Meanwhile, Epstein – who was standing behind Petty – was jittery and looked clearly distressed. Another highlight of the night came when a mohawked Eddie Vedder, of Pearl Jam, gave an entertaining 17-minute speech honoring the Ramones.

Later in the evening, the expanded Heartbreakers performed "Mary Jane's Last Dance" and "American Girl." Howie Epstein and Ron Blair took turns playing with the band, as they each performed on one song. But while Stan Lynch played the drums on both songs, Steve Ferrone – who was not inducted with the rest of the band – stood at the side of the stage, shaking a tambourine. Scott Thurston was also not inducted.

Backstage, the 51-year-old Petty told reporters, "It's very easy to be cynical about the Hall of Fame. But on the other hand, it's really a beautiful thing for someone like me. I dedicated my entire life to this music."

Just two months after his induction into the Rock and Roll Hall of Fame, Howie Epstein was fired from the Heartbreakers. At almost the same time, Epstein ended his 15-year relationship with Carlene Carter, who would leave New Mexico and move to Nashville to live with one of her daughters. (Carter later managed to break free from her addiction and would reestablish her music career.) Afterward, Epstein returned to his stately home in the suburbs of Santa Fe, where very few of the locals were aware of his presence. Despite his dismissal from the Heartbreakers, Epstein remained optimistic about his career. He was planning to record a solo album and take on some production work. He had also formed a local blues-rock group called the Bottomfeeders.

Beginning with a performance on June 27 in Grand Rapids, Michigan, Ron Blair returned to his former position in the Heartbreakers. Although Blair had quit the group nearly two decades earlier – in part because he was newly married and had a young child – he was now divorced and his son was grown.

The ten-week, 32-date summer tour gave Petty an opportunity to try out three new tracks from his upcoming album. A reviewer said of one of the shows: "The 51-year-old Petty, rail-thin in a purple velvet coat and black-rebel shirt and pants – with his long blond hair evoking other times and hippier places – was his typically bashful, amiable self, repeatedly and profusely thanking the crowd in tones of surprise and humility." Taking turns as the opening act on the tour were Jackson Browne and Brian Setzer.

▶ CHAPTER 31
AMERICA'S LAST DJ

In October 2002, Tom Petty would revisit his battle against the music industry with the release of the concept album, *The Last DJ*. The project was originally titled *The Golden Circle*, a reference to skyrocketing ticket prices, which became pervasive after the Eagles introduced the concept of $100 tickets in 1994 for their infamous Hell Freezes Over reunion tour. Just one year earlier in 1993, top-level acts like Paul McCartney, Bruce Springsteen, and the Grateful Dead were charging between $26 and $32.50 per seat, with little in the way of any additional, tacked-on service charges. Petty would later admit, "I would feel embarrassed charging 200 bucks for a ticket." However, David Crosby, who was touring at the time as a part of Crosby, Stills & Nash, would ignite a storm of controversy when he said in the press: "What they do in terms of the gigs and the pricing and the rest of it is completely out of our hands. Anybody who thinks it's too much money shouldn't come."

Produced by George Drakoulias, *The Last DJ* was a testament to Petty's resiliency as a recording artist. Although Howie Epstein did not perform on the album, returning bassist Ron Blair played on just two tracks. (Petty and Campbell played the bass on the remaining songs.)

The title track and first single, "The Last DJ," received only moderate radio airplay. Petty called the song a "work of fiction: It's a story about a D.J. who becomes so frustrated with his inability to play what he wants that he moves to Mexico and gets his freedom back. The song is sung by a narrator who's a fan of this D.J. When I wrote that song, I swear I didn't know much about Clear Channel, and I certainly wasn't aiming it at any particular corporation. The words 'Clear Channel' never come up in my song, and I learned more about them when I started being banned by 'em!"

Unhappy with the rise of narrow, specialized formats and tight playlists, Petty explained: "The radio today is just intimidating. And it's formatted to a point where, if you're on this [position] of the dial this is all you're going to hear all day." Recalling the golden age of top-40 radio in the 1960s, Petty reminisced: "I remember a time when you could hear everything on one station. It was so great to go from Frank Sinatra to the Yardbirds. You didn't think twice about it.... I was also fortunate to come up in a time when there wasn't any music press. You couldn't read about a record. You'd listen to it and make up your own mind. Things that were good stuck, and things that weren't fell by the wayside. Like, you'd hang onto your Beach Boys albums, but somehow manage to lose Herman's Hermits."

The album's other prevalent theme was, in Petty's words, "the celebration of mediocrity in America." Petty explained: "For so much of my life, I took rock and roll seriously. I wonder if people understand how much that meant. It was a renaissance period – artists were doing their great work. But you took it for granted that it was just going to go on and on. It was sad to see rock and roll shoot itself in the foot." Defending his frustration and outrage, Petty argued: "It may sound like I'm just some old guy bitching about how much better things were in my day. But the truth is, they were." In a 21st century radio industry driven by stock prices and dividends, one insider lamented, "I don't know how anybody can be passionate about music when their job is on the line. They're going to rely on research and numbers, so the passion for the music is in jeopardy."

Petty was also unhappy with the explosion of singing competitions like *American Idol* and *America's Got Talent*: "It's reached absurd levels. When you're creating your pop stars on a game show on TV, you know something's wrong. [You're] insulting people who have put their [lives] into their art." But Petty's former producer Jimmy Iovine felt otherwise as he spent three seasons mentoring contestants on *American Idol*. Likewise, Stevie Nicks appeared on the program as a guest mentor during the 2012 season.

Another track from the album, "Money Becomes King" blasted the introduction of "gold circle seating" at concert venues. By shelling out hundreds of dollars, VIPs were rewarded with the best seats in the house and added amenities such as exclusive tour merchandise and meet-and-greet sessions with the artists. Petty said at the time: "Rich people aren't fun to play to. You want people there who make average incomes, because they might appreciate it more. And a rock show is still just a rock show. I've never seen one that is worth $100."

After attacking radio conglomerates, record companies, advertising executives, and concert promoters, Petty admitted that recording artists shared some of the responsibility for the decline in the quality of rock music: "I don't think the industry is entirely to blame. Let's face it: The music industry has always been laughably corrupt, always. It's the artists themselves that often cause problems. Artists aren't necessarily business people. And they aren't necessarily aware of all the things that go on in their names. Some just want to make some music, but there is a lot of greed among artists as well."

Despite Petty's enthusiasm for *The Last DJ*, it was not embraced in many quarters. Petty later recounted the reaction to the album's central message: "Yeah, I got beaten up pretty good and halfway expected to be.... I knew it wasn't going to be popular at the record [labels]." But the album was also not popular at many radio stations. A music director at a New York City station explained: "My first reaction was, 'What is this guy doing?' How can he expect us to put a song on the air that basically says we're [junk]?"

Shortly after the album's release, *Rolling Stone* magazine published the list, "The Ten Things That Piss Off Tom Petty." Topping the list: "Radio is not even worth listening to.... But I was elated when my song ["The Last DJ"] was banned. I mean, nothing could have complimented me more than to hear they just banned it at such-and-such station because it's anti-radio. Now, in 2002 to have a song banned that doesn't have a dirty word, doesn't advocate violence – it's fascinating, you know. Like, what are you afraid of?"

*   *   *   *   *   *

Staged at the prestigious Royal Albert Hall in London, the Concert for George was a musical tribute to the fallen Beatle on the one-year anniversary of his death. Harrison's longtime friend Eric Clapton recalled: "In the spring of 2002, Brian [Roylance] came around for dinner and we started talking about George.... I ventured to remark that it was sad that there would be no memorial for George, at least in a music sense, and Brian said, 'Not unless you do something.' So that trap was sprung, and I happily walked into it. The program was a labor of love in which I threw myself. Over the next few months, Olivia [Harrison] and Brian and I planned the event, discussing who we would ask and what songs we would play. Olivia was the mastermind of the whole thing, and I simply assembled the rock part of the musical end.... The only minor difficulty arose over who should sing 'Something.'"

Tickets to the tribute concert quickly sold out, despite the nearly $250 admission charge. All of the proceeds were donated to a charity founded by Harrison in 1973, the Material World Charitable Foundation.

On the evening of November 29, 2002, the Concert for George opened with Eric Clapton offering a few words to the audience. He then introduced the evening's first musical act, legendary sitar player Ravi Shankar and his daughter, Anoushka. The house band included Paul McCartney and Ringo Starr. While the back of the stage was graced by a large framed monitor that displayed a series of Harrison portraits, the front of the stage was rimmed with hundreds of flower bouquets brought by fans.

Dressed in dark suits, Tom Petty and the Heartbreakers performed a pair of Beatles-era songs composed by Harrison, "Taxman" and "I Need You." The group was then joined on stage by fellow Traveling Wilburys member Jeff Lynne and Harrison's son, Dhani, for an upbeat rendition of "Handle With Care," which was the best-received performance of Petty's short set. (Petty had originally wanted to perform Harrison's favorite Wilburys track, "If You Belonged To Me.") Petty seemed genuinely elated to be on the stage, celebrating his close friend's legacy. The Heartbreakers were followed by Billy Preston and Eric Clapton, who performed "Isn't It A Pity," a song written by Harrison in 1966.

The concert ended with Joe Brown playing the ukulele – one of Harrison's favorite instruments – on a touching version of the pop standard, "I'll See You In My Dreams." Brown, one of Britain's first rockers, had toured on the same bill as the Beatles in 1962. Later, Brown served as the best man when Harrison married Olivia in 1978.

▶ CHAPTER 32
HOWIE: STRAIGHT INTO DARKNESS

In early 2003, longtime Heartbreakers bassist Howie Epstein became the mortal victim of his addictions. Despite numerous interventions by his friends, Epstein's drug abuse had not abated and his health continued to deteriorate. Epstein was also experiencing financial problems during this period and was the target of a lawsuit by the Chase Mortgage Company.

The day before he died, a heartsick Epstein was dealing with the loss of his beloved 16-year-old dog, Dingo. Epstein was also complaining of serious stomach pain and was taking antibiotics for a large abscess on his leg. After passing out in the bathroom of his new girlfriend's home, he was driven to St. Vincent Hospital in Santa Fe. He died the following day. Epstein was just 46.

Carlene Carter told the press: "I'm devastated. I loved him very much. My kids thought of Howie as their father." A subsequent autopsy blamed Epstein's death on a combination of cocaine and heroin poisoning.

In a profession where drug use is prevalent and an integral part of the culture, it is no surprise that the rock and roll highway has been littered with addiction and drug-related fatalities. While some artists like Ray Charles, Steven Tyler, and Eric Clapton had been able to beat heroin addiction, the same drug has been responsible for the deaths of rock greats such as Janis Joplin, Jim Morrison, and Sid Vicious.

A newspaper later reported: "Local friends of Epstein's said that, before his death, the musician had opened the doors of his [New Mexico] home to other musicians and addicts, some of whom allegedly took advantage of Epstein's generosity."

Epstein's former bandmates in the Heartbreakers were devastated but not surprised by his death. One of the songs played at Epstein's funeral, "Turn Turn Turn" by the Byrds, was based on the Book of Ecclesiastes.

While Benmont Tench and Stan Lynch both attended the service in Milwaukee, Tom Petty decided not to go. Instead, Petty later staged a tribute to Epstein in Los Angeles.

Meanwhile, Carlene Carter would continue to suffer a series of personal calamities. The same year she lost Epstein to drugs, she would also endure the deaths of her 45-year-old sister Rosey Nix Adams, her mother June Carter, and her stepfather Johnny Cash. Carter would sum up the tragic year in the autobiographical song, "The Bitter End." She later admitted, "At the time I was writing that song, I felt really bleak about the future because in an eight-month period I had lost so many people that meant the world to me: Mom, John, Rosey and Howie. I couldn't see what the future held for me. But it seemed no matter how much I tried to tear myself up, I couldn't. I'm glad I didn't." Eventually, Carter would also write a song about her relationship with Epstein, "Judgement Day."

Although Epstein's death made Petty consider disbanding the Heartbreakers, the tragedy brought the surviving members of the group closer to each other. Petty later admitted, "If Ron Blair hadn't been there to step back in, I personally would've called it a day as far as the Heartbreakers are concerned. I don't know about them, but they probably would've too. I couldn't have faced a new person filling that slot, it would've felt phony. I owe Ron a lot. From that point on the band got reinvigorated and got a new start."

A number of years before Epstein's demise, Petty had said, "Howie could make the best solo album of any of the Heartbreakers 'cause he's the best singer." But despite the fact that Epstein had spent years planning a solo album, he never found the time to complete the project. Although a large trove of Epstein's music went missing from his home studio following his death, a number of his early home demos and unreleased studio tracks were later issued by his family.

*   *   *   *   *   *

Beginning with an appearance in the 1978 film, *FM*, Tom Petty would occasionally dabble in the field of acting. Other roles would follow. Petty made a cameo appearance in the film *Made In Heaven*, portraying the owner of a gambling house. In the film, he uttered the memorable line, "You're the devil, Lucille." As Petty recalled, "I don't play a real nice guy. I've been asked a lot over the years to do parts. This one I only did because Tim Hutton kept asking me." Petty also had a bit role in the Kevin Kostner film, *The Postman*, portraying the former mayor of a post-apocalypse city. Later, Petty turned down a role in a film starring Billy Bob Thornton, *Daddy And Them*.

However, Petty had far better success on television. He made several appearances on a pair of HBO comedy programs starring Garry Shandling, in which he portrayed Shandling's real-life neighbor. On the final episode of *The Larry Sanders Show*, Petty nearly got into a violent brawl with actor Greg Kinnear.

But Petty did his best acting work as the voice of a cartoon character. In 2002, he appeared on *The Simpsons*. In the episode, "How I Spent My Strummer Vacation," Homer Simpson visited a rock and roll fantasy camp, where he was tutored on stage strutting by Mick Jagger, stage clothing by Lenny Kravitz, and lyric composition by Tom Petty. Petty's cartoon persona wrote an oddball song about a drunken girl behind the wheel of a car who contemplated the state of public schools. Later, Petty's character lost a toe in a stage accident.

Then in 2004, Petty provided the voice of Elroy "Lucky" Kleinschmidt on the prime-time cartoon series, *King Of The Hill*. Not a fan of modern television, Petty was initially unfamiliar with the exploits of the animated family led by patriarch Hank Hill. Petty recalled, "I think it was Billy Bob Thornton who turned me on to that. He had a bunch of tapes of it, and he said, 'Man, you're just going to love this.' I started watching it, and I just thought it was the greatest thing. Then it was just kind of a strange, cosmic connection; they called and wanted to know if I would come down and tape a show. So I jumped at that, and it turned out they liked the character so much they kind of wrote him into a lot of shows."

According to *King Of The Hill* co-creator Mike Judge, it was writer-producer John Altschuler who "had written this character named 'Lucky' and described him as looking like 'Tom Petty without the success.' And we thought, what if we tried to get Tom Petty? And [Petty] said, 'Yeah, I'll do it.' And he was great, just killed at the table read. Then he said, 'any time you want me to do it, I'll do it.'"

But Petty was surprised by the reaction at home: "My family went ape when I was asked to do an episode. It's as if I'd never accomplished anything in my life. For them, this is the absolute pinnacle of my career."

In a strange coincidence, Stephen Root – who provided the voices of two characters on the show, Buck Strickland and Bill Dauterive – was Petty's neighbor in Malibu. Additionally, Root was a Florida native who had attended the University of Florida in the early-1970s, during which time he occasionally saw Petty perform with Mudcrutch.

Over four episodes during his first season on the show, Petty portrayed a Florida-born redneck who retired after winning a $53,000 legal settlement for injuries sustained while slipping in a puddle of urine at a Costco store. Petty's character, Lucky, would refer to the payout as "my pee-pee money." Wearing a sleeveless t-shirt and sporting a bushy, 1970s-era mullet hairstyle, Lucky once camped out in front of a theater to be the first in line for tickets to a Foghat concert. Driving a beat-up pickup truck, Lucky dated and later married Hank Hill's niece, Luanne, whose voice was provided by actress Brittany Murphy.

Petty explained at the time: "Lucky is a fairly complex guy. He's really an idiot, but he's sort of a philosophical idiot. But he has a really good heart." However, one journalist described the character's persona as "a thorough white-trash stereotype with a simple mind and bizarre moral code. In lesser hands, this character could have caused great offense." In all, Petty would appear in 28 episodes from 2004 until the show's cancellation in 2009.

*   *   *   *   *   *

On June 22, 2003, Tom Petty experienced what he believed was "a close encounter of the third kind." But over the years, a number of other rockers have also reported encounters with UFOs. In 1974, John Lennon witnessed what he described as a flying saucer hovering outside of his apartment in New York City. He would mention the incident in the lyrics of his solo hit, "Nobody Told Me." Dave Davies, the co-founder of the Kinks, claimed in his autobiography that in 1982 he experienced multiple contacts with extraterrestrial beings. Jimi Hendrix once told a reporter for *The New York Times*, "There are other people in the solar system, you know, and they have the same feelings too." And Cat Stevens made a spectacular claim in 1973: "One night I was lying in bed and I saw this flying saucer shoot across the sky and stop over me. And it sucked me up in it. When it put me down, I shot up in bed. I know it wasn't a dream. It was real."

Meanwhile, when Tom Petty was driving along the Pacific coast in Malibu, he spotted three large, silver globes that were hovering near the ground. Panicked by the sight of the unexplained orbs – which he believed were UFOs – he rushed home. Returning to the scene with his wife, Dana, and a friend, Petty quickly realized the globes were actually large balloons tethered to the ground. The three balloons had been installed on the estate of music mogul Dick Clark to ward off members of the paparazzi who were flying overhead in helicopters, trying to snap photos of the outdoor wedding of actor Adam Sandler to model Jackie Titone. With his eyes still focused skyward, Petty attempted to turn his car around. But in the process, he struck another vehicle. Within seconds, a flustered Petty was swarmed by the dozens of photographers who were assembled nearby.

Following the accident, Petty gave up driving. Just like his father, Petty was accident-prone behind the wheel. Afterward, he was usually chauffeured around town by longtime Heartbreakers roadie, Alan "Bugs" Weidel. But driving a vehicle was a concern for many rockers over the years. Elvis Presley complained he could not drive a car in peace. Female fans would constantly crash into him, apologize and then ask for an autograph.

▶ CHAPTER 33
PETTY'S SAVING GRACE

In 2005, Tom Petty decided to spice up the Heartbreakers' stage show for an upcoming tour. He had been inspired to make the changes by Hollywood designer Saul Bass, who was best known for his work on the silver screen thrillers *Vertigo* and *Psycho*. Petty said at the time: "We've never had anything that exploded or anything. But production can be fun. In the type of places we're playing, these big outdoor shows, it's good to have something for the people a mile away watching the thing. And we've also incorporated the video in an unusual way into the act."

Hitting the road in June, Tom Petty and the Heartbreakers introduced a pair of tracks, "Turn This Car Around" and a song highlighted by a lengthy Benmont Tench piano solo, "Melinda." While on tour, Petty told *Rolling Stone*: "I'm 54, and girls are throwing their underwear at me.... The crowds are just manic – in Boston, they were singing so loud they actually drowned us out." Touring without the support of a new album, Petty chose to work with independent promoters around the country instead of contracting with the Clear Channel spin-off firm, Live Nation. As *Billboard* columnist Ray Waddell noted: "He could have played fewer dates, only played in major markets or stayed indoors and jacked up the price, but that's not the way [he wanted] to do it. There are a lot of things about this tour to admire."

Petty hired the Black Crowes as the opening act for a number of the dates. The group had been discovered and signed to Rick Rubin's Def American label in 1988 by Petty's producer George Drakoulias, who gave the unknown act a modest $5,000 advance. Drakoulias also changed the group's name from Mr. Crowe's Garden. When asked about the band, Petty joked, "For some reason, I have a special affinity for unattractive, pot-smoking musicians with Southern accents."

*　　　*　　　*　　　*　　　*　　　*

In December 2005, Tom Petty was awarded *Billboard* magazine's prestigious Century Award. Just thirteen years earlier in 1992, Petty presented the inaugural award to George Harrison. In Harrison's acceptance speech, he described the Traveling Wilburys as "the band that made me remember how much fun it was to play rock and roll."

In late-2005, Olivia Harrison asked Tom Petty and Jeff Lynne to be the presenters for Harrison's solo induction into the Rock and Roll Hall of Fame, the following spring. Although Petty was quick to oblige, Lynne had to be persuaded due to his disdain for public appearances.

With "Wilbury Twist" playing in the background, Petty and Lynne took the stage at the Waldorf Astoria in New York City. Standing at the podium, Petty offered a tribute to Harrison: "He just loved playing music with his friends. And he loved guitars. And he loved rock and roll. And he loved Carl Perkins. And he loved Little Richard. And he loved Dhani and Olivia. And he loved to stay up all night long and play the ukulele till dawn." While Petty's poignant speech lasted just a little over four minutes – which was very brief by Rock Hall standards – the somewhat reclusive Lynne followed Petty with just a 20-second statement. Olivia Harrison's selection of Petty – instead of the two surviving Beatles – was a surprise to many and demonstrated the close friendship that Petty and the former Beatle had cultivated in such a short time. (Much like the situation at the Concert for George tribute in 2002, many of the attendees at the Rock Hall induction lamented the absence of Bob Dylan.)

Later that evening, Petty and Lynne performed two songs with an all-star band that included Steve Ferrone, Scott Thurston, Steve Winwood, Jim Capaldi, Prince, and George Harrison's 26-year-old son, Dhani (who looked far younger than his age). After a faithful rendition of "Handle With Care," the highlight of the evening came when Prince delivered a blistering guitar solo during an extended version of "While My Guitar Gently Weeps," which amazed many in the audience.

The day after the Hall of Fame induction ceremony, Petty found himself starting another musical project. Petty recalled, "The performance went well, so on the trip back I said to [Jeff Lynne], 'We ought to do a track sometime.' Then, Mike [Campbell] and I went over to Jeff's house, showed him a tune, and he wanted to cut it right there in his studio. We didn't have a band, so Jeff said, 'You play drums don't you?' So I wound up being the drummer. Anyway, that first track went really nice, so we just pitched camp at Jeff's studio. I kept dragging out songs, and the next thing we knew, we'd recorded ten tracks. It was just the three of us. Jeff played bass, Mike played all the solos, and each one of us would fill in wherever we could on keyboard and guitar." Petty also forced Mike Campbell to break out of his traditional mold and had him play some blues-style slide guitar on a vintage Les Paul.

Petty said of the project: "It's not a real loud record or an all-out rock fest. It's quieter but not mellow. I wanted to make this for a long time. It's not a record I could have made in the '70s. I wasn't seasoned enough." But while recording the album, Petty began to ponder his legacy: "Lately I've been concerned with what I'll leave behind artistically. The biggest priority with the new record now is that I know this is here longer than me and that's more important than [it] being a hit record. Years ago you'd have to make sure you had one [track] that was a [hit] single. I don't think that pops up in my mind anymore. I'm a little more into the poetry and the lyrical images than I used to be. I don't want to waste a line, I want it to mean something and I want it to be the right line. With this record I knew that I wanted to have a sound that was cohesive. I didn't want to make a concept album but I wanted it to fit together sonically. The space is everything in a record. It's not anthemic at all. I'm real bored with [being] anthemic. I did that and I am not trying to do it again."

More importantly for Petty, the album reflected his personal serenity at the time: "It wouldn't have been a very good record if I just sat back and wrote about how happy I was. But I am pretty happy these days. I've gone through the dark tunnel and come out the other end.... I have a good family, my kids are doing well, and I have a young boy who just turned thirteen, and that's a whole movie on its own. I never really had any real family. My mom died when I was quite young, and my dad was never around much. And so when I married Dana, she and her mom and her brother lived down here, and they kind of adopted me into their family.... So I feel good having that kind of bond with a family."

Released in July 2006, *Highway Companion* was considered Petty's third solo album. Co-produced with Jeff Lynne and Mike Campbell, the album received only moderate radio airplay. The album's futuristic cover was designed by artist Robert Deyber, and pictured an astronaut and monkey glancing at a space rocket.

Calling the project a "midtempo gem," a *Rolling Stone* critic gave *Highway Companion* three-and-a-half stars and began his review with the comment: "In a career that has now reached its thirtieth year, Tom Petty has never made a bad album." On the other hand, a *Billboard* magazine reviewer called the album "a surprisingly moody affair" full of "melancholic road anthems."

The track "Saving Grace" (not the 1980 Dylan song of the same name) was a retro-sounding, blues-inspired tune that was an unlikely choice as the album's lead radio single. The album's other highlights included "Turn This Car Around" and "Flirting With Time." Another track, the Grammy-nominated "Square One," was originally featured on the soundtrack of the 2005 film, *Elizabethtown.*

Meanwhile, in April 2006, on the 30th anniversary of the Heartbreakers' founding, Petty hinted to a journalist that he was about to retire from the road after the completion of a summer tour. Instead, he would play only occasional dates because full-fledged tours had become too physically taxing. But after the news hit various media outlets, Petty backed off from his "retirement."

With Petty poised to launch a cross-country tour in June to promote *Highway Companion*, it was difficult to fault him for wanting to slow down or take an extended break. As drummer Steve Ferrone observed, "We go on the road with Tom and he is very enthusiastic; then after a while it starts to wear on him. Usually by the end of the tour even though we have had a great time, Tom says he will never do it again. But give him six months sitting at home and he'll start writing and then he'll want to get together and play." The 30th Anniversary Tour would hit nearly three dozen cities and feature a number of musical guests including Stevie Nicks, the Allman Brothers Band, Pearl Jam, Trey Anastasio (of the group Phish), the Black Crowes, and the Derek Trucks Band.

But Petty would soon find himself in yet another public battle. Going well beyond his 1981 fight with his own record company over the list price of the album *Hard Promises*, Petty went after scalpers who were profiting on the re-sale of concert tickets. Setting up a pre-sale system on his website, Petty offered fans the first shot at good seats. But following numerous complaints, Petty and Ticketmaster identified 1,400 tickets that were purchased by scalpers – and then voided the tickets! The unprecedented move shocked veteran scalpers who were accustomed to buying and selling concert tickets much like traders of a commodity on

Wall Street. Ticketmaster executive David Marcus commented: "It's a risk for an artist to cancel a sold ticket and have it put back on sale. It speaks volumes for Tom Petty and his management and their sincere interest in their fans."

Then on September 21, Petty performed in Gainesville at what was billed as the 30th Anniversary Concert. Surprisingly, Petty had not performed in his hometown for almost 13 years.

Earlier in the day, the city's mayor officially proclaimed the date, Tom Petty and the Heartbreakers Day. At a press conference attended by the entire group, a representative of the university apologized for not organizing a parade. Benmont Tench, who had purchased his family's home following the death of his father, told those in attendance, "I really, really love this town. It's really special. You need to know what you've got here." Steve Ferrone chimed in, "I come from a town somewhat like Gainesville.... [but] in Brighton [England], we don't have any alligators."

The concert at the O'Connell Center in Gainesville had sold out in just 10 minutes. A local reporter described the electrified atmosphere inside the venue: "They went berserk – stomping, screaming and causing a rumble that rivaled the neighboring [University of Florida stadium] on game day. The crowd started going nuts when the lights went down, and when the first chord of 'Listen To Her Heart' was played, the noise only intensified." Relaxed, wearing a loose, untucked aqua-blue silk shirt, an unbuttoned black vest with a shooting red heart on the back, and a multi-colored neckerchief, Petty gave a spirited performance. Before playing "Southern Accents," Petty announced to the crowd that he had not performed the song since the last time he was in Gainesville.

Stevie Nicks – who sang three duets with Petty that night – was presented with a gift after the concert. Nicks recalled: "Tom made me a little platinum sheriff's badge that had 24-karat gold and diamonds across the top and said 'To Our Honorary Heartbreaker, Stevie Nicks,' while on the reverse, it read 'To The Only Girl In Our Band.'"

While in Gainesville, Petty wanted to visit his friends, family, and old haunts, but was emotionally drained by the experience of returning to his hometown. Petty recalled, "It spooked me, really. It was nice but it was also overwhelming. You can't really walk down the street or talk to anybody because everybody was talking at once. At the concert I just hid in the bus until it was time to play."

Although he was an established rock superstar, Petty still managed to remain a relatively private person. In thousands of interviews, he rarely mentioned his first or second wife, his two daughters, or his stepson. Early in his career, Petty realized that fame was a double-edged sword and he constantly battled to keep his personal life out of the tabloids. Petty once said, "I never wanted to be a big show-biz personality. I think it's fine for people who like it, but it would terrify me to make my life so public. You get nervous because you go places and you start to draw a crowd.... But it's still embarrassing to be standing in line for a movie and everyone starts to shout." As Paul McCartney explained in a 2004 interview: "George [Harrison] once said that fame cost him his nervous system. I can understand that. Fame happened to us all when we were just kids, really. Being recognized wherever we went, that came really quick.... Until the whole world knew who we were. So there was nowhere, absolutely nowhere, we could go where we weren't instantly recognizable. And, whatever we did, even if we never made another record, we could never be unfamous again."

In the end, Petty's "retirement tour" grossed approximately $30 million. Also that year, Tom Petty and the Heartbreakers were invited to headline the Bonnaroo Festival in Tennessee. At the start of his performance, Petty announced to the 80,000 assembled concertgoers: "I'm Tom Petty and behind me are the Heartbreakers. We're going to have a good time tonight. I promise you that."

Around this time, a deejay in Delaware sparked a controversy when he suggested that Tom Petty's seminal track "Last Dance With Mary Jane" was duplicated both musically and thematically by the Red Hot Chili Peppers on their hit "Dani California." Petty said of the similarities between the two songs: "I don't know if they stole it or not. It's their cross to bear, not mine. That one does sound particularly close in meter and chord and even subject matter. I think it's odd that Rick Rubin produced both records and never noticed it when my gardener did. I won't sue, but I wouldn't mind if they cut me in for a piece." Meanwhile, the Strokes – who opened up for Petty in 2006 – openly admitted to lifting portions of "American Girl" on their 2001 hit track, "Last Nite."

▶ CHAPTER 34
THE DOCUMENTARY

In 2006, four years after Tom Petty and the Heartbreakers were inducted into the Rock and Roll Hall of Fame, the group was the subject of an exhibit at the lakefront museum in Cleveland. Most of the artifacts came from a storage closet at Petty's home in Malibu. "We left his house pinching ourselves," recalled Rock Hall curator Howard Kramer.

Among the pieces of memorabilia featured in the exhibit was Petty's birth certificate, which read: "Born at Alachia Hospital in Gainesville. 18 3/4 inch long; light blond hair; blue eyes." Other items included one of the large, red velvet hats worn by Petty in the video for "Don't Come Around Here No More;" a promotional Mudcrutch flyer designed by Tom Leadon; several inexpensive, spiral notebooks full of Petty's handwritten lyrics; the first version of the cover for *Full Moon Fever*, which was originally titled *Songs From The Garage* and featured a nighttime shot of Petty's garage; and five guitars, including Petty's prized 1968 Gibson acoustic model, which he had used to compose nearly all of his songs. But the most shocking item on display was Petty's financial statement from Shelter Records for the six-month period, "1-1-1975 to 6-30-1975," which reported a debt of $102,123.38 to the label and a mere $8.70 in earnings.

Also revealed in 2006, famed film director Peter Bogdanovich had started shooting a behind-the-scenes documentary of Tom Petty and the Heartbreakers. Bogdanovich had just completed a documentary of actor John Ford when fate would intervene. Petty's producer George Drakoulias, who was good friends with the director, asked Bogdanovich if he was interested in filming a documentary about Tom Petty.

Bogdanovich later recalled: "I had a four-hour meeting with Tom in November '05. We met in Malibu at a restaurant near his house, and I asked him to tell me the story of the band, in a thumbnail version. Shortly thereafter I was asked how I would tell the story, and I decided to do it as a narrative, going straightforward. We considered calling it 'An American Odyssey,' but thought that was a bit pretentious. But it is an odyssey, a trip, a journey, and chronologically is the best way to do it.... I did all the interviews myself. It was important that the interviewee be talking to me." But Bogdanovich warned at the time: "I'm not an expert on Tom Petty, I'm just a fan. But what really appeals to me is that he's a real American artist – an impressionist."

Petty was glad to be working with a topnotch filmmaker: "I didn't want this to go down the 'Behind the Music' rock-doc kind of thing. So many rock documentaries are so predictable and not very interesting. And I think our story was a unique one and I knew he would make an honest film."

For the project, Bogdanovich conducted more than 100 hours of interviews and viewed 400 hours of archival footage. He recalled, "I decided early on that we would have no narrator, but that [Petty] would tell the story." Missing from the film were new interviews with Stan Lynch, who declined Bogdanovich's repeated requests. Lynch explained: "I didn't talk to the Bogdanovich people. I just couldn't. It's like a part of my life I've actually... I won't say forgotten, because I actually still dream about it. It comes up in weird ways. But I really had to let go of it or else I would walk around constantly trying to tell people who I used to be."

The completed documentary would log in at 238 minutes – nearly four-hours – in length. At the onset, Petty agreed he "would have no say on the final cut" and despite his many objections, he "lost every argument" with Bogdanovich in the cutting room. As Petty recalled, "He was adamant that I couldn't tell him what to do." The film included interviews with Stevie Nicks, Eddie Vedder, George Harrison, Jeff Lynne, Rick Rubin, Roger McGuinn, Johnny Depp, Jackson Browne, and many others. Surprisingly, the film also included amateur film footage of Petty as a young child.

Released in October 2007, *Runnin' Down A Dream* was praised by both fans and critics. A *New York Times* reviewer wrote: "The movie looks back in cultural history to a time before 'rock stars were invented on game shows,' as Mr. Petty wryly observes. It also serves as a vivid reminder that Mr. Petty remains one of the coolest guys out of the South since William Faulkner." The documentary was also screened at a number of theaters across the country.

*   *   *   *   *   *

In one of his many tirades against modern radio, Tom Petty once said: "It would be great if deejays were actually hired on a sense of musical taste and knowledge, as well as being able to perform or whatever it is they do. There was a time when the deejay was selecting records.... Radio at its best is an artform, and in America, it has really been treated badly."

Eventually, someone offered Petty a solution. Lee Abrams, the chief creative officer of SiriusXM satellite radio, gave Petty his own radio show. Abrams recalled. "Tom obviously wasn't thrilled with the state of terrestrial radio.... So, I thought maybe he should show us how he'd like to do radio."

In 2004, Petty launched a weekly, hour-long radio show called *Tom Petty's Buried Treasure*. Recorded in a studio at his home, the program gave Petty the opportunity to dig deep into his personal music collection, which was heavy on British Invasion groups, classic electric blues, classic soul, 1960s garage rock, and 1970s classic rock. A huge proponent of the satellite radio format, Petty said at the time, "It's exciting because it's a new frontier in a lot of ways. It reminds me a little bit of when MTV came along; they're eager for programming, and they're so open to ideas."

*   *   *   *   *   *

In 2008, Tom Petty and the Heartbreakers were the recipients of an unexpected honor. The group was offered the opportunity to perform during the halftime of Super Bowl XLII, which pitted the undefeated New England Patriots against the underdog New York Giants. However, according to some reports, the Heartbreakers were the backup choice after the Eagles had turned down the invitation from the NFL.

Not surprisingly, Petty did not immediately accept the offer. But while Petty pondered whether the performance would be akin to taking on a commercial sponsor, his bandmates were eager to appear at the annual gridiron spectacle. After a quick band meeting, Petty accepted the invitation. As with all previous halftime performers, Tom Petty and the Heartbreakers were not paid for their appearance.

But after Petty agreed to perform, there were a few detractors who questioned his selection. A columnist for *The Houston Chronicle* was not pleased, as he judged the Heartbreakers by their achievements on the top-40 charts: "The NFL obviously thinks Tom Petty and the Heartbreakers are in the same league as McCartney, the Stones and U2. I don't.... Tom Petty and the Heartbreakers have never had a No. 1 record. Only three of their songs ever made the top 10."

Arriving in Arizona, Tom Petty and the Heartbreakers were surprised by the amount of preparation that was required for their brief performance. Hundreds of technicians and stagehands were hired to make sure the group's mini-concert on the Super Bowl stage went off without a hitch. After the group decided what to play, some of the songs had to be shortened for the television broadcast. Even though they were seasoned professionals, the Heartbreakers spent a full month practicing their short set.

At a press conference one day before the Big Game, Tom Petty was asked about his longtime pledge to avoid corporate sponsorship. He responded, "Well, when you play on TV, you have a sponsor. That's just the way it works, so we're just going to try and entertain the people and be sweet boys."

The Heartbreakers were selected to perform at the Super Bowl, in part, due to the Janet Jackson/Justin Timberlake fiasco in 2004, with the NFL wanting to rule out any possibility of a halftime controversy. Referencing that event, Ryan Seacrest announced during the pre-game show, "And word is Tom Petty's wardrobe is functioning. Thank goodness."

On game day, Petty was interviewed on the set of *NFL Total Access*, as he sat between football analysts Rich Eisen and Peyton Manning. Smiling for the cameras, just a few hours before his big performance, Petty looked unusually relaxed. Meanwhile, a number of other musical acts performed during the pre-game festivities including Willie Nelson, Sarah Evans, and Alicia Keys.

The game began after *American Idol* winner Jordin Sparks sang the National Anthem. Then after the first half of the game had been played, Tom Petty and the Heartbreakers waited on the New England Patriots' side of the field for the temporary stage to be constructed. With rain in the forecast, the stadium's retractable roof had been ordered closed by the NFL. Showing no signs of pre-concert jitters, the Heartbreakers were eager to begin. As one reporter observed: "Once given the go signal, the musicians quickly took the stage, picked up their instruments and started performing. They made playing a concert for about 100 million people look almost effortless."

In the darkened stadium, the halftime show began with a large red heart projected onto the stage. Moments later, the booming sound of a beating human heart shook the stadium. Dressed in dark suits, Tom Petty and the Heartbreakers quickly took the stage, which was shaped like the group's guitar-and-heart logo. As bright lights flashed across the stadium floor, a group of 1,600 pre-selected fans stormed the field and headed toward the front of the stage. With Petty appearing uncharacteristically nervous for the first minute or so, the group opened with a rousing, upbeat version of "American Girl." The group then continued with a straight-ahead rendition of "I Won't Back Down." After thanking the crowd and saying "God bless you," a smiling Petty gazed at the audience and strummed the opening notes of "Free Fallin'." The song turned into a massive sing-along and garnered the most applause of the night. Petty closed his performance with "Runnin' Down A Dream." In all, three of the four songs were taken from Petty's solo album, *Full Moon Fever*.

One music critic said of the 12-minute halftime performance: "There was no high-tech tomfoolery, just a [cool] lighted stage that looked like a Flying V guitar piercing a big red heart.... And there were no eye-candy dancers, just some very road-worn musicians in matching black suit coats." But another rock critic made a damaging claim against Petty. Thor Christensen of *The Dallas Morning News* wrote: "Tom Petty bills himself as an old-fashioned rock 'n' roller who takes a stand.... But Sunday, he backed down in his Super Bowl halftime show. It seems the rocker was lip-syncing." Amazingly, Petty was accused of sounding *too* good during his performance.

Two years later, when the Who were selected to perform at the Super Bowl, guitarist Pete Townshend contacted Petty to ask for his advice. Ironically, neither Townshend nor his bandmate Roger Daltrey had ever attended an NFL game.

▶ CHAPTER 35
THE MUDCRUTCH REUNION

Sometimes you can go home again, sometimes you can right a past wrong, and sometimes you can reunite with your true love. And if you happen to be a successful rocker named Tom Petty, sometimes you can reform a rock and roll band from your youth.

In early 2007, Petty fulfilled a goal that had been nagging at him for several years when he reformed his pre-Heartbreakers band, Mudcrutch. It was the Peter Bogdanovich documentary that gave Petty the impetus to reunite with his former bandmates from Gainesville. Petty explained: "The feeling got stronger as Peter and I were in the cutting room. At one point we had an hour-long thing just on Mudcrutch. I felt like there was some music there that got left behind." As Petty recounted, "I just had this random thought: 'I really liked that band, I wonder what it would be like to get them together.'" But Mike Campbell was not enthusiastic at first: "When Tom called me and said he wanted to do this, my first reaction was, why?"

Tom Leadon, Mudcrutch's rhythm guitarist, recalled how the band was resurrected: "I was driving home from getting groceries at Kroger's, and my cellphone rang. He said, 'Hey, it's your old pal Tom Petty.' My first thought was that it was one of my friends pulling my leg. I wasn't going to fall for that." But when Petty suggested putting the old band back together, Leadon was stunned: "I felt like a bolt of lightning went through my body." At the time, Leadon was working as a music teacher at the Jan Williams School near Nashville, having forgone his academic training as an electrical engineer.

Meanwhile, drummer Randall Marsh had returned to Florida after spending decades in California and expected the Mudcrutch reunion to be some sort of low-key affair. He recalled, "I was dumbfounded. I just presumed they'd been working on a movie and maybe had a few beers and Peter misconstrued some nostalgic idea." Recalling his time at the Mudcrutch Farm, Marsh explained: "When I think of the farm, I think of the front room and I think of us assembling in there, sitting in chairs and rehearsing. That's the first thing I think of because we did it so much."

Arriving in Los Angeles, Leadon and Marsh moved into Petty's home for a month. The reformed Mudcrutch consisted of Tom Petty, Mike Campbell, Benmont Tench, Tom Leadon, and Randall Marsh. Surprisingly, three former members of Mudcrutch were not asked to join the reconstituted group – Charlie Souza, Jim Lenahan, and Danny Roberts.

Petty reverted to his previous role as the band's bass player. As such, he enjoyed not having to be the focus of the group. Petty explained, "Mudcrutch is basically a West Coast rock band, the way it sounds. And for me, playing bass instead of guitar puts a different spin on things. It's an entirely new rhythm section from the Heartbreakers."

The Mudcrutch album was recorded in August 2007 at the Heartbreakers' rehearsal and storage space in the Van Nuys section of Los Angeles. Nicknamed "the Clubhouse," the former warehouse contained much of the group's musical gear. A visiting reporter from London was astounded by the room's precious contents: "Around us, there are racks (and racks and racks and racks) of guitars, including at least 10, three-quarter-size Rickenbackers ('Like John Lennon used to play'), a black Gibson 330 that is the only one of its kind in the world, five or six super-exotic Vox Teardrops, a hundred others just as noteworthy. There are cloth-covered amplifiers of the type seen standing behind the Beatles at their experimental stadium shows of the mid-1960s, and there's a grand piano covered in a commemorative Elvis rug. The walls are covered in vintage concert posters, and ancient record sleeves." In addition, the room featured a large artwork of a smiling Marilyn Monroe and – in a prominent spot – a pair of ukuleles given to Petty by George Harrison. Petty admitted, "Music runs my life. I'm embarrassed that I don't have any hobbies. I don't collect anything. Well, I collect guitars and records."

Before the start of the recording sessions, Petty reminded his Mudcrutch bandmates that they were *not* working on a "Tom Petty album." Petty recalled: "Everyone got involved, threw in something, and afterward I thought, 'Why in hell would I ever record any other way?'"

Mike Campbell recalled one memorable session: "Tom [Petty] brought in this song he'd just written. We started playing it, and when we got to the chorus, Leadon stepped up to the mike and sang the harmony. I don't know how he even knew the words yet." Recorded in a mere ten days, the album was produced by Petty, Campbell, and Ryan Ulyate, who had first worked with Petty on *Highway Companion.*

Mudcrutch's self-titled, 14-track album was released in April 2008. A small sticker on the cover proclaimed, "The Debut Album." The front cover featured a colorful but faceless human head that resembled a Civil War-era portrait. The project included two remakes: the Byrds' psychedelic-tinged "Lover Of The Bayou" and the Flying Burrito Brothers' country-rock arrangement of the truck-driving classic, "Six Days On The Road." Another track, "Queen Of The Go-Go Girls" chronicled the band's days at their old stomping ground, Dub's; the song had been written years earlier by Tom Leadon.

Although "Scare Easy" was issued as the debut single, the most memorable song on the album was "Crystal River." The track was named for a breathtaking nature preserve located about an hour south of Gainesville. At nine-and-a-half minutes long and full of extended guitar solos, "Crystal River" was not the type of song found on a Heartbreakers album. Mike Campbell said of the track, "Every time we tried to cut something out of it, it didn't feel right.... That stretched on partly because that was the first time we played together... and we were learning to interact with each other again. That take is literally the first time we ever played that song, on the first day. We were still getting used to the room, the sounds, getting comfortable with one another."

A full 33-years after the group had abruptly disbanded in the wake of a heated argument inside a Los Angeles recording studio, Mudcrutch began a short tour, playing 11 shows across California. Surprisingly, the group did not book a single date in Gainesville or anywhere in Florida.

Randall Marsh recalled the backstage tension before the first reunion show: "I kept telling myself, 'Take away the fame and celebrity, it's just another gig, just another band.' But before we went on, I was about to wet my pants." Similarly, Petty was unsure how audiences would react to an entire concert without hearing Heartbreakers standards like "American Girl" or "Refugee." However, at the group's first performance, "the material was so immediately accessible that nobody in the audience seemed to mind. Well, almost nobody; there was one woman who timidly blurted out a request for 'Breakdown' a couple of times, backing down after noticing the disapproving murmuring around her."

At the Fillmore Auditorium in San Francisco, an excited Petty told the crowd: "Having the band back together is beyond our wildest dreams. We've made a new album and we're going to play every track on the album." Performing on a stage adorned with layered Persian rugs and little else, Petty looked completely at ease.

Meanwhile, Mike Campbell regarded the tour as a pleasant respite: "One of the problems with the Heartbreakers is too many hits. It's a real struggle to inject new music into those shows. There's very little room for spontaneity and discovery. This band is all about that. As a musician, that's just a gift." Shortly after the completion of the tour, Petty released the four-track Mudcrutch concert album, *Extended Play Live*. Satisfied with the success of their reunion album and subsequent tour, the members of Mudcrutch were hoping to embark on a second tour later in the year.

After taking a week off to rest, Petty, Campbell, and Tench returned to their day gigs and began rehearsing for an upcoming Heartbreakers tour. During the three-month summer tour – which featured Steve Winwood as the opening act – Petty frequently performed an obscure track, the bluesy "Sweet William," which was the B-side of the group's 1999 single, "Room At The Top." At a number of shows, Tom Leadon was a guest musician on a pair of Mudcrutch songs.

*   *   *   *   *   *

In 2009, Tom Petty and the Heartbreakers decided to chronicle their many years on the road. The four-CD boxed set, *The Live Anthology*, was a collection of 48 concert tracks from three decades of work, spanning 1978 to 2007. (A deluxe edition included a fifth bonus disc.) Wisely, the Heartbreakers had recorded many of their performances over the years.

After producer Ryan Ulyate organized a library of 3,509 songs from 169 of the group's concerts, he sat down and listened to every track. After giving each of the tracks a numerical rating, Ulyate spent months reviewing the songs with Petty and Campbell. Ulyate recalled, "If it didn't grab us in the first minute, then it didn't make the short list."

The tracks were issued as they were originally performed without any overdubs or fixes. Satisfied with his long body of work, Petty declared at the time: "I never thought I'd make any money. I actually had the opposite viewpoint – I was willing to sacrifice the paycheck and the nice car for the pleasure of doing this."

▶ CHAPTER 36
GOT MY MOJO WORKING

A "mojo" is commonly defined as a magical charm used in voodoo ceremonies. The word is also prevalent in the lyrics of songs by bluesmen such as Muddy Waters and Blind Lemon Jefferson. In an Austin Powers film, actor Mike Myers' character went back in time to battle Dr. Evil over a stolen "mojo," which was the source of Powers' manly appeal. But Tom Petty had his own definition of the term: "Mojo is power. You've got your mojo working. Things are happening for you."

As the first Heartbreakers album in eight years, *Mojo* signaled a significant stylistic detour for the group. Petty was inspired to return to his love of the blues, in part, after appearing onstage with singer-songwriter J.J. Cale. Petty recalled at the time, "Every rehearsal for years started with blues. It's how we sound after hours. I thought, 'we should stay where we naturally play.'" Mike Campbell – who was greatly influenced in his early years by Chicago-born blues guitarist Michael Bloomfield – explained, "Growing up in Florida, we listened to a lot of blues, Muddy Waters, Howlin' Wolf, Jimmy Reed, Lightnin' Hopkins. And that's still the stuff we listen to when we're on break. And then there's the influence of the British [blues]. So this is just a hybrid of all the things we've been influenced by."

But Petty was not entirely confident about his vocal abilities: "I used to be a little insecure about whether I could sing the blues authentically. I can do my version of it, and this has our stamp on it. It would be an empty exercise if we weren't bringing something to the party." In setting his goals for the album, Petty explained: "I had this picture in my mind of making a record that had something in common spiritually with the Chess blues records, even the English blues bands of the late-'60s: [John] Mayall, Peter Green. That's the stuff that really just kills me.... I don't think we could have made this record in the '80s. I don't think our heads were in that spot."

Just like the sessions for the Mudcrutch reunion album, *Mojo* was recorded in an informal environment at the group's Clubhouse in Van Nuys. The project was essentially a live album, with the members of the group sitting side-by-side as they performed. Campbell explained, "We didn't want to do overdubs. So it was all live off the floor [including] all the solos and most of the vocals. We played without headphones, except for Tom, he had a little earplug so he could hear his vocal. But we were all in the same room, and we just played together." The project was co-produced by Petty, Campbell, and Ryan Ulyate.

On the album, Mike Campbell played a very rare and expensive guitar – a 1959 Les Paul Standard Sunburst. Campbell admitted at the time: "I've always wanted one, but it's taken me so long because only 600 were originally made – and around 100 of those have been destroyed or lost. There's something magical about that sound; it's what Eric Clapton, Jimmy Page and Peter Green used in the early days. A friend of mine who sells vintage guitars called me and told me he wanted to buy a house and was willing to part with his Les Paul. I paid half now and will pay the rest after the tour."

But Petty was also captivated by the instrument. Campbell recalled, "I remember [Tom] sitting down, and he had a twinkle in his eye. He said, 'Let's make that guitar the sound of this album.'" With Campbell finally given the opportunity to demonstrate his prowess on the electric guitar, one reviewer suggested, "For this album, the band should have renamed themselves Mike Campbell & The Heartbreakers." Later, Campbell decided against taking the instrument – which was valued at more than $250,000 – on the road.

A surprise hit, *Mojo* debuted at number-two on *Billboard* magazine's album chart in June 2010. The project's highlights included "I Should Have Known It," "Jefferson Jericho Blues," and "Good Enough." But the album's most talked-about selection was "Running Man's Bible." Petty said of the song, "I'd always wanted to deal with Howie's death, and there's some of that in there. It's one of those embarrassingly revealing songs. It just crept into my mind one day. I was playing the guitar, and it started falling out, and I wrote it down as quick as I could." Another track, "U.S. 41" sounded like an undiscovered Canned Heat song and mentioned Tom Petty's mysterious grandfather, William "Pulpwood" Petty.

Despite *Mojo's* strong early sales, the album represented a major departure from the group's traditional sound. When asked at the time to predict how concert audiences would react to the group's new material, Petty responded, "I have a feeling that they'll stay in their seats and enjoy it, but I don't give a damn if everyone goes to the bathroom.... I'm not going to be just a song-and-dance man. I'm gonna play what I want to play. I know I should always give people a good dose of what they came to hear, because I'm not playing at the corner bar.... But we also refuse to become one of those groups that only live in the past." The 40-date *Mojo* tour hit the road in May 2010 and featured a number of notable opening acts, including ZZ Top, Joe Cocker, and Crosby, Stills & Nash.

Meanwhile, in 2011, radio giant Cumulus Media unceremoniously fired veteran deejay Jim Ladd, who had inspired Petty's controversial hit, "The Last DJ." Ladd, who had been behind the microphone at KLOS in Los Angeles for the previous 14 years, told *Rolling Stone* magazine, "It's really bad news. It was people in my profession that first played Tom Petty, first played the Doors. But the people programming stations [now] are not music people – they're business people." That same week, Clear Channel Communications also laid off hundreds of staffers.

Also in 2011, Tom Petty and the Heartbreakers started working on their followup album, *Hypnotic Eye*. Co-produced by Petty and Ryan Ulyate, the album would take three years to record. The project marked Petty's return to his classic rock and roll sound.

*   *   *   *   *   *

During this period, Tom Petty became more concerned about his overall health – which meant trying yet again to quit smoking. But after years of touring, Petty was coping with the physical ravages of the rock and roll road. Like many veteran musicians, Petty had lost a significant amount of his hearing and was also afflicted with a constant buzzing in his ears. Additionally, his right knee had been surgically repaired and his left foot was riddled with arthritis. As Petty admitted, "I have to survive on medication the rest of my life in order to walk. That's something I can deal with, I suppose.... I feel sometimes like an ex-football player." And decades after smashing his left hand against a wall, Petty continued to experience pain from the injury.

With Petty deciding to cut down on touring, he became more selective about which cities to visit. Just days before the start of a world tour in 2012, Tom Petty and the Heartbreakers suffered a minor calamity. While rehearsing at Culver Studios in Los Angeles, five of the band's guitars were stolen, including Petty's prized, 1967 12-string blonde Rickenbacker. Although Petty had offered a "no questioned asked" reward, police quickly solved the case and the instruments were returned.

Meanwhile, two decades had passed since Tom Petty and the Heartbreakers last performed in Britain (not counting the group's brief appearance at the Concert for George tribute in 2002). The group belatedly returned in June 2012 for a performance at the Isle of Wight Festival. As a warm-up for their headlining slot on the first night of the three-day event, the Heartbreakers scheduled two concerts at the legendary Royal Albert Hall in London.

Petty was concerned that a British festival-style audience might not be receptive to his meat-and-potatoes, Heartland brand of rock and roll. But most of the 55,000 spectators – who were mired in a muddy, rain-swamped field – had waited years for the Heartbreakers to make a return trek to the U.K. Starting their set with "Listen To Her Heart" and continuing with a strong catalog of proven rock standards, the Heartbreakers were greeted by an appreciative audience.

The following year, Tom Petty and The Heartbreakers made a second appearance at the Bonnaroo Festival. The group co-headlined the annual event along with Paul McCartney and Mumford & Sons.

▶ CLOSING TIME

In 1983, 32-year-old Tom Petty stated, "If I ever get tired of playing live that'll probably be the end of my career in music." Then three decades later at age 62, Petty looked back on his long career and mused: "A reliable car, a place to live and a job playing music, that was my goal, it was my entire dream. The rest of it just came in increments. Things started to move really fast and didn't seem to stop for the longest time. Suddenly, you look around, and all this great stuff has happened. I was just trying to get to the next gig, or the next record. It's kind of still the same." Echoing the sentiment, Los Angeles deejay Jim Ladd observed that Petty and his bandmates "started in a garage in Gainesville, Florida, and stuck it out through all the hard times, and they never lost sight of their goal, which was, I think for them, not to be celebrities but to be great musicians."

Over an extended career filled with twists and turns, Petty has maintained a high level of integrity as a musician, bandleader, and businessman. In retrospect, Petty admitted: "All I've ever done is written songs and made records and done concerts. I don't think I've ever sold my soul or anything. I think I avoided cashing in more than most of my peers." But over the years, Petty had managed to achieve something quite rare in rock and roll, as he sustained a creative streak that kept his music vibrant and relevant, despite changes in popular tastes.

As he matured and outlasted nearly all of his musical contemporaries, Petty revealed, "My kids say that I am really cool as an old man. Aging has been good for me because it's made me wiser, and I'm more fun in general. I used to be so revved up all the time, and I'm not as bad as I used to be. I used to get so angry. I still have my moments, though, where I can get like that, especially with business. I can get really pissed off with that. Every day there are more fires to be put out, more things that have to be dealt with, and I really don't want to spend my time doing that. With everything else I think I am more at peace. At least I hope I am. I really don't want any more drama."

But as Petty became an elder statesman of American rock and roll, he began to contemplate his own mortality: "I've got so much music inside that I want to get out. I'm just trying to find the vehicles and the time to get that music out and to keep making more."

▶ SELECTED BIBLIOGRAPHY

Aledort, Andy. (1995, August). Chartbreaker. *Guitar School.*

Allman, Gregg; & Light, Alan. (2012). *My Cross to Bear.* New York: William Morrow.

Balfour, Victoria. (1986). *Rock Wives.* New York: Beech Tree Books.

Bartosek, John. (1973, June 24). Music is life for Gainesville's 'Mudcrutch.' *The Gainesville Sun.*

Bell, Max. (1980, March 15). Call Tom Petty the new Springsteen and he'll cut you! *New Musical Express.*

Berkery, Patrick. (2008, May). Stan Lynch. *Modern Drummer.*

Benarde, Scott R. (2003). *Stars of David.* Hanover, NH: Brandeis University Press.

Bianchi, Mike. (2008 February 5). Perseverance pays off for Tom and Tom. *The Orlando Sentinel.*

Blake, Mark. (2012, July). He knew he was right. *Q.*

Block, Melissa. (2013, March 8). Dave Grohl finds music's human element – in a machine. *All Things Considered.* Philadelphia: NPR.

Bogdanovich, Peter [Director]. (2007). *Runnin' Down a Dream.* Warner Brothers.

Bogdanovich, Peter. (2007, October 12). *Runnin' Down a Dream.* Press conference presented by the New York Film Festival, New York.

Brown, Mick. (2007, September 8). Stevie Nicks: A survivor's story. *The (London) Telegraph.*

Carr, Daphne. (2008, January 16). Tom Petty's Los Angeles. *L.A. Weekly.*

Cash, Johnny. (1997). *Cash: The Autobiography.* San Francisco: HarperSanFrancisco.

Cash, Rosanne. (2010). *Composed: A Memoir.* New York: Viking.

Chancellor, Jennifer. (2010, September 19). Before the Heartbreakers, Tom Petty had Tulsa ties. *Tulsa World.*

Christian, Pam. (1978, October). Derringer pops off. *Reader's Magazine.*

Clapton, Eric. (2007). *Clapton: The Autobiography.* New York: Broadway Books.

Collins, Dianne. (1987, May-June). Petty little thing called love. *Rock Express.*

Corcoran, Michael. (1989, August). Raised on promises. *Spin.*

Crowe, Cameron. (1978, October 19). Tom Petty's gonna get it – his way. *Rolling Stone.*

Dean, Bill. (2007, August 19). Forever fascinated: Tom Petty's love for rock 'n' roll began the day he met Elvis in Ocala. *The Ocala Star-Banner.*

Dean, Bill. (2008, April 29). Mudcrutch reunites for album. *The Gainesville Sun.*

DeCurtis, Anthony. (1986, March 27). Dylan down under. *Rolling Stone.*

DeCurtis, Anthony. (1987, May 7). Tom Petty's new LP: Back to basics. *Rolling Stone.*

Demorest, Stephen. (1978, August). Tom Petty: Animus americus unpoliticus. *Creem.*

Derogatis, Jim. (2003, April 13). Damn the torpedoes. *The Chicago Sun Times.*

DeWitt, Howard A. (2001). *Stranger in Town: The Musical life of Del Shannon.* Dubuque, IA: Kendall/Hunt Publishing.

DeYoung, Bill. (1984, July 20). Stan Lynch, the homebody Heartbreaker. *The Gainesville Sun.*

DeYoung, Bill. (1985, May 6). Breaking form: Tom Petty's change of heart. *Music.*

DeYoung, Bill. (1995, November 21). The beat of a different drum: Stan Lynch finds life's just fine after Tom Petty and The Heartbreakers. *The Gainesville Sun.*

DeYoung, Bill. (1987, July 24). TP, Heartbreakers bring it on home with Florida tour. *The Gainesville Sun.*

DeYoung, Bill. (1990, January 31). Tom Petty grew up runnin' for a dream. *The Gainesville Sun.*

DeYoung, Bill. (1990, July 13). Tom Petty: Full steam ahead. *Goldmine.*

DeYoung, Bill. (1992, August 2). The evolution of a rock star. *The Gainesville Sun.*

DeYoung, Bill. (1995, November 21). The beat of a different drum: Stan Lynch finds life's just fine after Tom Petty and the Heartbreakers. *The Gainesville Sun.*

di Perna, Alan. (1999, April). Tom Petty: American boy. *Pulse.*

Dye, Robert; & Trost, Isaiah. (2003, March 10). Rock and roll animals. *Guitar World Acoustic.*
Dylan, Bob, (2004). *Chronicles: Volume One.* New York: Simon & Schuster.
Erickson, Steve. (2008, June). Time stops for no one. *Relix.*
Farber, Jim. (1999, April 18). Tom Petty gets personal. *The New York Daily News.*
Felder, Don; & Holden, Wendy. (2008). *Heaven and Hell: My Life in the Eagles.* Hoboken, NJ: John Wiley & Sons.
Flanagan, Bill. (1986). *Written in My Soul.* Chicago: Contemporary Books.
Flanagan, Bill. (1986, April). Tom Petty pulls together: The Southern soul of a Hollywood rocker. *Musician.*
Flanagan, Bill. (1990, April). The Heartbreakers highway. *Musician.*
Flanagan, Bill. (1994, December). Frontman: Tom Petty. *Musician.*
Flans, Robyn. (1984, February). Stan Lynch: Heartbreaking rhythm. *Modern Drummer.*
Fong-Torres, Ben. (2010, April 25). Go after what you love. *Parade.*
Freff. (1985, June). Tom Petty & Dave Stewart?! *Musician.*
Fricke, David. (2009, December 10). It's good to be king. *Rolling Stone.*
Galante Block, Debbie; & Rosen, Craig. (2006, March 25). Getting at the essence of the Heartbreakers. *Billboard.*
Garbarini, Vic. (1987, November). The essential Jimmy Iovine. *Musician.*
Gardner, Thom. (1977, November/December). Tom Petty. *Back Door Man.*
Geldof, Bob. (1988). *Is That it?* New York: Ballantine.
George-Warren, Holly. (2000, September). Tom Petty. *Oxford American.*
George-Warren, Holly (Ed.). (2005). *Farm Aid: A Song for America.* New York: Rodale.
Gilmore, Mikal. (1977, June 30). Tom Petty's rock fervor. *Rolling Stone.*
Gilmore, Mikal. (1980, February 21). Tom Petty's real-life nightmares. *Rolling Stone.*
Goldberg, Danny. (2008). *Bumping into Geniuses.* New York: Gotham Books.
Goldberg, Michael. (1986, January 16). Back on the road. *Rolling Stone.*
Gotz, David M. (1980, February). Interview: Petty gets his torpedoes together and damns ahead to the airwaves. *Record Review.*
Graustark, Barbary; & Coppola, Vincent. (1980, January 7). Rock's new heartbreak kid. *Newsweek.*
Gross, Terry. (2008, February 1). Tom Petty knows 'how it feels.' *Fresh Air.* Philadelphia: NPR.
Guerra, Tom. (2008, March). Mike Campbell. *ToneQuest Report.*
Gundersen, Edna. (1990, February 9). Petty at his peak. *USA Today.*
Gundersen, Edna. Gundersen, Edna. (2006, July 25). Tom Petty: Into the great wide open. *USA Today.*
Harris, Carol Ann. (2007). *Storms: My Life With Lindsey Buckingham and Fleetwood Mac.* Chicago: Chicago Review Press.
Hiatt, Brian. (2005, August 11). Petty rules road. *Rolling Stone.*
Hiatt, Brian. (2011, September 15). The private life of George Harrison. *Rolling Stone.*
Hilburn, Robert. (1987, May 24). A Petty mood: A classic rocker's passion is refreshed. *The Los Angeles Times.*
Hilburn, Robert. (2002, March 15). No backing down. *The Los Angeles Times.*
Hogan, Richard. (1981, August 31). Tom Petty makes 'Hard Promises' to rock & roll. *Circus.*
Hurwitz, Matt. (2007, June 11). Wilburys set to travel again. *USA Today.*
Jackson, Blair. (1978, April 7). Tom Petty and the Heartbreakers – it's only rock 'n' roll (and that's the point). *BAM.*
Jackson, Blair. (1979, December). Tom Petty's rock victory. *BAM.*
Jackson, Blair. (1981, August). Just a popular rock 'n' roll band. *Trouser Press.*
Jackson, Blair. (1983, January 28). There's a lot more to the Heartbreakers than Tom Petty. *BAM.*
Kelp, Larry. (1980). Don't call him blondie. *Relix.*
Kot, Greg. (1999, April 29). Tom Petty and the Heartbreakers: Echo. *Rolling Stone.*
Kot, Greg. (2002, November 17). Tom Petty disillusioned but still loves the music. *The Chicago Tribune.*
Kot, Greg. (2010, June 1). Tom Petty, the interview: 'I wanted to rough it up.' *The Chicago Tribune.*
Kubernik, Harvey. (1980, March 8). The trials of Tom Petty: Petty gets it. *Melody Maker.*

Lanham, Tom. (1994, December). Petty on the inside. *Pulse.*
Liben, Michael P. (1979, February). Tom Petty – Heartbreaker at home & a broad. *New Wave Rock.*
Light, Alan. (2006, August 10). Steady Petty. *Rolling Stone.*
Linder, Greg. (1978, October 20). Tom Petty: A mystery man unveiled. *Reader's Magazine.*
Lloyd, Robert. (1991, October). Flying lessons: Tom Petty takes his bearings. *L.A. Style.*
Luckman, Michael. (2005). *Alien Rock: The Rock 'n' Roll Extraterrestrial Connection.* New York: Pocket Books.
Marks, Craig; & Tannenbaum, Rob. (2011). *I Want My MTV.* New York: Dutton.
Marsh, Dave. (1980, June-July). The critics vs. Tom Petty. *Musician.*
Marsh, Dave. (1981, July). Tom Petty. *Musician.*
Matthews, Tom. (2010, November 22). Heart Breaker. *Milwaukee Magazine.*
McShane, Rod. (1977, August). Tom Petty. *Dark Star.*
Mettler, Mike. (2010, June-July-August). Mojo workin'. *Sound + Vision.*
Miller, William F. (1995, May). Steve Ferrone: Subtlety mastered. *Modern Drummer.*
Miller, Eric T. (2003, January/February). If I had my way, I'd tear the building down. *Magnet.*
"More than a pretty face." (1977). *Melody Maker.*
Morse, Steve. (1980, March). Blonde on blonde. Trouser Press.
Moseley, Willie G. (2002, October). Chris Hillman: Bluegrass, bass, and back again. *Vintage Guitar.*
Neal, Chris. (2007, September/October). Keyboardist Benmont Tench of Tom Petty and the Heartbreakers. *Performing Songwriter.*
Newman, Melinda. (2005, December 3). Tom Petty: A portrait of the artist. *Billboard.*
Nicks, Stevie; & Stewart, Dave [Directors]. (2013). *Stevie Nicks: In Your Dreams.* Virgil Films and Entertainment.
Obrecht, Jas. (1986, August). Tom Petty: The dying art of rhythm guitar. *Guitar Player.*
O'Dell, Chris; & Ketcham, Katherine. (2009). *Miss O'Dell.* New York: Touchstone.
Palmer, Robert. (1985, March 25). A new album by Petty and the Heartbreakers. *The New York Times.*
Pang, Kevin. (2009, September 8). Mike Judge looks back over 13 years of 'King of the Hill.' *The Chicago Tribune.*
Passy, Charles. (2002, March 19). Petty never forgot family, neighbors in Gainesville. *The Palm Beach Post.*
Peeples, Stephen. (1977, October 9). Tom Petty and the Heartbreakers: Hogtown boys make good. *Rock Around The World.*
Petty, Tom. (2002, January 17). Remembering George. *Rolling Stone.*
Philips, Chuck. (1992, April 5). Petty's secret Warners deal isn't for petty cash. *The Los Angeles Times.*
Pond, Steve. (1981, July 23). Tom Petty: A rock & roll hero keeps fighting on. *Rolling Stone.*
Pryor, Sam. (2010, August). Steve Ferrone: Tapping into 40 years of groove. *Drum! Magazine.*
Ransom, Kevin. (1995, March). Profile: Mike Campbell. *Guitar Player.*
Rensin, David. (1982, September). 20 questions: Tom Petty. *Playboy.*
Ressner, Jeffrey. (1991. October). Tom Petty: Traveling Heartbreaker. *CD Review.*
Robertson, Sandy. (1985, April 20). Petty prime. *Sounds.*
Rogers, Ray. (1988, July). A storm called Stevie. *Interview.*
Rose, Joseph. (1978, February). Tom Petty and the Elvis Presley connection. *Hit Parader.*
Rosen, Craig. (2006, March 25). Tom Petty & The Heartbreakers. *Billboard.*
Rosen, Steven. (1985, Summer). Tom Petty and the Heartbreakers: Even the winners get lucky sometime. *International Musicians and Recording World.*
Rowland, Mark. (1987, September). Heartbreaker straight ahead. *Musician.*
Rowland, Mark. (1990, March). The quiet Wilbury. *Musician.*
Rowland, Mark. (1997, January). Beck meets Petty: Rockin', writin', survivin' in L.A. *Musician.*
Scaggs, Austin. (2006, May 18). Petty on the edge. *Rolling Stone.*
Schaults, Janine. (2010, June 2). The making of *Mojo. The Chicago Tribune.*
Schenkman, Richard (Director and Producer). (1986). *Southern Accents.* MTV.
Schlenker, Dave. (2005, December). Grapevine: Tom Petty takes it home. *Gainesville Magazine.*

Schruers, Fred. (1995, May 4). Tom Petty on the road: This is how it feels. *Rolling Stone.*
Schruers, Fred. (1999, July 7). Tom Petty: The *Rolling Stone* interview. *Rolling Stone.*
Scoppa, Bud. (1985, August). Tom Petty's year (or two) of living dangerously. *Record.*
Scoppa, Bud. (1987, June 1). Winging it with Petty & Campbell. *Music Connection.*
Scoppa, Bud. (1987, August). Tom Petty & The Heartbreakers: Less is more, more or less. *Creem.*
Scopa, Bud. (2007, September). The inside story of the Traveling Wilburys: Rock's greatest ever supergroup. *Uncut.*
Secor, Ketch. (2010, Fall). Runnin' down a dream. *The Exeter Bulletin.*
Shapiro, Susin. (1977, April 9). The heartbreak kid. *Sounds.*
Sharp, Ken. (2012, December). Mojo man. *Bass Player.*
Shelton, Robert. (2011). *No Direction Home: The Life and Music of Bob Dylan.* Milwaukee: Hal Leonard Corporation.
Simmons, Sylvie. (1989, June 14). Moonlighting. *Raw.*
Simmons, Sylvie. (2006, October). Rock of ages. *Mojo.*
Simmons, Sylvie. (2009, September). The real slowhand. *Mojo.*
Simmons, Silvie. (2010, July 10). Revolution! *Mojo.*
Simon, Scott. (2007, November 17). 'Running Down' a New Petty Documentary. *Weekend Edition.* New York: NPR.
Smith, Joe. (1988). *Off the Record: An Oral History of Popular Music.* New York: Warner Books.
Snow, Mat. (2010, January). The bard of blue collar rock has led the Heartbreakers to glory on through tragedy. *Mojo.*
Synder, John. (1976, December 10). Tommy Petty leaves home again: A rock roller out of time. *The Gainesville Sun.*
Sounes, Howard. (2001). *Down the Highway: The Life of Bob Dylan.* New York: Grove Press.
Steigner, Nancy. (1986, July 16). *Judge Benjamin Tench.* University of Florida Oral History Program.
Stewart, Dave. (2008). *The Dave Stewart Songbook: The Stories Behind the Songs, Volume One.* Encinitas, CA: Surfdog.
Stock, Tom. (1978, August). Tom Petty's Back. *Beat Instrumental.*
Strauss, Neil. (2006, July 13). Tom Petty's last dance. *Rolling Stone.*
Sweeting, Adam. (1981, June 13). Tuning up the criminal kind. *Melody Maker.*
Sweeting, Adam. (2004, May). Southern Accents. *Uncut.*
Terrell, Steve. (2004, March 12). Overdose suspected in death of local musician. *The Santa Fe New Mexican.*
Thompson, Art. (1999, May). Heartbreaker hideout in the studio with Tom Petty & Mike Campbell. *Guitar Player.*
Thompson, Art. (2006, July). 30 years & counting. *Guitar Player.*
"Tom Petty." (2007, January). *Classic Rock.*
Tom Petty and the Heartbreakers. (1999). *Behind the Music.* New York: VH1.
Tragash, Jennifer. (2007, October 10). Petty's long-term impact. *The Gainesville Sun.*
Trynka, Paul. (2007). *Iggy Pop: Open Up and Bleed.* New York: Broadway Books.
Udovitch, Mim; & Wild, David. (2002, January 17). Remembering George. *Rolling Stone.*
Uhelszki, Jaan. (1999, June). Echo chamber. *Guitar Magazine.*
Uhelszki, Jaan. (2006, July/August). Tom Petty: Anatomy of a rockstar. *Harp.*
Uhelszki, Jaan. (2012, June). Tom Petty: Won't back down. *Uncut.*
Wallace, Alice. (2006, September 20). Memories of Petty: How singer found way in area. *The Gainesville Sun.*
Whitburn, Joel. (2008). *Rock Tracks 1981-2008.* Menomonee Falls, WI: Record Research.
Whitburn, Joel. (2009). *Top Pop Singles 1955-2008.* Menomonee Falls, WI: Record Research.
Wild, David. (1991, August 8). Over the hump. *Rolling Stone.*
Willman, Chris. (2010, September-October). The great wide open. *M Music & Musicians.*
Wixen, Randall D. (2009). *The Plain and Simple Guide to Music Publishing (2nd ed.).* Milwaukee: Hal Leonard.
Zimmer, Dave. (1989, May 5). Once in a full moon. *BAM.*

▶ NOTES

INTRODUCTION
1. "one of rock music's most..." ~ Sauro, Tony. (2008, May 1). Tom Petty revisits Mudcrutch. *The Stockton Record.*
2. "a surlier version of the..." ~ Boucher, Geoff. (2006, December 31). Happily not retired. *The Los Angeles Times.*
3. "I found him so in..." ~ Bogdanovich, Peter. (2007, October 12). *Runnin' Down a Dream.* Press conference presented by the New York Film Festival, New York.
4. "He admits he's neither the..." ~ Soren, Tabitha. (1995, October 5). Veteran rocker into the great wide open: Tom Petty to play homecoming show. *The Tuscaloosa News.*
5. "It's easy to take Tom..." ~ Gardner, Elysa. (1994, November 3). Recordings: American boys. *Rolling Stone.*
6. "people told Tommy he'd never..." ~ Bianchi, Mike. (2008 February 5). Perseverance pays off for Tom and Tom. *The Orlando Sentinel.*
7. "I didn't get into this..." ~ Schruers, Fred. (1995, May 4). Tom Petty on the road: This is how it feels. *Rolling Stone.*
8. "I developed a problem with..." ~ Fong-Torres, Ben. (2010, April 25). Go after what you love. *Parade.*
9. "Tom's the kind of proud..." ~ Wild, David. (1991, August 8). Over the hump. *Rolling Stone.*
10. "When I was coming up..." ~ Thompson, Art. (1999, May). Heartbreaker hideout in the studio with Tom Petty & Mike Campbell. *Guitar Player.*
11. "People talk about how he..." ~ Wild, David. (1991, August 8). Over the hump. *Rolling Stone.*

CHAPTER 1: RAISED IN GAINESVILLE
1. Raised in an unremarkable working-class..." ~ Rizzo, Frank. (1984, November 16). Rockers recall their first musical memories. *The Winnipeg Free Press.*
2. "My dad's mother was..." ~ Schruers, Fred. (1995, May 4). Tom Petty on the road: This is how it feels. *Rolling Stone.*
3. "They were attacked on a..." ~ George-Warren, Holly. (2000, September). Tom Petty. *Oxford American.*
4. "How they hooked up I..." ~ Schruers, Fred. (1995, May 4). Tom Petty on the road: This is how it feels. *Rolling Stone.*
5. "It was a cinder-block..." ~ "Tom Petty's *Pet Sounds.*" (1994, November 6). *Newsweek.*
6. "I never felt safe as..." ~ Uhelszki, Jaan. (2006, July/August). Tom Petty: Anatomy of a rockstar. *Harp.*
7. "were called seceders, runaways, renegades" ~ DeYoung, Bill. (1992, August 16). Greetings from Gainesville, Florida. *The Gainesville Sun.*
8. "There's two parts of Gainesville..." ~ Marsh, Dave. (1981, July). Tom Petty. *Musician.*
9. "The Other Florida" ~ Harris, David. (1974, February 14). Hogtown justice. *Rolling Stone.*
10. "The climate was hot and..." ~ Felder, Don; & Holden, Wendy. (2008). *Heaven and Hell: My Life in the Eagles.* Hoboken, NJ: John Wiley & Sons.

CHAPTER 2: ELVIS & TOM
1. "a quiet Southern boy with..." ~ Wallace, Alice. (2006, September 20). Memories of Petty: How singer found way in area. *The Gainesville Sun.*
2. "I was a very poor athlete..." ~ "Tom Petty." (2008, January 31). Super Bowl news conference.

3. "when you grow up there..." ~ Archdeacon, Tom. (2008, February 1). Through the arch: Tom Petty couldn't root for the Buckeyes. *The Dayton Daily News.*
4. "Everything became pretty clear at..." ~ Newman, Melinda. (2005, December 3). Tom Petty: A portrait of the artist. *Billboard.*
5. "Girls, I'll see y'all backstage..." ~ Gary, Corsair. (2008, June 17). Elvis wasn't a star when he came to Ocala in 1955. *The Villages Daily Sun.*
6. "Teenagers screaming 'We want Elvis'..." ~ Marshall, Barbara. (2012, December 22). When Elvis came to town. *The Palm Beach Post.*
7. "He talked Southern, like he..." ~ Marshall, Barbara. (2012, December 22). When Elvis came to town. *The Palm Beach Post.*
8. "One day my uncle, who..." ~ Shapiro, Susin. (1977, April 9). The heartbreak kid. *Sounds.*
9. "He got home and told..." ~ DeYoung, Bill. (1990, January 31). Tom Petty grew up runnin' for a dream. *The Gainesville Sun.*
10. "This guy who lived down..." ~ Rose, Joseph. (1978, February). Tom Petty and the Elvis Presley connection. *Hit Parader.*
11. "By the sixth grade, we'd..." ~ DeYoung, Bill. (1990, January 31). Tom Petty grew up runnin' for a dream. *The Gainesville Sun.*
12. "I can't tell you how..." ~ Corcoran, Michael. (1989, August). Raised on promises. *Spin.*
13. "And that was the end..." ~ Wild, David. (1991, August 8). Over the hump. *Rolling Stone.*
14. Just ten-years-old at the time..." ~ Rose, Joseph. (1978, February). Tom Petty and the Elvis Presley connection. *Hit Parader.*
15. "He was completely, completely enthralled..." ~ Dean, Bill. (2007, August 19). Forever fascinated: Tom Petty's love for rock 'n' roll began the day he met Elvis in Ocala. *The Ocala Star-Banner.*
16. "It's a strange thing to..." ~ Fricke, David. (2009, December 10). It's good to be king. *Rolling Stone.*
17. "Music was a safe place..." ~ Kot, Greg. (2002, November 17). Tom Petty disillusioned but still loves the music. *The Chicago Tribune.*
18. "When I met Elvis, we..." ~ Petty, Tom. (2006, August). What I've learned. *Esquire Magazine.*
19. "When I was really young..." ~ George-Warren, Holly. (2000, September). Tom Petty. *Oxford American.*
20. "We were country people, and..." ~ Snow, Mat. (2010, January). The bard of blue collar rock has led the Heartbreakers to glory on through tragedy. *Mojo.*
21. "Before I knew it, I..." ~ Felder, Don; & Holden, Wendy. (2008). *Heaven and Hell: My Life in the Eagles.* Hoboken, NJ: John Wiley & Sons.

CHAPTER 3: THE BRITISH INVASION HITS GAINESVILLE

1. "They came out and just..." ~ Bosso, Joe. (2004, May). American idols. *Guitar World.*
2. "The rise of Beatlemania coincided..." – Pallandino, Grace. (1996). *Teenagers: An American history.* New York: Basic Books.
3. "It was the Escorts, Gregg..." ~ Bosso, Joe. (2004, May). American idols. *Guitar World.*
4. "Once I found the guitar..." ~ Benarde, Scott. (1991, October 24). Meet the Heartbreakers: Boys in Tom Petty's band. *The Tuscaloosa News.*
5. "which made me the freak..." ~ Blake, Mark. (2012, July). He knew he was right. *Q.*
6. "They threw me out of..." ~ Shapiro, Susin. (1977, April 9). The heartbreak kid. *Sounds.*
7. "That was a time of..." ~ Passy, Charles. (2002, March 19). Petty never forgot family, neighbors in Gainesville. *The Palm Beach Post.*
8. "He was very abusive." ~ I... Fong-Torres, Ben. (2010, April 25). Go after what you love. *Parade.*
9. "[She] was a complete angel" ~ Fong-Torres, Ben. (2010, April 25). Go after what you love. *Parade.*
10. "My mother... never stood up..." ~ Uhelszki, Jaan. (2012, June). Tom Petty: Won't back down. *Uncut.*

11. "I basically just studied Lennon's..." ~ Obrecht, Jas. (1986, August). Tom Petty: The dying art of rhythm guitar. *Guitar Player.*
12. "The Beatles came out. And..." ~ Hilburn, Robert. (1977, April 26). S.F. smitten by Heartbreakers. *The Los Angeles Times.*
13. "In the mid-Sixties, the British..." ~ Petty, Tom. (2010. December 9). The best of the British Invasion. *Rolling Stone.*

CHAPTER 4: SO YOU WANNA BE A ROCK & ROLL STAR

1. "some song came on, I..." ~ Soren, Tabitha. (1995, October 5). Veteran rocker Into the great wide open: Tom Petty to play homecoming show. *The Tuscaloosa News.*
2. "enormous Sears amplifier with six..." ~ Lloyd, Robert. (1991, October). Flying lessons: Tom Petty takes his bearings. *L.A. Style.*
3. "[We] went to the dance..." ~ Lloyd, Robert. (1991, October). Flying lessons: Tom Petty takes his bearings. *L.A. Style.*
4. "The girl wasn't impressed. After..." ~ Soren, Tabitha. (1995, October 5). Veteran rocker Into the great wide open: Tom Petty to play homecoming show. *The Tuscaloosa News.*
5. "My mom was flabbergasted at..." ~ Newman, Melinda. (2005, December 3). Tom Petty: A portrait of the artist. *Billboard.*
6. "Those frat parties were wild..." ~ Felder, Don; & Holden, Wendy. (2008). *Heaven and Hell: My Life in the Eagles.* Hoboken, NJ: John Wiley & Sons.
7. "was one of the guys... that..." ~ Beaton, Matthew. (2011, August). Tom Petty: The enigma. *Gainesville Today.*
8. "It was not yet cool..." ~ Densmore, John. (1990). *Riders on the Storm: My Life with Jim Morrison and the Doors.* New York: Delacorte Press.
9. "I could hear loud music..." ~ Tragash, Jennifer. (2007, October 10). Petty's long-term impact. *The Gainesville Sun.*
10. Although he would usually remain... ~ Schruers, Fred. (1995, May 4). Tom Petty on the road: This is how it feels. *Rolling Stone.*
11. "We realized Tom was the..." ~ Wallace, Alice. (2006, September 20). Memories of Petty: How singer found way in area. *The Gainesville Sun.*
12. In these motel rooms, young... ~ Pond, Steve. (1981, July 23). Tom Petty: A rock & roll hero keeps fighting on. *Rolling Stone.*
13. "There's no money in it..." ~ "Tom Petty." *The Tonight Show.* (1999, June 10). Interview, with Jay Leno. NBC.
14. "his art teacher at Gainesville..." ~ Bianchi, Mike. (2008 February 5). Perseverance pays off for Tom and Tom. *The Orlando Sentinel.*
15. "Rock is more fun." ~ Graustark, Barbary; & Coppola, Vincent. (1980, January 7). Rock's new heartbreak kid. *Newsweek.*
16. "He came in one day..." ~ Gray Streeter, Leslie. (2006, October 1). Homecoming for a Heartbreaker: Gainesville welcomes native son Tom Petty. *The Palm Beach Post.*
17. "Once I got in a band..." ~ Demorest, Stephen. (1978, August). Tom Petty: Animus americus unpoliticus. *Creem.*
18. "High school was the most..." ~ Bartosek, John. (1973, June 24). Music is life for Gainesville's 'Mudcrutch.' *The Gainesville Sun.*
19. "Gainesville was the only place..." ~ Hellegaard, James. (1993, September 5). Remember 1968?: City was hotbed of protest. *The Gainesville Sun.*
20. "Daddy, if you'll just leave..." ~ DeYoung, Bill. (1992, August 2). The evolution of a rock star. *The Gainesville Sun.*
21. "I thought he was going..." ~ Tom Petty and the Heartbreakers. (1999). *Behind the Music.* New York: VH1.
22. "My father was a very..." ~ Snow, Mat. (2010, January). The bard of blue collar rock has led the Heartbreakers to glory on through tragedy. *Mojo.*
23. "My father used to have..." ~ Gross, Terry. (2008, February 1). Tom Petty knows 'how it feels.' *Fresh Air.* Philadelphia: NPR.

24. "Jacksonville was a transient town..." ~ Edmonds, Ben; & Uhelszki, Jaan. (1997, November). How the South rose again: The soaring flight and tragic fall of Lynyrd Skynyrd. *Mojo.*
25. "There was something in the..." ~ Norman, Michael. (1999, June 13). Rock's everyman Petty believes in his music. *The Cleveland Plain Dealer.*
26. "I got to see the..." ~ Petty, Tom. (2011). The Byrds. *Rolling Stone: 100 greatest artists of all time.*

CHAPTER 5: HERE COMES MUDCRUTCH

1. "I think we liked it..." ~ DeYoung, Bill. (1990, January 31). Tom Petty grew up runnin' for a dream. *The Gainesville Sun.*
2. "the band with the worst..." ~ Hogan, Richard. (1981, August 31). Tom Petty makes 'Hard Promises' to rock & roll. *Circus.*
3. "I took my tuition and..." ~ Schruers, Fred. (1995, May 4). Tom Petty on the road: This is how it feels. *Rolling Stone.*
4. "My dad was a big..." ~ Guerra, Tom. (2008, March). Mike Campbell. *ToneQuest Report.*
5. Picking up the guitar at... ~ "Dylan merges with Petty's band during tour. (1986, July 12). *St. Joseph News-Press.*
6. "My mom got me my..." ~ Guerra, Tom. (2008, April). Runnin' down a dream: Mike Campbell. *Premier Guitar.*
7. "I went to a friend's..." ~ Guerra, Tom. (2008, April). Runnin' down a dream: Mike Campbell. *Premier Guitar.*
8. "Back then we didn't have..."~ Guerra, Tom. (2008, April). Runnin' down a dream: Mike Campbell. *Premier Guitar.*
9. "The stuff that got me..." ~ Hunter, Dave. (1999, June). Mike Campbell: Anything that's rock'n'roll.
10. "Our families were just scraping..." ~ Hogan, Richard. (1981, August 31). Tom Petty makes 'Hard Promises' to rock & roll. *Circus.*
11. "I think [my] attraction to..." ~ Benarde, Scott R. (2003). *Stars of David.* Hanover, NH: Brandeis University Press.
12. "I remember playing in the..." ~ DeYoung, Bill. (1995, November 21). The beat of a different drum: Stan Lynch finds life's just fine after Tom Petty and the Heartbreakers. *The Gainesville Sun.*
13. "I was gigging pretty heavily..." ~ Berkery, Patrick. (2008, May). Stan Lynch. *Modern Drummer.*
14. "I used to get in..." ~ Jackson, Blair. (1983, January 28). There's a lot more to the Heartbreakers than Tom Petty. *BAM.*
15. "Look man, you can call..." ~ Jackson, Blair. (1983, January 28). There's a lot more to the Heartbreakers than Tom Petty. *BAM.*
16. "Then sometime in 1964, my..." ~ Sharp, Ken. (2012, December). Mojo man. *Bass Player.*
17. "After I got back to..." ~ Sharp, Ken. (2012, December). Mojo man. *Bass Player.*
18. "Around 1968, my dad got..." ~ Sharp, Ken. (2012, December). Mojo man. *Bass Player.*
19. "I got into a band..." ~ Sharp, Ken. (2012, December). Mojo man. *Bass Player.*
20. "They were into a different..." ~ DeYoung, Bill. (1990, August 8). For one former Heartbreaker, breaking up was too easy to do. *The Gainesville Sun.*
21. "Tom used to impress me..." ~ DeYoung, Bill. (1990, August 8). For one former Heartbreaker, breaking up was too easy to do. *The Gainesville Sun.*
22. "like the Who, or a..." ~ DeYoung, Bill. (1990, August 8). For one former Heartbreaker, breaking up was too easy to do. *The Gainesville Sun.*
23. "Janice was so gorgeous, and..." ~ Allman, Gregg; & Light, Alan. (2012). *My Cross to Bear.* New York: William Morrow.

CHAPTER 6: THE MUDCRUTCH FARM

1. "became the hangout for every..." ~ DeYoung, Bill. (1987, July 24). TP, Heartbreakers bring it on home with Florida tour. *The Gainesville Sun.*

2. "My transportation was not..." ~ Edwards, Gavin. (2008, May 1). Tom Petty reunites Mudcrutch. *Rolling Stone.*
3. "We played there for several..." ~ Locey, Bill. (2008, April 17). Tom Petty takes a run at the charts with his first band. *The Ventura County Star.*
4. "more like a heavy metal..." ~ Demorest, Stephen. (1978, August). Tom Petty: Animus americus unpoliticus. *Creem.*
5. "[My brother] Bernie told me..." ~ DeYoung, Bill. (1990, July 13). Tom Petty: Full steam ahead. *Goldmine.*
6. "We had never really been..." ~ Thompson, Art. (2006, July). 30 years & counting. *Guitar Player.*
7. "There was a point with..." ~ DeYoung, Bill. (1987, July 24). TP, Heartbreakers bring it on home with Florida tour. *The Gainesville Sun.*
8. "It got very hard to..." ~ DeYoung, Bill. (1987, July 24). TP, Heartbreakers bring it on home with Florida tour. *The Gainesville Sun.*
9. "We didn't have a TV..." ~ Boucher, Geoff. (2008, April 27). Tom Petty returns to his roots with Mudcrutch. *The Los Angeles Times.*
10. "I started playing piano when..." ~ Allan, Marc D. (1991, September 10). Heartbreakers' talented keyboardist pulls no strings: He prefers guitars. *The Indianapolis Star.*
11. "I'd hear the Beatles on..." ~ Macias, Chris. (1999, August 29). Everybody is a star: In Tom Petty and the Heartbreakers, each band member gets a chance to shine. *The Sacramento Bee.*
12. "He was an older kid..." ~ Rodgers, Larry. (1999, September 24). Tom Petty, Heartbreakers too stubborn to back down. *The Spartanburg Herald-Journal.*
13. At age 12 in 1965 ~ Steigner, Nancy. (1986, July 16). *Judge Benjamin Tench.* University of Florida Oral History Program.
14. "I don't think I ever..." ~ Secor, Ketch. (2010, Fall). Runnin' down a dream. *The Exeter Bulletin.*
15. "There was a bit of..." ~ Secor, Ketch. (2010, Fall). Runnin' down a dream. *The Exeter Bulletin.*
16. "Our mission was to prove..." ~ Hogan, Richard. (1981, August 31). Tom Petty makes 'Hard Promises' to rock & roll. *Circus.*
17. But the group was not ~ http://nicholsandnonsense.blogspot.com/2013/05/grumps-corner-inaugural-post.html.
18. "The guy who started my..." ~ Macias, Chris. (1999, August 29). Everybody is a star: In Tom Petty and the Heartbreakers, each band member gets a chance to shine. *The Sacramento Bee.*

CHAPTER 7: RESTLESS IN GAINESVILLE
1. "It would depend on the..." ~ Morse, Steve. (1980, March). *Blonde on blonde.* Trouser Press.
2. "I remember we drove one..." ~ McLeese, Don. (1983, March 29). Tom Petty: On his own terms. *The (Gannet-Westchester) Herald-Statesman.*
3. "Wherever you turned there were..." ~ McShane, Rod. (1977, August). Tom Petty. *Dark Star.*
4. "We went to the record..." ~ DeYoung, Bill. (1987, July 24). TP, Heartbreakers bring it on home with Florida tour. *The Gainesville Sun.*
5. "About a year before we..." ~ DeYoung, Bill. (1987, July 24). TP, Heartbreakers bring it on home with Florida tour. *The Gainesville Sun.*
6. "Everybody started to leave because..." ~ Morse, Steve. (1980, March). Blonde on blonde. *Trouser Press.*
7. "Most people come to Florida..." ~ Corcoran, Michael. (1989, August). Raised on promises. *Spin.*
8. "I stayed behind because there..." ~ Schruers, Fred. (1995, May 4). Tom Petty on the road: This is how it feels. *Rolling Stone.*
9. "Driving to L.A. was the..." ~ Corcoran, Michael. (1989, August). Raised on promises. *Spin.*
10. "There's something magical about it..." ~ di Perna, Alan. (1999, April). Tom Petty: American boy. *Pulse.*
11. "We made our first rounds..." ~ Scaggs, Austin. (2006, May 18). Petty on the edge. *Rolling*

Stone.
12. "We told them we drove..." ~ Corcoran, Michael. (1989, August). Raised on promises. *Spin.*
13. "I remember going into MGM..." ~ Newman, Melinda. (2005, December 3). Tom Petty: A portrait of the artist. *Billboard.*
14. "It was not a sure..." ~ Wallace, Alice. (2006, September 20). Memories of Petty: How singer found way in area. *The Gainesville Sun.*
15. "could pass for" Petty's "twin sister" ~ Wild, David. (1991, August 8). Over the hump. *Rolling Stone.*
16. "That was the first time..." ~ Simmons, Sylvie. (2009, September). The real slowhand. *Mojo.*
17. "a bearlike man who didn't..." ~ O'Dell, Chris; & Ketcham, Katherine. (2009). *Miss O'Dell.* New York: Touchstone.
18. "I was so proud of..." ~ O'Dell, Chris; & Ketcham, Katherine. (2009). *Miss O'Dell.* New York: Touchstone.
19. "(Leon's) idea was to give..." ~ Easterling, Mike. (2009, November 12). Feels like religion. *Urban Tulsa Weekly.*
20. But after traveling just two... ~ Sweeting, Adam. (1981, June 13). Tuning up the criminal kind. *Melody Maker.*
21. "Cordell was a great guy..." ~ Marsh, Dave. (1981, July). Tom Petty. *Musician.*
22. "it was a different time..." ~ Guerra, Tom. (2008, April). Runnin' down a dream: Mike Campbell. *Premier Guitar.*
23. "In the early '70s my..." ~ Wixen, Randall D. (2009). *The Plain and Simple Guide to Music Publishing (2nd ed.).* Milwaukee: Hal Leonard.
24. "It's an awkward situation when..." ~ Rowland, Mark. (1987, September). Heartbreaker straight ahead. *Musician.*
25. "It wasn't so long ago..." ~ Goodman, Fred. (1992, January). Big deals: How money fever is changing the music industry. *Musician.*
26. "we all had two grand..." ~ Schruers, Fred. (1999, July 7). Tom Petty: The *Rolling Stone* interview. *Rolling Stone.*
27. "Jane was with me. And..." ~ Schruers, Fred. (1999, July 7). Tom Petty: The *Rolling Stone* interview. *Rolling Stone.*

CHAPTER 8: CALIFORNIA DREAMING

1. "There were too many cooks..." ~ Wild, David. (1991, August 8). Over the hump. *Rolling Stone.*
2. "There were personal things, and..." ~ DeYoung, Bill. (1990, July 13). Tom Petty: Full steam ahead. *Goldmine.*
3. "We did half an album..." ~ DeYoung, Bill. (1995, March 3). For Al Kooper, turning 50 was a good excuse for celebrating. *The Gainesville Sun.*
4. "good reggae cut" ~ "Single reviews: First time around." (1975, February 15). *Billboard.*
5. "I was living in Hollywood..." ~ Rowland, Mark. (1987, September). Heartbreaker straight ahead. *Musician.*
6. "Leon, who I'd never met..." ~ Simmons, Sylvie. (2006, October). Rock of ages. *Mojo.*
7. "[Russell] kept me on salary..." ~ Rowland, Mark. (1987, September). Heartbreaker straight ahead. *Musician.*
8. "It was a real crazy..." ~ Kendall, Paul. (1977, June). Four guys with a passion. *Zigzag.*
9. "I tried making an album..." ~ Kelp, Larry. (1980). Don't call him blondie. *Relix.*
10. "for $40 a month..." ~ Flans, Robyn. (1984, February). Stan Lynch: Heartbreaking rhythm. *Modern Drummer.*
11. "quit when he found himself..." ~ Flans, Robyn. (1984, February). Stan Lynch: Heartbreaking rhythm. *Modern Drummer.*
12. "I was working with this..." ~ Berkery, Patrick. (2008, May). Stan Lynch. *Modern Drummer.*
13. "literally ran into each other..." ~ DeYoung, Bill. (1984, July 20). Stan Lynch, the homebody Heartbreaker. *The Gainesville Sun.*
14. "What happened was a friend..." ~ Kendall, Paul. (1977, June). Four guys with a passion.

Zigzag.
15. "I called Tom and I..." ~ Rosen, Craig. (2006, March 25). Tom Petty & The Heartbreakers. *Billboard.*
16. "I knew everybody in the..." ~ Crowe, Cameron. (1978, October 19). Tom Petty's gonna get it – his way. *Rolling Stone.*
17. "I have a record deal..." ~ Newman, Melinda. (2005, December 3). Tom Petty: A portrait of the artist. *Billboard.*
18. "The whole reason my name..." ~ Marsh, Dave. (1981, July). Tom Petty. *Musician.*
19. "We were spendin' every day..." ~ Scoppa, Bud. (1987, June 1). Winging it with Petty & Campbell. *Music Connection.*

CHAPTER 9: HERE COMES THE HEARTBREAKERS

1. "They were building a studio..." ~ Demorest, Stephen. (1978, August). Tom Petty: Animus americus unpoliticus. *Creem.*
2. "The engineers were *proudly* on..." ~ Simmons, Sylvie. (2006, October). Rock of ages. *Mojo.*
3. "When we did it, we'd..." ~ Marsh, Dave. (1981, July). Tom Petty. *Musician.*
4. "We went and listened to..." ~ Rosen, Craig. (2006, March 25). Tom Petty & The Heartbreakers. *Billboard.*
5. "album was a real curiosity..." ~ Marsh, Dave. (1981, July). Tom Petty. *Musician.*
6. "another punk rock, black leather..." ~ "Album reviews: Pop." (1976, December 4). *Billboard.*
7. "When I did that album..." ~ McShane, Rod. (1977, August). Tom Petty. *Dark Star.*
8. "I've heard this story about..." ~ DeRogatis, Jim. (2003). *Milk It!* Cambridge, MA: DaCapo Press.
9. The story may have been... ~ Crowe, Cameron. (1978, October 19). Tom Petty's gonna get it – his way *Rolling Stone.*
10. "maybe the reason it's taken..." ~ Hogan, Richard. (1981, August 31). Tom Petty makes 'Hard Promises' to rock & roll. *Circus.*
11. "I've found you can save..." ~ Jackson, Blair. (1983, January 28). There's a lot more to the Heartbreakers than Tom Petty. *BAM.*
12. "I had a bad temper..." ~ Blake, Mark. (2012, July). He knew he was right. *Q.*
13. "I had a tough childhood..." ~ Fricke, David. (2009, December 10). It's good to be king. *Rolling Stone.*
14. "We were walking into our..." ~ Crowe, Cameron. (1978, October 19). Tom Petty's gonna get it – his way *Rolling Stone.*
15. "Those were wonderful days, though..." ~ Corcoran, Michael. (1989, August). Raised on promises. *Spin.*
16. "I liked punk but I..." ~ Blake, Mark. (2012, July). He knew he was right. *Q.*
17. "an Oklahoman" ~ Savage, William W. (1998). *Singing Cowboys and All That Jazz: A Short History of Popular Music in Oklahoma.* Norman, OK: The University of Oklahoma Press.
18. "A lot of people used..." ~ Chancellor, Jennifer. (2010, September 19). Before the Heartbreakers, Tom Petty had Tulsa ties. *Tulsa World.*

CHAPTER 10: THE DEBUT ALBUM

1. "Petty was the most reserved..." ~ Zimmerman, Lee. (2008, July 10). Hailing the Heartbreakers. *The Broward-Palm Beach New Times.*
2. "Since I've been back here..." ~ Synder, John. (1976, December 10). Tommy Petty leaves home again: A rock roller out of time. *The Gainesville Sun.*
3. Not surprisingly, Petty heard "Breakdown" ~ Schenkman, Richard (Director and Producer). (1986). *Southern Accents.* MTV.
4. "I wrote 'Breakdown' in the..." ~ Obrecht, Jas. (1986, August). Tom Petty: The dying art of rhythm guitar. *Guitar Player.*
5. "When I came up with..." ~ Aledort, Andy. (1995, August). Chartbreaker. *Guitar School.*
6. "Yeah, the *Live 'Leg* is..." ~ Girard, Jim. (1977, December 22). Tom Petty: Present and future. *Scene.*

7. "We had enough buzz to..." ~ Newman, Melinda. (2005, December 3). Tom Petty: A portrait of the artist. *Billboard.*
8. "When he sings his 'Fooled..." ~ Gilmore, Mikal. (1977, June 30). Tom Petty's rock fervor. *Rolling Stone.*

CHAPTER 11: AMERICAN GIRL

1. "'American Girl' would have made ..." ~ Jackson, Blair. (1978, April 7). Tom Petty and the Heartbreakers – it's only rock 'n' roll (and that's the point). *BAM.*
2. "I wrote 'American Girl' really..." ~ Girard, Jim. (1977, December 22). Tom Petty present and future: Whatever we do, it'll rock. *(Cleveland) Scene.*
3. "my sorry attempt to sound..." ~ Deggans, Eric. (2008, June 2). Legendary rocker Bo Diddley dies at 79. *The Tampa Bay Times.*
4. "Just before the band left..." ~ McShane, Rod. (1977, August). Tom Petty. *Dark Star.*
5. "a classic rock 'n' roll..." ~ Hilburn, Robert. (1977, April 26). S.F. smitten by Heartbreakers. *The Los Angeles Times.*
6. "You can quote me on..." ~ Shapiro, Susin. (1977, April 9). The heartbreak kid. *Sounds.*
7. "The next thing I knew..." ~ Flans, Robyn. (1984, February). Stan Lynch: Heartbreaking rhythm. *Modern Drummer.*
8. "There were riots 15 minutes..." ~ Peeples, Stephen. (1977, October 9). Tom Petty and the Heartbreakers: Hogtown boys make good. *Rock Around The World.*
9. "the first time I heard..." ~ Aparicio, Nestor. (1991, April 4). Former Byrd Roger McGuinn giving fame a fresh sound. *The Baltimore Sun.*
10. "He rang up the office..." ~ Linder, Greg. (1978, October 20). Tom Petty: A mystery man unveiled. *Reader's Magazine.*
11. "Tom Petty was a real..." ~ Einarson, John. (2005). *Mr. Tambourine Man: The Life and Legacy of the Byrds' Gene Clark.* San Francisco: Backbeat.
12. "We've always been cast in..." ~ Bell, Max. (1980, March 15). Call Tom Petty the new Springsteen and he'll cut you! *New Musical Express.*
13. "The problem with doing a..." ~ Hoffman, Per. (1991, September). *Guitar World.* Melody maker.
14. "We went around Europe, then..." ~ Waddell, Ray. (2006, March 25). Heartbreakers bring consistency and passion to shows. *Billboard.*
15. "one of the most in-demand..." ~ "More than a pretty face." (1977). *Melody Maker.*
16. After the Heartbreakers were stripped-searched... ~ Jackson, Blair. (1978, April 7). Tom Petty and the Heartbreakers – It's only rock 'n' roll (and that's the point). *BAM.*
17. "the European tour gave them..." ~ Jackson, Blair. (1978, April 7). Tom Petty and the Heartbreakers – It's only rock 'n' roll (and that's the point). *BAM.*
18. "We got on the covers..." ~ Newman, Melinda. (2005, December 3). Tom Petty: A portrait of the artist. *Billboard.*
19. "big hotel rooms and lots..." ~ DeYoung, Bill. (1984, July 20). Stan Lynch, the homebody Heartbreaker. *The Gainesville Sun.*
20. "We probably would've been dropped..." ~ Uhelszki, Jaan. (2012, June). Tom Petty: Won't back down. *Uncut.*
21. "We got to this gig..." ~ Fricke, David. (2009, December 10). It's good to be king. *Rolling Stone.*
22. "One night with the Doobie..." ~ Fricke, David. (2009, December 10). It's good to be king. *Rolling Stone.*
23. "Tom's a good example of..." ~ Christian, Pam. (1978, October). Derringer pops off. *Reader's Magazine.*
24. "We knew the first album..." ~ Jackson, Blair. (1978, April 7). Tom Petty and the Heartbreakers – It's only rock 'n' roll (and that's the point). *BAM.*
25. "It was a surreal day, it..." ~ Gardner, Thom. (1977, November/December). Tom Petty. *Back Door Man.*

CHAPTER 12: TOM PETTY: SINGER & SONGWRITER

1. "I'm not careful about my..." ~ Gotz, David M. (1980, February). Interview: Petty gets his torpedoes together and damns ahead to the airwaves. *Record Review.*
2. "Tom's always been a style..." ~ DeYoung, Bill. (1984 July 20). Stan Lynch, the homebody Heartbreaker. *The Gainesville Sun.*
3. "[Petty] was the only guy..." ~ Hogan, Richard. (1981, August 31). Tom Petty makes 'Hard Promises' to rock & roll. *Circus.*
4. "The first time I tried..." ~ Fong-Torres, Ben. (2010, April 25). Go after what you love. *Parade.*
5. "Songwriting is a hard thing..." ~ Dye, Robert; & Trost, Isaiah. (2003, March 10). Rock and roll animals. *Guitar World Acoustic.*
6. "[after a concert] I don't..." ~ Rowland, Mark. (1997, January). Beck meets Petty: Rockin', writin', survivin' in L.A. *Musician.*
7. "I find that the less..." ~ Rowland, Mark. (1997, January). Beck meets Petty: Rockin', writin', survivin' in L.A. *Musician.*
8. "You're in the bathroom when..." ~ Lanham, Tom. (1994, December). Petty on the inside. *Pulse.*
9. "He'll come up with real..." ~ Flans, Robyn. (1984, February). Stan Lynch: Heartbreaking rhythm. *Modern Drummer.*
10. "Tom's trip is based around..." ~ Ransom, Kevin. (1995, March). Profile: Mike Campbell. *Guitar Player.*
11. "I've seen songs come in..." ~ Flans, Robyn. (1984, February). Stan Lynch: Heartbreaking rhythm. *Modern Drummer.*
12. "I'm real good with ambiguity..." ~ di Perna, Alan. (1999, April). Tom Petty: American boy. *Pulse.*
13. "There's times I'll hear a..." ~ Hogan, Richard. (1981, August 31). Tom Petty makes 'Hard Promises' to rock & roll. *Circus.*
14. "I never was a big..." ~ Rotman, Natalie. (2009, November 30). Tom Petty releases 'Live Anthology' disc set. *The Seattle Times.*
15. "Tom doesn't want to sing..." ~ Neal, Chris. (2007, September/October). Keyboardist Benmont Tench of Tom Petty and the Heartbreakers. *Performing Songwriter.*
16. "Petty's stories were distilled in..." ~ Galante Block, Debbie; & Rosen, Craig. (2006, March 25). Getting at the essence of the Heartbreakers. *Billboard.*
17. "We tend to work from..." ~ Mettler, Mike. (2010, June-July-August). Mojo workin'. *Sound + Vision.*
18. "I'm pretty rough on myself..." ~ Fricke, David. (2009, December 10). It's good to be king. *Rolling Stone.*
19. "I have to go to..." ~ Rowland, Mark. (1987, September). Heartbreaker straight ahead. *Musician.*
20. "[Petty's] stuff is deceptively simple..." ~ Zaleski, Annie. (2011, October 17). Happy birthday, Tom Petty! Musicians talk about why he still rules at age 61. *Alternative Press.*
21. "Once have a good song..." ~ DeYoung, Bill. (1985, May 6). Breaking form: Tom Petty's change of heart. *Music.*

CHAPTER 13: YOU'RE GONNA GET IT

1. "when we got back ABC..." ~ Stock, Tom. (1978, August). Tom Petty's Back. *Beat Instrumental.*
2. "well, he doesn't do outside..." ~ Sharp, Ken. (2013, January). The dream team. *Goldmine.*
3. "The Neve boards were considered..." ~ Block, Melissa. (2013, March 8). Dave Grohl finds music's human element – in a machine. *All Things Considered.* Philadelphia: NPR.
4. "I was trying to make..." ~ DeYoung, Bill. (1993, October 29). Memories are made of this. *The Gainesville Sun.*
5. "My wife Jane had gone..." ~ DeYoung, Bill. (1993, October 29). Memories are made of this. *The Gainesville Sun.*

6. "The only good rock 'n' roll..." ~ Linder, Greg. (1978, October 20). Tom Petty: A mystery man unveiled. *Reader's Magazine.*
7. "I actually *danced* with [the..." ~ Linder, Greg. (1978, October 20). Tom Petty: A mystery man unveiled. *Reader's Magazine.*
8. "I didn't want to do..." ~ Gotz, David M. (1979, August). *Record Review* interview: Tom Petty. *Record Review.*
9. "We haven't played bars in..." ~ Liben, Michael P. (1979, February). Tom Petty – Heartbreaker at home & a broad. *New Wave Rock.*
10. Around this time, Tom Petty... ~ Morse, Steve. (1980, March). Blonde on blonde. *Trouser Press.*
11. "I have a real heavy..." ~ Marsh, Dave. (1981, July). Tom Petty. *Musician.*
12. "I've noticed that I can't..." ~ Rensin, David. (1982, September). 20 questions: Tom Petty. *Playboy.*

CHAPTER 14: I FOUGHT THE LAW

1. "I heard Tom Petty's first..." ~ Garbarini, Vic. (1987, November). The essential Jimmy Iovine. *Musician.*
2. "The first two songs he..." ~ Rosen, Craig. (2006, March 25). Tom Petty & The Heartbreakers. *Billboard.*
3. "At the time, Iovine had..." ~ Scoppa, Bud. (1985, August). Tom Petty's year (or two) of living dangerously. *Record.*
4. "He put a contract in..." ~ Dylan, Bob, (2004). *Chronicles: Volume One.* New York: Simon & Schuster.
5. "it is no secret that..." ~ Jackson, Blair. (1979, December). Tom Petty's rock victory. *BAM.*
6. "It was the principle: the..." ~ Gilmore, Mikal. (1980, February 21). Tom Petty's real-life nightmares. *Rolling Stone.*
7. "When word got around that..." ~ Jackson, Blair. (1979, December). Tom Petty's rock victory. *BAM.*
8. "I thought they were idiots..." ~ Berkery, Patrick. (2008, May). Stan Lynch. *Modern Drummer.*
9. "That's when I thought I..." ~ Gilmore, Mikal. (1980, February 21). Tom Petty's real-life nightmares. *Rolling Stone.*
10. "If I lost, we were..." ~ Marsh, Dave. (1981, July). Tom Petty. *Musician.*
11. "In Jimmy's defense, he was..." ~ Berkery, Patrick. (2008, May). Stan Lynch. *Modern Drummer.*
12. "When we started doing..." ~ DeYoung, Bill. (1990, August 8). For one former Heartbreaker, breaking up was too easy to do. *The Gainesville Sun.*
13. "We'd be working in the..." ~ Marsh, Dave. (1981, July). Tom Petty. *Musician.*
14. "Eventually I convinced the judge..." ~ Bell, Max. (1980, March 15). Call Tom Petty the new Springsteen and he'll cut you! *New Musical Express.*
15. "Have legal hassles and bankruptcy torpedoed this rocker's career?" ~ "Have legal hassles and bankruptcy torpedoed this rocker's career?" (1979, December 11). *Circus,* [front cover].
16. "I intended Backstreet to be..." ~ Gilmore, Mikal. (1980, February 21). Tom Petty's real-life nightmares. *Rolling Stone.*
17. "Tom Petty fought the law..." ~ Bell, Max. (1980, March 15). Call Tom Petty the new Springsteen and he'll cut you! *New Musical Express.*
18. "Something like this builds you..." ~ Jackson, Blair. (1979, December). Tom Petty's rock victory. *BAM.*

CHAPTER 15: TORPEDO ROCK & ROLL

1. "We all have torpedoes to..." ~ Jackson, Blair. (1979, December). Tom Petty's rock victory. *BAM.*
2. "I was afraid to put..." ~ Marsh, Dave. (1981, July). Tom Petty. *Musician.*
3. "Jimmy Iovine told me, 'People'll..." ~ Jackson, Blair. (1979, December). Tom Petty's rock victory. *BAM.*

4. "Elliot came in and said..." ~ Flanagan, Bill. (1990, April). The Heartbreakers highway. *Musician.*
5. "The Rickenbacker is rich and..." ~ Thompson, Art. (1999, May). Heartbreaker hideout in the studio with Tom Petty & Mike Campbell. *Guitar Player.*
6. "I just didn't want to..." ~ Schruers, Fred. (1995, May 4). Tom Petty on the road: This is how it feels. *Rolling Stone.*
7. Initially, the members of the Heartbreakers..." ~ Goldberg, Danny. (2008). *Bumping into Geniuses.* New York: Gotham Books.
8. "I thought it was a..." ~ Thompson, Art. (1999, May). Heartbreaker hideout in the studio with Tom Petty & Mike Campbell. *Guitar Player.*
9. "It was something my dad..." ~ DeYoung, Bill. (1993, October 29). Memories are made of this. *The Gainesville Sun.*
10. "We're always hearing that we're..." ~ Graustark, Barbary; & Coppola, Vincent. (1980, January 7). Rock's new heartbreak kid. *Newsweek.*
11. "almost broke up the band..." ~ Flans, Robyn. (1984, February). Stan Lynch: Heartbreaking rhythm. *Modern Drummer.*
12. "It took four weeks to..." ~ Garbarini, Vic. (1987, November). The essential Jimmy Iovine. *Musician.*
13. "We played 'Refugee' 200 times..." ~ Scoppa, Bud. (1987, June 1). Winging it with Petty & Campbell. *Music Connection.*
14. "We made a video for..." ~ Marks, Craig; & Tannenbaum, Rob. (2011). *I Want My MTV.* New York: Dutton.
15. "During the first week of..." ~ Pond, Steve. (1981, July 23). Tom Petty: A rock & roll hero keeps fighting on. *Rolling Stone.*
16. "unable to speak after the..." ~ Pond, Steve. (1981, July 23). Tom Petty: A rock & roll hero keeps fighting on. *Rolling Stone.*
17. "Being on the cover of..." ~ Woodward, Fred; & Wenner, Jann S. (1998). *Rolling Stone: The complete covers,* 1967-1997. New York: Harry N. Abrams.
18. "a genuine love song in..." ~ Marsh, Dave. (1980, June-July). The critics vs. Tom Petty. *Musician.*
19. "I got the idea for..." ~ DeYoung, Bill. (1993, October 29). Memories are made of this. *The Gainesville Sun.*
20. "It had nothing to do..." ~ Gotz, David M. (1980, February). Interview: Petty gets his torpedoes together and damns ahead to the airwaves. *Record Review.*
21. "I wanted to write anthems..." ~ Bell, Max. (1980, March 15). Call Tom Petty the new Springsteen and he'll cut you! *New Musical Express.*
22. "I was offered the cover..." ~ Kubernik, Harvey. (1980, March 8). The trials of Tom Petty: Petty gets it. *Melody Maker.*
23. "His way of playing the..." ~ Obrecht, Jas. (1986, August). Mike Campbell with the Heartbreakers. *Guitar Player.*

CHAPTER 16: HARD PROMISES
1. "His death hurt real bad..." ~ Rensin, David. (1982, September). 20 questions: Tom Petty. Playboy.
2. "I hope we're not remembered..." ~ Pond, Steve. (1981, July 23). Tom Petty: A rock & roll hero keeps fighting on. *Rolling Stone.*
3. "I was fighting the record..." ~ Woodward, Fred; & Wenner, Jann S. (1998). *Rolling Stone: The complete covers,* 1967-1997. New York: Harry N. Abrams.
4. "I took a huge stand..." ~ Howell, Peter. (1991, June 29). For Tom Petty rock scene still a heartbreaker. *The Toronto Star.*
5. "If they'd have listened to..." ~ Derogatis, Jim. (2003, April 13). Damn the torpedoes. *The Chicago Sun Times.*
6. "That was a song that..." ~ Hilburn, Robert. (2002, March 15). No backing down. *The Los Angeles Times.*

7. "They were *not* supportive when..." ~ Rogers, Ray. (1988, July). A storm called Stevie. *Interview.*
8. After completing a grueling but... ~ Harris, Carol Ann. (2007). *Storms: My Life With Lindsey Buckingham and Fleetwood Mac.* Chicago: Chicago Review Press.
9. "she had a vivid stage..." ~ Goldberg, Danny. (2008). *Bumping into Geniuses.* New York: Gotham Books.
10. "I got Petty to come..." ~ Goldberg, Danny. (2008). *Bumping into Geniuses.* New York: Gotham Books.
11. "A week later Jimmy have..." ~ Goldberg, Danny. (2008). *Bumping into Geniuses.* New York: Gotham Books.
12. "I first met Tom in..." ~ Osborn, Dave. (2012, April 25). Tom Petty, Florida's native rocker, still pulls in respect, and full houses, nearly 40 years after his debut. *The Naples Daily News.*
13. "Near the end of the..." ~ Shannon, Bob; & Javna, John. (1986). *Behind the Hits.* New York: Warner Books.
14. "She came into the studio..." ~ Jackson, Blair. (1981, August). Just a popular rock 'n' roll band. *Trouser Press.*
15. "When Stevie heard it, she..." ~ Jackson, Blair. (1981, August). Just a popular rock 'n' roll band. *Trouser Press.*
16. "When I first saw it..." ~ Hoye, Jacob (Ed.). (2001). *MTV: Uncensored.* New York: Pocket Books.
17. "for *Hard Promises*, we did..." ~ Marks, Craig; & Tannenbaum, Rob. (2011). *I Want My MTV.* New York: Dutton.
18. "This taste of loneliness is..." ~ Cohen, Debra Rae. (1981, July 23). From golden boy to grown-up. *Rolling Stone.*
19. "Iovine immediately says, 'It's..." ~ Berkery, Patrick. (2008, May). Stan Lynch. *Modern Drummer.*
20. "It had not escaped Tom..." ~ Goldberg, Danny. (2008). *Bumping into Geniuses.* New York: Gotham Books.
21. "I remember being shut down..." ~ Snider, Mike. (2009, December 20). Tom Petty's live legacy gets the mega-box-set treatment. *USA Today.*
22. "[WLUP] came to me and..." ~ Sweeting, Adam. (1981, June 13). Tuning up the criminal kind. *Melody Maker.*
23. "Petty's backup band, the Heartbreakers..." ~ DeWitt, Howard A. (2001). *Stranger in Town: The Musical life of Del Shannon.* Dubuque, IA: Kendall/Hunt Publishing.

CHAPTER 17: GOODBYE RON, HELLO HOWIE

1. "couldn't get back on the..." ~ DeYoung, Bill. (1990, August 8). For one former Heartbreaker, breaking up was too easy to do. *The Gainesville Sun.*
2. "The first couple of years..." ~ DeYoung, Bill. (1990, August 8). For one former Heartbreaker, breaking up was too easy to do. *The Gainesville Sun.*
3. "At the time, it was..." ~ DeYoung, Bill. (1990, August 8). For one former Heartbreaker, breaking up was too easy to do. *The Gainesville Sun.*
4. "When he first quit, he..." ~ Strauss, Neil. (2006, July 13). Tom Petty's last dance. *Rolling Stone.*
5. "Sam Epstein, was a top..." ~ Jackson, Blair. (1983, January 28). There's a lot more to the Heartbreakers than Tom Petty. *BAM.*
6. "there was little parental restraint..." ~ Matthews, Tom. (2010, November 22). Heart Breaker. *Milwaukee Magazine.*
7. "The funny thing is... the..." ~ Jackson, Blair. (1983, January 28). There's a lot more to the Heartbreakers than Tom Petty. *BAM.*
8. "I was a terrible drunk..." ~ Matthews, Tom. (2010, November 22). Heart Breaker. *Milwaukee Magazine.*
9. "Howie was the sane one..." ~ Matthews, Tom. (2010, November 22). Heart Breaker. *Milwaukee Magazine.*

10. "He played the bass, and" ~ Petty, Tom. (2003, April 3). Howie Epstein. *Rolling Stone.*
11. "When I asked Howie to..." ~ Petty, Tom. (2003, April 3). Howie Epstein. *Rolling Stone.*
12. "I was definitely happy when..." ~ Flanagan, Bill. (1990, April). The Heartbreakers highway. *Musician.*
13. "It really was a spontaneous..." ~ Gans, David. (1984, February). Tom Petty: Pride and passion. *Hit Parader.*
14. "We're playing in front of..." ~ Matthews, Tom. (2010, November 22). Heart Breaker. *Milwaukee Magazine.*
15. "I think that I'm a..." ~ Flanagan, Bill. (1986). *Written in My Soul.* Chicago: Contemporary Books.
16. "In the old days, when..." ~ Jackson, Blair. (1983, January 28). There's a lot more to the Heartbreakers than Tom Petty. *BAM.*

CHAPTER 18: LONG AFTER DARK

1. "When it came to my..." ~ Schoemer, Karen. (1991, October 30). Petty moves into his own. *The Gainesville Sun.*
2. "We've probably been the most..." ~ Morse, Steve. (1983, March 24). Tom Petty: A survivor. *The Boston Globe.*
3. "[It's] the most misunderstood song..." ~ Flanagan, Bill. (1986). *Written in My Soul.* Chicago: Contemporary Books.
4. "I think that those [musicians]..." ~ Derogatis, Jim. (2003, April 13). Damn the torpedoes. *The Chicago Sun Times.*
5. "The solo in the middle..." ~ Obrecht, Jas. (1986, August). Mike Campbell with the Heartbreakers. *Guitar Player.*
6. "I've always admired those Clint..." ~ DeYoung, Bill. (1983, February 4). Be it ever so humble: Tom Petty talks about home. *The Gainesville Sun.*
7. "I thought let's just get..." ~ Rotman, Natalie. (2009, November 30). Tom Petty releases 'Live Anthology' disc set. *The Seattle Times.*
8. "There was a minute-long..." ~ Marks, Craig; & Tannenbaum, Rob. (2011). *I Want My MTV.* New York: Dutton.
9. "I didn't even want to..." ~ Hilburn, Robert. (1987, May 24). A Petty mood: A classic rocker's passion is refreshed. *The Los Angeles Times.*
10. "L.A. is not nearly as..." ~ Morse, Steve. (1983, March 24). Tom Petty: A survivor. *The Boston Globe.*
11. "We played a little country..." ~ DeYoung, Bill. (1983, February 4). Be it ever so humble: Tom Petty talks about home. *The Gainesville Sun.*
12. "After that last tour, I..." ~ Robert, Palmer. (1985, March 25). A new album by Petty and the Heartbreakers. *The New York Times.*
13. "I just needed time off..." ~ Hilburn, Robert. (1985, March 31). Tom Petty tries his hand at Southern rock. *The Los Angeles Times.*
14. "It was reaching a point..." ~ Gilmore, Mikal. (1986, July 17). Positively Dylan. *Rolling Stone.*
15. "It took us all getting..." ~ Robertson, Sandy. (1985, April 20). Petty prime. *Sounds.*

CHAPTER 19: PETTY'S SOUTHERN ROOTS

1. "It's always taken us a..." ~ Palmer, Robert. (1985, March 25). A new album by Petty and the Heartbreakers. *The New York Times.*
2. "For a while I thought..." ~ DeYoung, Bill. (1985, May 6). Breaking form: Tom Petty's change of heart. *Music.*
3. "drugs had entered the picture" ~ Tom Petty and the Heartbreakers. (1999). *Behind the Music.* New York: VH1.
4. "It was kind of like..." ~ Taylor, Jonathon. (1986, June 22). Tom Petty: Good ol' boy making good music. *The Chicago Tribune.*
5. "Tom was dancing with the..." ~ Sweeting, Adam. (2004, May). Southern Accents. *Uncut.*

6. "My manager and I were..." ~ Hilburn, Robert. (1985, March 31). Tom Petty tries his hand at Southern rock. *The Los Angeles Times.*
7. While recuperating in a hospital... ~ Blake, Mark. (2012, July). He knew he was right. *Q.*
8. "When I broke my hand..." ~ Scoppa, Bud. (1985, August). Tom Petty's year (or two) of living dangerously. *Record.*
9. "I know he didn't mean..." ~ Hochanadel, Michael. (1985, June 15). Petty, Heartbreakers 'fresh' for SPAC show. *The Schenectady Gazette.*
10. "Breaking my hand was unfortunate..." ~ Rosen, Steven. (1985, Summer). Tom Petty and the Heartbreakers: Even the winners get lucky sometime. *International Musicians and Recording World.*
11. "I hope I don't have..." ~ Rosen, Steven. (1985, Summer). Tom Petty and the Heartbreakers: Even the winners get lucky sometime. *International Musicians and Recording World.*
12 "There were three important songs..." ~ Hill, Dave. (1989, May 5). Petty's bourgeois songs. *The (London) Independent.*
13. "We had lived in California..." ~ Hilburn, Robert. (2002, March 15). No backing down. *The Los Angeles Times.*
14. "Coming back after spending time..." ~ Taylor, Jonathon. (1986, June 22). Tom Petty: Good ol' boy making good music. *The Chicago Tribune.*
15. "Here is Petty at his..." ~ Millman, Joyce. (1985, May 23). Tom Petty's rebel yell. *Rolling Stone.*
16. "When I read the reviews..." ~ Smith, Joe. (1988). *Off the Record: An Oral History of Popular Music.* New York: Warner Books.
17. "If you go down to..." ~ Flanagan, Bill. (1986, April). Tom Petty pulls together: The Southern soul of a Hollywood rocker. *Musician.*
18. "We recorded it first in..." ~ Flanagan, Bill. (1986, April). Tom Petty pulls together: The Southern soul of a Hollywood rocker. *Musician.*
19. "I want to be your..." ~ Stewart, Dave. (2008). *The Dave Stewart Songbook: The Stories Behind the Songs, Volume One.* Encinitas, CA: Surfdog.
20. Walsh and Nicks would reconcile... ~ Brown, Mick. (2007, September 8). Stevie Nicks: A survivor's story. *The (London) Telegraph.*
21. "Tom Petty came down and..." ~ Stewart, Dave. (2008). *The Dave Stewart Songbook: The Stories Behind the Songs, Volume One.* Encinitas, CA: Surfdog.
22. "He said to Jimmy, 'I..." ~ Stewart, Dave. (2008). *The Dave Stewart Songbook: The Stories Behind the Songs, Volume One.* Encinitas, CA: Surfdog.
23. "Even though I was deeply..." ~ Stewart, Dave. (2008). *The Dave Stewart Songbook: The Stories Behind the Songs, Volume One.* Encinitas, CA: Surfdog.
24. "wearin' like a Kentucky general's..." ~ Scoppa, Bud. (1985, August). Tom Petty's year (or two) of living dangerously. *Record.*
25. "I wanted to make a..." ~ Derogatis, Jim. (2003, April 13). Damn the torpedoes. *The Chicago Sun Times.*
26. "When we wrote that, it..." ~ Flanagan, Bill. (1986, April). Tom Petty pulls together: The Southern soul of a Hollywood rocker. *Musician.*
27. "I just got carried away..." ~ Flanagan, Bill. (1986, April). Tom Petty pulls together: The Southern soul of a Hollywood rocker. *Musician.*
28. "It was my idea to..." ~ Freff. (1985, June). Tom Petty & Dave Stewart?! *Musician.*
29. "There were two camps when... ~ DeYoung, Bill. (1985, May 6). Breaking form: Tom Petty's change of heart. *Music.*
30. "The director [Jeff Stein] and..." ~ Robertson, Sandy. (1985, April 20). Petty prime. *Sounds.*
31. "admitted [to] experiencing 'Paradise Syndrome'..." ~ Scott, Paul. (2013, August 4). How pop's most toxic love affair cast a shadow over SIX marriages. *The Daily Mail.*
32. "[MTV] actually made me edit..." ~ Newman, Melinda. (2005, December 3). Tom Petty: A portrait of the artist. *Billboard.*
33. "A visual image doesn't have..." ~ Gore, Tipper. (1986). *Raising PG Kids in an X-Rated Society.* Nashville: Abingdon Press.

34. "Mike [Campbell] didn't like it..." ~ Newman, Melinda. (2005, December 3). Tom Petty: A portrait of the artist. *Billboard*.
35. "It's never going to be..." ~ Goldberg, Michael. (1986, January 16). Back on the road. *Rolling Stone*.
36. "I remember hiring all those..." ~ Schruers, Fred. (1995, May 4). Tom Petty on the road: This is how it feels. *Rolling Stone*.
37. "now sports 1965 Byrds' granny..." ~ Marlowe, Jon. (1985, July 18). Off the record: Byrd-watching with Tom Petty. *The Miami News*.
38. "insensitivity" ~ George, Nelson. (1986, May 10). Rhythm & blues. *Billboard*.
39. "One of those guys in..." ~ Scoppa, Bud. (1987, August). Tom Petty & The Heartbreakers: Less is more, more or less. *Creem*.
40. "I had received a call..." ~ Cash, Rosanne. (2010). *Composed: A Memoir*. New York: Viking.
41. "When I re-signed there wasn't..." ~ Rowland, Mark. (1987, September). Heartbreaker straight ahead. *Musician*.

CHAPTER 20: LIVE AID & FARM AID

1. "Paul didn't ask me to..." ~ Jones, Dylan. (2013). The Eighties: One Day, One Decade. London: Preface.
2. "I had called Dylan through..." ~ Geldof, Bob. (1988). *Is That it?* New York: Ballantine.
3. "crass, stupid and nationalistic" ~ Geldof, Bob. (1988). *Is that it?* New York: Ballantine.
4. "We spent a week rehearsing..." ~ Goldberg, Michael. (1986, January 16). Back on the road. *Rolling Stone*.
5. "There was nobody in the..." ~ George-Warren, Holly (Ed.). (2005). *Farm Aid: A Song for America*. New York: Rodale.
6. "When we went to the..." ~ Goldberg, Michael. (1986, January 16). Back on the road. *Rolling Stone*.
7. "Live Aid and Farm Aid..." ~ Gilmore, Mikal. (1985, October 13). Behind the glasses, Dylan at 44 looking scruffy but ready. *The Los Angeles Herald-Examiner*.

CHAPTER 21: DYLAN & PETTY

1. "Are you kidding? Put me..." ~ Goldberg, Michael. (1986, January 16). Back on the road. *Rolling Stone*.
2. "I was a little nervous..." ~ Rowland, Mark. (1987, September). Heartbreaker straight ahead. *Musician*.
3. "[Dylan would say], 'Here's the..." ~ Bream, Jon. (1986, June 22). The many faces of Bob Dylan. *The (Minneapolis-St.Paul) Star Tribune*.
4. "after the under-rehearsed band..." ~ DeCurtis, Anthony. (1986, March 27). Dylan down under. *Rolling Stone*.
5. "According to some reviews, the..." ~ Gilmore, Mikal. (1986, July 17). Positively Dylan. *Rolling Stone*.
6. "It was an interesting thing..." ~ Flanagan, Bill. (1986, April). Tom Petty pulls together: The Southern soul of a Hollywood rocker. *Musician*.
7. "I got to sing 'Knockin..." ~ White, Timothy. (1990). *Rock Lives*. New York: Henry Holt and Company.
8. While in New Zealand, Bob... ~ Sounes, Howard. (2001). *Down the Highway: The Life of Bob Dylan*. New York: Grove Press.
9. "Everyone's always saying to me..." ~ Gilmore, Mikal. (1986, July 17). Positively Dylan. *Rolling Stone*.
10. "With the rehearsals and the..." ~ Obrecht, Jas. (1986, August). Tom Petty: The dying art of rhythm guitar. *Guitar Player*.
11. "With singers, he used little..." ~ Scoppa, Bud. (1987, June 1). Winging it with Petty & Campbell. *Music Connection*.
12. "It's a sure bet that..." ~ Tucker, Ken. (1986, July 21). Music: Dylan and Petty at Spectrum. *The Philadelphia Inquirer*.

13. "one of the most forgettable..." ~ Sounes, Howard. (2001). *Down the Highway: The Life of Bob Dylan*. New York: Grove Press.
14. "As a matter of fact..." ~ Flanagan, Bill. (1986, April). Tom Petty pulls together: The Southern soul of a Hollywood rocker. *Musician*.
15. "If the audience wanted a..." ~ Taylor, Jonathon. (1986, June 15). Bob Dylan plus Tom Petty adds up to tour de force for concert. *The Chicago Tribune*.
16. "he somehow thought it was..." ~ Simmons, Sylvie. (2006, October). Rock of ages. *Mojo*.
17. "Garcia had attended a Dylan-Petty..." ~ Jackson, Blair. (2000). *Garcia: An American Life*. New York: Penguin.
18. "I gotta say, when we..." ~ Potter, Mitch. (1989, June 11). Tom Petty: Mellowing of a rebel. *The Toronto Star*.
19. "We started playing around at..." ~ Zimmer, Dave. (1989, May 5). Once in a full moon. *BAM*.
20. "I remember coming home with..." ~ Sharp, Ken. (2013, January). The dream team. *Goldmine*.
21. "He was very nervous about..." ~ Corcoran, Michael. (1989, August). Raised on promises. *Spin*.
22. "While they were mixing [the..." ~ Sharp, Ken. (2013, January). The dream team. *Goldmine*.
23. "All the songs were written..." ~ Morse, Steve. (1989, May 4). Tom Petty's year off wasn't to be. *The Boston Globe*.
24. "About a year later I..." ~ Wild, David. (1991, August 8). Over the hump. *Rolling Stone*.
25. "Brian Epstein got a chuckle..." ~ Goldman, Albert. (1992). *Sound bites*. New York: Turtle Bay Books.
26. "I really have turned down..." ~ Miller, Eric T. (2003, January/February). If I had my way, I'd tear the building down. *Magnet*.
27. "[Mellencamp] said a turning point..." ~ Light, Alan. (2007, January 22). Changes in Mellencamp country. *The New York Times*.
28. "They called me and asked..." ~ Matthews, Tom. (2010, November 22). Heart Breaker. *Milwaukee Magazine*. (1987, May 7). *Lodi News-Sentinel*.
29. "We have seen so many..." ~ Densmore, John. (2013). *Unhinged: The Doors, Jim Morrison's Legacy Goes on Trial*. North Charleston, SCL Percussive Press.
30. "I remember reading about Petty..." ~ Densmore, John. (2013). *Unhinged: The Doors, Jim Morrison's Legacy Goes on Trial*. North Charleston, SCL Percussive Press.

CHAPTER 22: REFUGEE: THE HOUSE FIRE

1. "It started out that Bob..." ~ Holan, Marc. (1987, June 19). Tom Petty & The Heartbreakers: America's hardest working band. *Scene*.
2. "We didn't tinker with this..." ~ Rowland, Mark. (1987, September). Heartbreaker straight ahead. *Musician*.
3. "Our engineer, Don Smith, would..." ~ Rowland, Mark. (1987, September). Heartbreaker straight ahead. *Musician*.
4. "there's two or three songs..." ~ Rowland, Mark. (1987, September). Heartbreaker straight ahead. *Musician*.
5. "a small plane that actually..." ~ DeYoung, Bill. (1987, April 17). Tom Petty & the Heartbreakers' new album is a rocker. *The Gainesville Sun*.
6. "We were just taking names..." ~ DeCurtis, Anthony. (1987, May 7). Tom Petty's new LP: Back to basics. *Rolling Stone*.
7. "we weren't puttin' him down..." ~ Scoppa, Bud. (1987, June 1). Winging it with Petty & Campbell. *Music Connection*.
8. "Tallulah Bankhead and [televangelist] Jerry..." ~ Mars, Melanie. (1987, June 24). Dylan influence obvious in Petty concert. *The [Washington, Pennsylvania] Observer-Reporter*.
9. "On 'All Mixed Up,' we..." ~ Scoppa, Bud. (1987, August). Tom Petty & The Heartbreakers: Less is more, more or less. *Creem*.
10. In an odd series of events... ~ Nicks, Stevie; & Stewart, Dave [Directors]. (2013). *Stevie Nicks: In Your Dreams*. Virgil Films and Entertainment.

11. "I was really glad to..." ~ Uhelszki, Jaan. (1999, June). Echo chamber. *Guitar Magazine*.
12. "The band is pretty weirded..." ~ Racine, Marty. (May 29, 1987). For Petty, troubles don't stop the music. *The Houston Chronicle*.
13. "The funny thing was I..." ~ Uhelszki, Jaan. (1999, June). Echo chamber. *Guitar Magazine*.

CHAPTER 23: HANDLE WITH CARE

1. "I took Dylan to see..." ~ Flanagan, Bill. (1990, April). The Heartbreakers highway. *Musician*.
2. "In these first four shows..." ~ Dylan, Bob, (2004). *Chronicles: Volume One*. New York: Simon & Schuster.
3. "We were pretty worn out..." ~ Uhelszki, Jaan. (2012, June). Tom Petty: Won't back down. *Uncut*.
4. "I just thought, okay, it's..." ~ Simmons, Sylvie. (2006, October). Rock of ages. *Mojo*.
5. "By the time we got..." ~ Hilburn, Robert. (1987, May 24). A Petty mood: A classic rocker's passion is refreshed. *The Los Angeles Times*.
6. "I'd been on an eighteen..." ~ Dylan, Bob, (2004). *Chronicles: Volume One*. New York: Simon & Schuster.
7. "I first met him in..." ~ Udovitch, Mim; & Wild, David. (2002, January 17). Remembering George. *Rolling Stone*.
8. "I reminded him that we'd..." ~ Udovitch, Mim; & Wild, David. (2002, January 17). Remembering George. *Rolling Stone*.
9. "I went back to L.A..." ~ Udovitch, Mim; & Wild, David. (2002, January 17). Remembering George. *Rolling Stone*.
10. "We weren't even thinking about..." ~ Zimmer, Dave. (1989, May 5). Once in a full moon. *BAM*.
11. "I agreed because I was..." ~ Nash, Jesse. (1989, November). Roy Orbison. *Music Express*.
12. "when Roy started to go..." ~ Amburn, Ellis. (1990). *Dark Star: The Roy Orbison Story*. New York: Carol Publishing Group.
13. "His songs had songs within..." ~ Dylan, Bob, (2004). *Chronicles: Volume One*. New York: Simon & Schuster.
14. "The people who walked out..." ~ Shelton, Robert. (2011). *No Direction Home: The Life and Music of Bob Dylan*. Milwaukee: Hal Leonard Corporation.
15. "George, in his late twenties..." ~ Shapiro, Marc. (2005). *All Things Must Pass: The Life of George Harrison*. London: Virgin.
16. "We were three-quarters of..." ~ Scopa, Bud. (2007, September). The inside story of the Traveling Wilburys: Rock's greatest ever supergroup. *Uncut*.
17. "So [Jeff Lynne] had Roy..." ~ Zimmer, Dave. (1989, May 5). Once in a full moon. *BAM*. 17. "Tom called me down to..." ~ Guerra, Tom. (2008, March). Mike Campbell. *ToneQuest Report*.
18. "'Handle With Care' was finished..." ~ Scoppa, Bud. (2007, September). The inside story of the Traveling Wilburys. *Uncut*.
19. "The record company said, 'Oh..." ~ Rowland, Mark. (1990, March). The quiet Wilbury. *Musician*.
20. "He and Jeff used to..." ~ Hurwitz, Matt. (2007, June 11). Wilburys set to travel again. *USA Today*.
21. "We all jumped in a..." ~ Zimmer, Dave. (1989, May 5). Once in a full moon. *BAM*.
22. "We didn't ask any of..." ~ Ashton, Martin. (1989, February 24). Last testament, blue angel, *BAM*.
23. "It was kind of weird..." ~ Stewart, Dave. (2008). *The Dave Stewart Songbook: The Stories Behind the Songs, Volume One*. Encinitas, CA: Surfdog.
24. "Well, they treated me equally..." ~ di Perna, Alan. (1999, April). Tom Petty: American boy. *Pulse*.
25. "We got everyone to agree..." ~ Rowland, Mark. (1990, March). The quiet Wilbury. *Musician*.
26. "We'd start out every day..." ~ Scopa, Bud. (2007, September). The inside story of the Traveling Wilburys: Rock's greatest ever supergroup. *Uncut*.

27. "We usually went by a..." ~ Rowland, Mark. (1990, March). The quiet Wilbury. *Musician*.
28. "Supergroups are almost always a..." ~ Milward, John. (1989, May 4). Petty and the Wilburys: Supergroup success story. *The Philadelphia Inquirer*.
29. "Just getting some famous people..." ~ Rowland, Mark. (1990, March). The quiet Wilbury. *Musician*.
30. "We definitely didn't want to..." ~ Bauder, David. (1988, December 14). Legends joined to become "Traveling Wilburys." *The Fort Scott (Kansas) Tribune*.
31. "each of the five mythical..." ~ Holden, Stephen. (1988, November 16). The pop life: Those Wilbury boys. *The New York Times*.
32. "I wanna be a mega-star. I..." ~ Balfour, Victoria. (1986). *Rock Wives*. New York: Beech Tree Books.
33. "My domestic life was in..." ~ Gold, Adam. (2011, September 29). Nick Lowe: The Cream interview. *Nashville Scene*.
34. "I definitely won't get married..." ~ Balfour, Victoria. (1986). *Rock Wives*. New York: Beech Tree Books.
35. Before moving into their renovated... ~ Wild, David. (1991, August 8). Over the hump. *Rolling Stone*.
36. "kind of a cross between..." ~ "Tom Petty's *Pet Sounds*." (1994, November 6). *Newsweek*.

CHAPTER 24: SONGS FROM THE GARAGE

1. "My life changed, the whole..." ~ Schruers, Fred. (1995, May 4). Tom Petty on the road: This is how it feels. *Rolling Stone*.
2. "I think there was some..." ~ Mitchell, Rick. (1989, July 9). Veteran rocker has never sounded better. *The Houston Chronicle*.
3. "[Benmont Tench] used to say..." ~ Holan, Marc. (1991, September 6). A conversation with Tom Petty. *Scene*.
4. "It's the only time in..." ~ Newman, Melinda. (2005, December 3). Tom Petty: A portrait of the artist. *Billboard*.
5. "I carried a tape around..." ~ Gundersen, Edna. (1990, February 9). Petty at his peak. *USA Today*.
6. "We had Tom Petty on..." ~ Moseley, Willie G. (2002, October). Chris Hillman: Bluegrass, bass, and back again. *Vintage Guitar*.
7. "My daughter thought I wrote..." ~ DeYoung, Bill. (1989, April 26). Tom Petty presents a solo album. *The Gainesville Sun*.
8. "*Full Moon Fever* isn't Petty's..." ~ Guterman, Jimmy. (1989, May 4). Tom Petty's solo effort: An infectious 'fever.' *Rolling Stone*.
9. "The album seemed a turning..." ~ Simmons, Sylvie. (1989, June 14). Moonlighting. *Raw*.
10. "It was sort of deliberate..." ~ Simmons, Sylvie. (1989, June 14). Moonlighting. *Raw*.
11. "acoustic wall of sound..." ~ Dye, Robert; & Trost, Isaiah. (2003, March 10). Rock and roll animals. *Guitar World Acoustic*.
12. "a deeply inspired, very Harrison-esque..." ~ Aledort, Andy. (1995, August). Chartbreaker. *Guitar School*.
13. "'I Won't Back Down' is..." ~ Uhelszki, Jaan. (2006, July/August). Tom Petty: Anatomy of a rockstar. *Harp*.
14. When Harrison arrived at the... ~ Guerra, Tom. (2008, March). Mike Campbell. *ToneQuest Report*.
15. "It was George's idea to..." ~ Fricke, David. (2009, December 10). It's good to be king. *Rolling Stone*.
16. "To me American music was..." ~ Simmons, Sylvie. (2006, October). Rock of ages. *Mojo*.
17. The track would set a... ~ Whitburn, Joel. (2008). *Rock Tracks 1981-2008*. Menomonee Falls, WI: Record Research.
18. "I don't think we had..." ~ Newman, Melinda. (2005, December 3). Tom Petty: A portrait of the artist. *Billboard*.
19. "That was the first time..." ~ Wild, David. (1991, August 8). Over the hump. *Rolling Stone*.

20. "cattle horns, a suit of..." ~ Willman, Chris. (1989, July 27). Petty & Heartbreakers take a classic stance. *The Los Angeles Times.*
21. "For the first time in..." ~ Wild, David. (1991, August 8). Over the hump. *Rolling Stone.*
22. "Axl said, 'I know this...'" ~ Flanagan, Bill. (1990, April). The Heartbreakers highway. *Musician.*
23. "All my blood rushed into..." ~ Motley Crue; & Strauss, Neil. (2002). *The Dirt.* New York: HarperEntertainment.
24. "Well, you know us. We..." ~ Flanagan, Bill. (1990, April). The Heartbreakers highway. *Musician.*
25. "The Heartbreakers want to stay..." ~ Flanagan, Bill. (1990, April). The Heartbreakers highway. *Musician.*
26. "We don't have any plans..." ~ Holan, Mark. (1989, June 8). Of full moons and Wilburys. *Scene.*
27. "A lot of money was..." ~ Wild, David. (1991, August 8). Over the hump. *Rolling Stone.*
28. "I wish we had played..." ~ McCormick, Neil. (2012, June 16). Tom Petty: A rock star for the ages. *The Daily Telegraph.*
29. "promoters kept calling and calling" ~ Flanagan, Bill. (1990, April). The Heartbreakers highway. *Musician.*

CHAPTER 25: RETURN OF THE TRAVELING WILBURYS

1. "along with songwriters like Tom..." ~ Schoemer, Karen. (1992, January 19). John Mellencamp's carnival. *The New York Times.*
2. "The way Roy saw life..." ~ Zimmer, Dave. (1989, May 5). Once in a full moon. *BAM.*
3. "I always felt like he..." ~ Lanham, Tom. (1994, December). Petty on the inside. *Pulse.*
4. "You can't replace Roy Orbison..." ~ Rowland, Mark. (1990, March). The quiet Wilbury. *Musician.*
5. "That was George's idea..." ~ Hurwitz, Matt. (2007, June 11). Wilburys set to travel again. *USA Today.*
6. "People don't listen to records..." ~ Rowland, Mark. (1997, January). Beck meets Petty: Rockin', writin', survivin' in L.A. *Musician.*
7. "There's no telling what kind..." ~ Gundersen, Edna. (1990, November 7). On 'Vol. 3,' the Traveling Wilburys enjoy the ride. *USA Today.*
8. "It was Roy's presence [that]..." ~ Sounes, Howard. (2001). *Down the Highway: The Life of Bob Dylan.* New York: Grove Press.
9. "Last time, it was a..." ~ Gundersen, Edna. (1990, November 7). On 'Vol. 3,' the Traveling Wilburys enjoy the ride. *USA Today.*
10. "[it] stays close to 1950's..." ~ Pareles, Jon. (1990, November 4). Shake, rattle and growing old with the Wilburys. *The New York Times.*
11. "We had to switch them..." ~ Holan, Marc. (1991, September 6). A conversation with Tom Petty. *Scene.*
12. "The others were all released..." ~ Ressner, Jeffrey. (1991, October). Tom Petty: Traveling Heartbreaker. *CD Review.*

CHAPTER 26: THE TIMES THEY ARE A-CHANGING

1. "I think it was probably..." ~ Sharp, Ken. (2013, January). The dream team. *Goldmine.*
2. "They dug Jeff. It was..." ~ Ressner, Jeffrey. (1991, October). Tom Petty: Traveling Heartbreaker. *CD Review.*
3. "Maybe it was a case..." ~ Flanagan, Bill. (1994, November). Into the great wide open. *Mojo.*
4. "full of hazy references, half-baked..." ~ Racine, Marty. (1991, June 30). Mediocrity from Tom Petty. *The Houston Chronicle.*
5. "We just wanted to capture..." ~ Goldstein, Patrick. (1991, August 25). Tom Petty is mad as a hatter in 'Wide Open' video. *The Los Angeles Times.*
6. Petty had made the decision... ~ Newman, Melinda. (2005, December 3). Tom Petty: A portrait of the artist. *Billboard.*

7. "estimated $20-million, six-album pact" ~ Philips, Chuck. (1992, April 5). Petty's secret Warners deal isn't for petty cash. *The Los Angeles Times.*
8. "because he was disappointed with..." ~ Philips, Chuck. (1992, April 5). Petty's secret Warners deal isn't for petty cash. *The Los Angeles Times.*
9. "Although short in stature, Mo..." ~ Goldberg, Danny. (2008). *Bumping into Geniuses.* New York: Gotham Books.
10. An unhappy Stan Lynch flew... ~ Carr, Daphne. (2008, January 16). Tom Petty's Los Angeles. *L.A. Weekly.*
11. "I avoid being on those..." ~ Thomas, Brett. (1994, September 18). Tom terrific. *The (Sydney, Australia) Sun Herald.*
12. "I was actually listening to..." ~ Berkery, Patrick. (2008, May). Stan Lynch. *Modern Drummer.*
13. "one of the most revolting..." ~ Russell, Deborah. (1994, January 14). The eye: Dead beat. *Billboard.*

CHAPTER 27: RICK RUBIN & WILDFLOWERS
1. While growing up in Long... ~ Hirschberg, Lynn. (1997, September 2). The music man. *The New York Times.*
2. Ironically, during this period Petty... ~ Zanes, Warren. (2008). *Revolutions in Sound: Warner Brothers Records, the First Fifty Years.* San Francisco: Chronicle Books.
3. "Mike had met Rick and..." ~ Flanagan, Bill. (1994, December). Frontman: Tom Petty. *Musician.*
4. "He did drive me a..." ~ Jackson, Alan. (1994, October 14). Too busy being big to be Petty. *The Times of London.*
5. "Tom Petty's *Wildflowers* would be..." ~ Wilde, Jon. (2005, April). Renaissance Maniac. *Uncut.*
6. "*Wildflowers* took a massively long..." ~ Lanham, Tom. (1994, December). Petty on the inside. *Pulse.*
7. "*Wildflowers* covered really everything that..." ~ Newman, Melinda. (2005, December 3). Tom Petty: A portrait of the artist. *Billboard.*
8. "I wasn't getting along with..." ~ Simmons, Sylvie. (2006, October). Rock of ages. *Mojo.*
9. "The studios were screwed up..." ~ Gundersen, Edna. (1994, November 15). Purely Petty: No backing down from rock's edge. *USA Today.*
10. "[Petty] ruminates about love, loneliness..." ~ Halvonik, Steve. (1994, November 4). Tom Petty: 'Wildflowers.' *The Pittsburgh Post-Gazette.*
11. "Tom is aware of this..." ~ Catlin, Roger. (1995, March 30). Petty's rocking the joint (joint?). *The Hartford Courant.*
12. "I don't want to be..." ~ Catlin, Roger. (1995, March 30). Petty's rocking the joint (joint?). *The Hartford Courant.*
13. "I enjoy a good joint..." ~ Rensin, David. (1982, September). 20 questions: Tom Petty. *Playboy.*
14. "no bones about his displeasure..." ~ DeYoung, Bill. (1995, November 21). The beat of a different drum: Stan Lynch finds life's just fine after Tom Petty and The Heartbreakers. *The Gainesville Sun.*
15. "It's gotten to the point..." ~ Jackson, Blair. (1983, January 28). There's a lot more to the Heartbreakers than Tom Petty. *BAM.*
16. "He wanted to do a..." ~ Soren, Tabitha. (1995, October 5). Veteran rocker Into the great wide open: Tom Petty to play homecoming show. *The Tuscaloosa News.*
17. "Over time, people have such..." ~ DeYoung, Bill. (1994, October 22). Drummer Stan Lynch leaves Tom Petty's band. *The Ocala Star-Banner.*
18. "Stan and I always had..." ~ Schruers, Fred. (1995, May 4). Tom Petty on the road: This is how it feels. *Rolling Stone.*
19. "I introduced myself as Stan..." ~ Troyanek, Madelyn. (2005, April 10). Former rock and roll star lives the quiet life on the beach, finds success as hit song writer. *The St. Augustine*

Record.
20. "Am I a fool to..." ~ DeYoung, Bill. (1995, November 21). The beat of a different drum: Stan Lynch finds life's just fine after Tom Petty and the Heartbreakers. *The Gainesville Sun.*
21. "I'm pissed at myself for..." ~ Berkery, Patrick. (2008, May). Stan Lynch. *Modern Drummer.*
22. "He came very close to..." ~ Morse, Steve. (1995, December 1). Many-sided boxes: Petty and Cocker collections go beyond the hits. *The Boston Globe.*
23. "Growing up in Brighton, I..." ~ Pryor, Sam. (2010, August). Steve Ferrone: Tapping into 40 years of groove. *Drum! Magazine.*
24. "I used to be with..." ~ Miller, William F. (1995, May). Steve Ferrone: Subtlety mastered. *Modern Drummer.*
25. "I really just screwed around..." ~ Keefe, Brent. (2012, August). Feeling it. *Drummer.*
26. "That was one of the..." ~ Miller, William F. (1995, May). Steve Ferrone: Subtlety mastered. *Modern Drummer.*
27. "It was all very straightforward..." ~ Miller, William F. (1995, May). Steve Ferrone: Subtlety mastered. *Modern Drummer.*
28. "a few days later, Thurston..." ~ Trynka, Paul. (2007). *Iggy Pop: Open Up and Bleed.* New York: Broadway Books.
29. "Eventually, Thurston got used to..." ~ Trynka, Paul. (2007). *Iggy Pop: Open Up and Bleed.* New York: Broadway Books.
30. "always saw himself as a..." ~ Schruers, Fred. (1999, July 7). Tom Petty: The *Rolling Stone* interview. *Rolling Stone.*
31. "It was the best look..." ~ Matthews, Tom. (2010, November 22). Heart Breaker. *Milwaukee Magazine.*
32. "I look over the set..." ~ Schruers, Fred. (1995, May 4). Tom Petty on the road: This is how it feels. *Rolling Stone.*
33. "young people at the show..." ~ Catlin, Roger. (1995, April 2). Tom Petty reaffirms his universal appeal. *The Hartford Courant.*
34. "We actually had two teenage..." ~ Schruers, Fred. (1995, May 4). Tom Petty on the road: This is how it feels. *Rolling Stone.*
35. "I've never even gone to..." ~ Miller, Eric T. (2003, January/February). If I had my way, I'd tear the building down. *Magnet.*

CHAPTER 28: OUT IN THE COLD

1. "For a long time, I..." ~ Rensin, David. (1982, September). 20 questions: Tom Petty. *Playboy.*
2. "You've got to always remember..." ~ Balfour, Victoria. (1986). *Rock Wives.* New York: Beech Tree Books.
3. "I was living in a..." ~ Strauss, Neil. (2006, July 13). Tom Petty's last dance. *Rolling Stone.*
4. "After the long tour we..." ~ di Perna, Alan. (1999, April). Tom Petty: American boy. *Pulse.*
5. "It was a challenge – how..." ~ Farber, Jim. (1999, April 18). Tom Petty gets personal. *The New York Daily News.*
6. "an affection for California and..." ~ Puterbaugh, Parke. (1996, September 5). She's the one: Tom Petty and the Heartbreakers. *Rolling Stone.*

CHAPTER 29: HELLO, MY NAME IS JOHNNY CASH

1. "[Rubin] came in one day..." ~ Simmons, Silvie. (2010, July 10). Revolution! *Mojo.*
2. "I took note of Bob..." ~ Cash, Johnny. (1997). *Cash: The Autobiography.* San Francisco: HarperSanFrancisco.
3. "the ultimate hippie, bald on..." ~ Cash, Johnny. (1997). *Cash: The Autobiography.* San Francisco: HarperSanFrancisco.
4. "According to the media at..." ~ Cash, Johnny. (1997). *Cash: The Autobiography.* San Francisco: HarperSanFrancisco.
5. "There'd be June telling me..." ~ Simmons, Silvie. (2010, July 10). Revolution! *Mojo.*
6. "It was like being in..." ~ Ellis, Bill. (1999, August 6). Heartbreakers stick to what they like: Rousing classic rock. *The Memphis Commercial Appeal.*

7. "It felt like God was..." ~ Simmons, Silvie. (2010, July 10). Revolution! *Mojo*.
8. "I just want to play..." ~ Selvin, Joel. (1997, January 9). Petty ready to play. *The San Francisco Chronicle*.
9. "Buddy Holly to John Mayall..." ~ Elwood, Philip. (1997, January 12). Petty preaches gospel of rock 'n' roll. *The San Francisco Chronicle*.
10. "The second night was maybe..." ~ Joel, Selvin. (1997, February 16). They've had enough: Just for now. *The San Francisco Chronicle*.
11. "I started writing the album..." ~ Farber, Jim. (1999, April 18). Tom Petty gets personal. *The New York Daily News*.
12. "It was a long process..." ~ Hughley, Marty. (1999, August 27). Heart to heart with a 'Breaker: Benmont Tench shares his love for the music. *The Oregonian*.
13. "We thought on this one..." ~ McCollum, Brian. (1999, April 11). Rock success is a simple matter for Tom Petty. *The Detroit Free Press*.
14. "Musically, this record is an..." ~ Norman, Michael. (1999, June 13). Rock's everyman Petty believes in his music. *The Cleveland Plain Dealer*.
15. "Petty and the Heartbreakers define..." ~ Kot, Greg. (1999, April 29). Tom Petty and the Heartbreakers: Echo. *Rolling Stone*.
16. "That *Echo* album was one..." ~ Hilburn, Robert. (2002, March 15). No backing down. *The Los Angeles Times*.
17. "It was hard for him..." ~ Graff, Gary. (2002, June 28). Tom Petty: Rock star just glad to be a member of the band. *The Cleveland Plain Dealer*.
18. "She had a boss who..." ~ Farber, Jim. (1999, April 18). Tom Petty gets personal. *The New York Daily News*.
19. "one of the most depressing..." ~ Gundersen, Edna. (2006, July 25). Tom Petty: Into the great wide open. *USA Today*.
20. "I just started making up..." ~ Uhelszki, Jaan. (1999, June). Echo chamber. *Guitar Magazine*.
21. "I'm really pissed that Howie..." ~ Matthews, Tom. (2010, November 22). Heart Breaker. *Milwaukee Magazine*.
22. "Going through with that was..." ~ Schruers, Fred. (1999, July 7). Tom Petty: The *Rolling Stone* interview. *Rolling Stone*.

CHAPTER 30: HAVE LOVE, WILL TRAVEL

1. "[Little Richard] was really nervous..." ~ Kot, Greg. (2001, July 20). Tom petty, regular rocker. *The Chicago Tribune*.
2. Building a home studio in... ~ Uhelszki, Jaan. (2012, June). Tom Petty: Won't back down. *Uncut*.
3. "It's been an ongoing issue..." ~ Kot, Greg. (2001, July 20). Tom Petty, regular rocker. *The Chicago Tribune*.
4. "I was mostly just amazed..." ~ Thompson, Art. (2006, July). The heart of the matter: Mike Campbell on crafting the Heartbreakers' guitar sounds. *Guitar Player*.
5. "We never thought we were..." ~ Hiatt, Brian. (2011, September 15). The private life of George Harrison. *Rolling Stone*.
6. "It's such a shame that..." ~ Fitzpatrick, Rob. (2009, November 15). New Tom Petty album *The Live Anthology*. *The Times of London*.
7. "My daughter Adria used to..." ~ Petty, Tom. (2002, January 17). Remembering George. *Rolling Stone*.
8. "We only had to work..." ~ Eliscu, Jenny; & Scaggs, Austin. (2002, April 25). Petty, Heads, Ramones lead Hall of Fame class of 2002. *Rolling Stone*.
9. "A little bag of dust..." ~ Matthews, Tom. (2010, November 22). Heart Breaker. *Milwaukee Magazine*.
10. "It's very easy to be..." ~ Moody, Nekesa Mumbi. (2002, March 19). Ramones, Petty among those ushered into the Rock Hall. *The Bowling Green (Kentucky) Daily News*.
11. "The 51-year-old Petty..." ~ Sauro, Tony. (2002, September 2). With Tom Petty, the only change is for the better. *The Stockton Record*.

CHAPTER 31: AMERICA'S LAST DJ

1. "I would feel embarrassed charging..." ~ Hiatt, Brian. (2005, August 11). Petty rules road. *Rolling Stone.*
2. "What they do in terms..." ~ Lindquist, David. (2002, February 17). American dreamers. *Indianapolis Star.*
3. "work of fiction: It's a..." ~ Derogatis, Jim. (2003, April 13). Damn the torpedoes. *The Chicago Sun Times.*
4. "The radio today is just..." ~ Rowland, Mark. (1997, January). Beck meets Petty: Rockin', writin', survivin' in L.A. *Musician.*
5. "I remember a time when..." ~ Thompson, Art. (1999, May). Heartbreaker hideout in the studio with Tom Petty & Mike Campbell. *Guitar Player.*
6. "the celebration of mediocrity in..." ~ Wild, David. (2002, March 28). Petty, aim, fire! *Rolling Stone.*
7. "For so much of my..." ~ Fricke, David. (2009, December 10). It's good to be king. *Rolling Stone.*
8. "It may sound like I'm..." ~ Farber, Jim. (2002, October 6). Fighting the good fight. *The New York Daily News.*
9. "I don't know how anybody..." ~ Stark, Phyllis. (1999, December 4). Do MDs still call the shots at radio? *Billboard.*
10. "It's reached absurd levels. When..." ~ Moon, Tom. (2002, October 8). Tom Petty lays out his case in song. *The Baltimore Sun.*
11. "Rich people aren't fun to..." ~ Morse, Steve. (2002, October 6). Tom Petty's peeved – and on a new CD, he won't back down. *The Boston Globe.*
12. "I don't think the industry..." ~ Wild, David. (2002, November 14). The ten things that piss off Tom Petty. *Rolling Stone.*
13. "Yeah, I got beaten up..." ~ Gundersen, Edna. (2006, July 25). Tom Petty: Into the great wide open. *USA Today.*
14. "My first reaction was, 'What..." ~ Bauder, David. (2002, October 12). For the love of rock, Tom Petty is on a roll. *The Akron Beacon Journal.*
15. "Radio is not even worth..." ~ Wild, David. (2002, November 14). The ten things that piss off Tom Petty. *Rolling Stone.*
16. "In the spring of 2002..." ~ Clapton, Eric. (2007). *Clapton: The Autobiography.* New York: Broadway Books.

CHAPTER 32: HOWIE: STRAIGHT INTO DARKNESS

1. "Local friends of Epstein's said..." ~ Terrell, Steve. (2004, March 12). Overdose suspected in death of local musician. *The Santa Fe New Mexican.*
2. "I'm devastated. I loved him..." ~ Terrell, Steve. (2003, February 25). Overdose Suspected in Death of Local Musician. *The Santa Fe New Mexican.*
3. Epstein was also experiencing financial... ~ Terrell, Steve. (2004, March 12). Overdose suspected in death of local musician. *The Santa Fe New Mexican.*
4. "At the time I was..." ~ Himes, Geoffrey. (2009, January 16). From a 'Bitter End' to new beginnings: After a period of loss, Carlene Carter finds a sweet place in her life. *The Washington Post.*
5. "If Ron Blair hadn't been..." ~ Kot, Greg. (2010, June 1). Tom Petty, the interview: 'I wanted to rough it up.' *The Chicago Tribune.*
6. "Howie could make the best..." ~ Flanagan, Bill. (1990, April). The Heartbreakers highway. *Musician.*
7. "I don't play a real..." ~ Collins, Dianne. (1987, May-June). Petty little thing called love. *Rock Express.*
8. "I think it was Billy..." ~ Schlenker, Dave. (2005, December). Grapevine: Tom Petty takes it home. *Gainesville Magazine.*
9. "had written this character named..." ~ Pang, Kevin. (2009, September 8). Mike Judge looks back over 13 years of 'King of the Hill.' *The Chicago Tribune.*

10. "My family went ape when..." ~ Gundersen, Edna. (2002, October 17). Petty runs down, and over, American dream. USA Today.
11. "Lucky is a fairly complex..." ~ Schlenker, Dave. (2005, December). Grapevine: Tom Petty takes it home. *Gainesville Magazine.*
12. "a thorough white-trash stereotype..." ~ Spurgeon, Ashley. (2012 January 5). Spurgeon's general warning: (Five) four things I like about Tom Petty. *Nashville Scene.*
13. "There are other people in..." ~ Luckman, Michael. (2005). *Alien Rock: The Rock 'n' Roll Extraterrestrial Connection.* New York: Pocket Books.
14. "One night I was lying..." ~ Luckman, Michael. (2005). *Alien Rock: The Rock 'n' Roll Extraterrestrial Connection.* New York: Pocket Books.
15. Meanwhile, when Tom Petty was... ~ Uhelszki, Jaan. (2006, July/August). Tom Petty: Anatomy of a rockstar. *Harp.*

CHAPTER 33: PETTY'S SAVING GRACE
1. "We've never had anything that..." ~ Waddell, Ray. (2005, August 13). Veteran Petty production team keeps focus on music. *Billboard.*
2. "I'm 54, and girls are..." ~ Hiatt, Brian. (2005, August 11). Petty rules road. *Rolling Stone.*
3. "He could have played fewer..." ~ Lewis, Randy. (2005, August 1). Tom Petty's bucking the big-bucks trend. *The Los Angeles Times.*
4. "For some reason, I have..." ~ Miller. Andrew. (2005, July 6). Flying high again. *Scene.*
5. "The performance went well, so..." ~ Thompson, Art. (2006, July). 30 years & counting. *Guitar Player.*
6. "It's not a real loud..." ~ Gundersen, Edna. (2006, July 25). Tom Petty: Into the great wide open. *USA Today.*
7. "Lately I've been concerned with..." ~ Uhelszki, Jaan. (2006, July/August). Tom Petty: Anatomy of a rockstar. *Harp.*
8. "It wouldn't have been a..." ~ Strauss, Neil. (2006, July 13). Tom Petty's last dance. *Rolling Stone.*
9. "In a career that has..." ~ Light, Alan. (2006, August 10). Steady Petty. *Rolling Stone.*
10. "We go on the road..." ~ Pryor, Sam. (2010, August). Steve Ferrone: Tapping into 40 years of groove. *Drum! Magazine.*
11. "It's a risk for an..." ~ Waddell, Ray. (2006, May 20). Scalper showdown. *Billboard.*
12. "They went berserk – stomping, screaming..." ~ Schlenker, Dave. (2006, September 22). No heartbreak at Petty's Gainesville homecoming. *The Ocala Star-Banner.*
13. "Tom made me a little..." ~ Nicks, Stevie. (2011). *100 Greatest artists of all time.* New York: Rolling Stone.
14. "It spooked me, really. It..." ~ Boucher, Geoff. (2006, December 31). Happily not retired. *The Los Angeles Times.*
15. "I never wanted to be..." ~ Jackson, Blair. (1981, August). Just a popular rock 'n' roll band. *Trouser Press.*
16. "George [Harrison] once said that..." ~ Wilde, Jon. (2004, July). McCartney: My life in the shadow of the Beatles. *Uncut.*
17. "I don't know if they..." ~ Gundersen, Edna. (2006, July 25). Tom Petty: Into the great wide open. *USA Today.*
18. The Strokes – who opened up... ~ Strauss, Neil. (2006, July 13). Tom Petty's last dance. *Rolling Stone.*

CHAPTER 34: THE DOCUMENTARY
1. "We left his house pinching..." ~ Millicia, Joe. (2006, July 5). Rock Hall pays tribute to Tom Petty. *The Akron Beacon Journal.*
2. "I had a four-hour meeting..." ~ Johnson, Barry. (2008, January 19). Reel music fest: Interview with Peter Bogdanovich. *The Oregonian.*
3. "I'm not an expert on..." ~ Scaggs, Austin. (2006, April 20). Petty's last summer tour? *Rolling*

Stone.

4. "I didn't want this go..." ~ Simon, Scott. (2007, November 17). 'Running Down' a New Petty Documentary. *Weekend Edition.* New York: NPR.
5. "I decided early on that..." ~ Bogdanovich, Peter. (2007, October 12). *Runnin' Down a Dream.* Press conference presented by the New York Film Festival, New York.
6. "I didn't talk to the..." ~ Berkery, Patrick. (2008, May). Stan Lynch. *Modern Drummer.*
7. "would have no say on..." ~ Erickson, Steve. (2008, June). Time stops for no one. *Relix.*
8. "He was adamant that I..." ~ Erickson, Steve. (2008, June). Time stops for no one. *Relix.*
9. "also serves as a vivid..." ~ Carr, David. (2007, October 10. Big screen embraces hot muse: Rock stars. *The New York Times.*
10. "It would be great if..." ~ Miller, Eric T. (2003, January/February). If I had my way, I'd tear the building down. *Magnet.*
11. "Tom obviously wasn't thrilled with..." ~ Boyle, Mike. (2006, March 25). 'The Last DJ' gets in the last word. *Billboard.*
12. "It's exciting because it's a..." ~ Schlenker, Dave. (2005, December). Grapevine: Tom Petty takes it home. *Gainesville Magazine.*
13. But according to some reports... ~ Patton, Gregg. (2008, February 2). Commentary: Petty whine about show for halftime. *The Sarasota Herald-Tribune.*
14. "The NFL obviously thinks Tom..." ~ Hoffman, Ken. (2007, December 6). Rock 'n' roll is sure Petty sometimes. *The Houston Chronicle.*
15. "Well, when you play on..." ~ Schmuck, Peter. (2008, February 1). Rolling out rock. *The Baltimore Sun.*
16. "Once given the go signal..." ~ Lang, Derrik J. (2008, February 4). Tom Petty plays it cool at Super Bowl. *USA Today.*
17. "There was no high-tech tomfoolery..." ~ DeRogatis, Jim. (2008, February 4). Halftime belongs to the Heartbreakers. *The Chicago Sun-Times.*
18. "Tom Petty bills himself as..." ~ Christensen, Thor. (2008, February 4). Petty smooth. *The Dallas Morning News.*

CHAPTER 35: THE MUDCRUTCH REUNION

1. "The feeling got stronger as..." ~ Erickson, Steve. (2008, June). Time stops for no one. *Relix.*
2. "I just had this random..." ~ Light, Alan. (2008, April 20). Running down a dream deferred. *The New York Times.*
3. "When Tom called me and..." ~ Light, Alan. (2008, April 20). Running down a dream deferred. *The New York Times.*
4. "I was driving home from..." ~ Light, Alan. (2008, April 20). Running down a dream deferred. *The New York Times.*
5. "I felt like a bolt..." ~ Boucher, Geoff. (2008, April 27), Tom Petty returns to his roots with Mudcrutch. *The Los Angeles Times.*
6. "I was dumbfounded. I just..." ~ Baron, Josh. (2008, June). Turning back the clock. *Relix.*
7. "When I think of the..." ~ Dean, Bill. (2008, April 29). Mudcrutch reunites for album. *The Gainesville Sun.*
8. "Mudcrutch is basically a West..." ~ Kot, Greg. (2010, June 1). Tom Petty, the interview: 'I wanted to rough it up.' *The Chicago Tribune.*
9. "Around us, there are racks ..." ~ Fitzpatrick, Rob. (2009, November 15). New Tom Petty album *The Live Anthology. The Times of London.*
10. "Music runs my life. I'm..." ~ Gundersen, Edna. (1994, November 15). Purely Petty: No backing down from rock's edge. *USA Today.*
11. "Everyone got involved, threw in..." ~ Kot, Greg. (2010, June 1). Tom Petty, the interview: 'I wanted to rough it up.' *The Chicago Tribune.*
12. "Tom [Petty] brought in this..." ~ Light, Alan. (2008, April 20). Running down a dream deferred. *The New York Times.*
13. "Every time we tried to..." ~ "Meet Tom Petty's 'new' old band." (2008, April 17). *Entertainment Weekly.*

271 - Notes

14. "I kept telling myself, 'Take..." ~ Baron, Josh. (2008, June). Turning back the clock. *Relix*.
15. "the material was so immediately..." ~ "Meet Tom Petty's 'new' old band." (2008, April 17). *Entertainment Weekly*.
16. "Having the band back together..." ~ Selvin, Joel. (2008, April 18). Tom Petty resurrects Mudcrutch. *The San Francisco Chronicle*.
17. "One of the problems with..." ~ Gottlieb, Jed. (2008, May 4). Mudcrutch makes tracks: Tom Petty reconvenes Heartbreakers' predecessor. *The Boston Herald*.
18. "If it didn't grab us..." ~ Snider, Mike. (2009, December 20). Tom Petty's live legacy gets the mega-box-set treatment. *USA Today*.
19. "I never thought I'd make..." ~ Fitzpatrick, Rob. (2009, November 15). New Tom Petty album the Live Anthology. *The Times of London*.

CHAPTER 36: GOT MY MOJO WORKING

1. "Mojo is power. You've got..." ~ Schaults, Janine. (2010, June 2). The making of *Mojo*. *The Chicago Tribune*.
2. "Every rehearsal for years started..." ~ Gundersen, Edna. (2010, June 10). With *Mojo*, Tom Petty happily sings the blues. *USA Today*.
3. "Growing up in Florida, we..." ~ Sterdan, Darryl. (2010, June 6). Guitar inspires Petty's *Mojo*. *The Toronto Sun*.
4. "I used to be a..." ~ Gundersen, Edna. (2010, June 10). With *Mojo*, Tom Petty happily sings the blues. *USA Today*.
5. "I had this picture in..." ~ Lewis, Randy. (2010, June 11). Tom Petty's got his *Mojo* working. *The Los Angeles Times*.
6. "We didn't want to do..." ~ Sterdan, Darryl. (2010, June 6). Guitar inspires Petty's *Mojo*. *The Toronto Sun*.
7. "I've always wanted one, but..." ~ Bandyke, Martin. (2010, July 22). Five questions with Mike Campbell, guitarist for the Heartbreakers. *The Detroit Free Press*.
8. "I remember [Tom] sitting down..." ~ Durchholz, Daniel. (2010, July 15). Heartbreakers jettison frills to find their 'Mojo.' *The St. Louis Post-Dispatch*.
9. "For this album, the band..." ~ Hathaway, Josh. (2010, June 17). Tom Petty & The Heartbreakers – Mojo. *The Seattle Post-Intelligencer*.
10. "I'd always wanted to deal..." ~ Scaggs, Austin. (2010, July 8). Q&A: Tom Petty. *Rolling Stone*.
11. "I have a feeling that..." ~ Willman, Chris. (2010, September-October). The great wide open. *M Music & Musicians*.
12. "It's really bad news. It..." ~ Knopper, Steve. (2011, November 24). Rock radio takes another hit. *Rolling Stone*.
13. "I have to survive on..." ~ Lloyd, Robert. (1991, October). Flying lessons: Tom Petty takes his bearings. *L.A. Style*.

CLOSING TIME

1. "If I ever get tired of..." ~ Jackson, Blair. (1983, January 28). There's a lot more to the Heartbreakers than Tom Petty. *BAM*.
2. "A reliable car, a place..." ~ McCormick, Neil. (2012, June 16). Tom Petty: A rock star for the ages. *The Daily Telegraph*.
3. "[The Heartbreakers] started in a..." ~ Lewis, Randy. (2010, June 11). Tom Petty's got his *Mojo* working. *The Los Angeles Times*.
4. "All I've ever done is..." ~ Miller, Eric T. (2003, January/February). If I had my way, I'd tear the building down. *Magnet*.
5. "My kids say that I..." ~ "Tom Petty." (2007, January). *Classic Rock*.
6. "I've got so much music..." ~ Rodgers, Larry. (2008, February 3). Runnin' down the dream. *The Arizona Republic*.

▶ INDEX

Winterland Ballroom, 85
Winwood, Steve, 220, 234
WKRP, 117
WLS (Chicago), 28
WLUP (Chicago), 107
WMET (Chicago), 107
Wolf, Howlin', 237
Wolfman Jack, 83
Wood, Ronnie, 137
Woodstock, 28, 38, 42, 112
Wozniak, Steve, 112-113
Wrecking Crew, 50
Wright, Frank Lloyd, 163
Wynette, Tammy, 104

Y

Yakus, Shelley, 87, 88
Yardbirds, 210
Young, Neil, 3, 81, 132, 141, 179

Z

Zanes, Warren, 79
Zappa, Frank, 41
Zombies, 198
Zuckerberg, Mark, 42
ZZ Top, 239

CPSIA information can be obtained at www.ICGtesting.com
Printed in the USA
BVOW04s0903040914

365458BV00021B/479/P